Look

for Our Mother
and Our Father

Anonymous

Nada y
Nadie
Publisher

ISBN: 978-0-692-00924-6

Nada y
Nadie
Publisher

Address inquiries to:
Nada y Nadie
nada-y-nadie@hotmail.com

For my children, and everyone else's.

The Creator acts through all of us, and those who are aware, act well. I could call this book *Half Way There*, because clearly I am. I have seen the illusion of my culture, but have not yet replaced it with reality; I am still of my culture. I am not *there*, aware as I act of the act of the Creator; I have not the mercy and compassion of the person who has walked the spiritual path.

And so, though this book is an act of creation, I cannot say I have written well: On the lie of my culture, I clearly see the truth, but someone wiser would have had more understanding and compassion in their speech. And because of my failings, I ask the Creator to help those who read my words to read well and hear the Creator's message.

The Earth is our Mother, and I revere and love her. I cry that she is hurt, and I know she cries for the suffering of her children. Yet I know, too, that she has great power to heal, herself and her children, if we just give her the chance.

For my Mother and my Father, for all my brothers and sisters, and for our children, I pray to the Great Spirit and hope that we may all learn to act well.

Contents

War & Colonization

Wisdom

Introduction to
Look
for Our Mother
and Our Father

Introduction

All of my life, people have commented on my ability to see things holistically: to look at the big picture; to put the puzzle together; to see how things interrelate. Here is my holistic look at our culture, my panoramic view, and it's not the view you usually see.

If someone rejects my methodology, so be it – I reject their need for methodology. If someone questions my logic, that's fair – I question their faith in logic. Please understand from the start that these essays are not an argument, nor a hypothesis, nor an intellectual exercise, nor a scholarly discussion; I am simply putting forth what I see. If someone feels I have not offered a rigorous argument with ample substantiation, I would say they are reading through the lenses of a culture which has defined "rigorous argument" and "ample substantiation" to perpetuate the status quo, not to search for truth. As, I hope, you will see in the pages that follow, these are simply tools of our culture, tools which limit what we view. I write from my heart, and any substantiation I haven't provided can be found in the world and in life. In the end, either the essays reach you, or they don't.

*   *   *

Many people in the U.S.A. believe this is the greatest country ever, a shining light of freedom and democracy and everything that is right in the world. If incest and pollution and rape and child pornography are rampant, we can overlook that, because we also have the Constitution of the United States and what we believe to be a superior standard of living.

People in this country do not wonder, "Six hundred years ago, the native peoples who inhabited these lands didn't have all of our problems."

Instead, they think, "We live in an advanced, complex society, so of course we have problems that other peoples didn't have. People are working on solutions to the problems that can be solved, and many of our problems are just an unfortunate part of life, a part of human nature, common to every culture on the planet. Eventually, we will move beyond the flaws in our society, because we are constantly trying to move forward."

The people of this country think we are the most medically advanced society in history, and so they do not say, "Today, millions of animals will be subjected to extreme pain in laboratory experiments, in an attempt to find cures for diseases, and over the decades billions of animals have died and billions of dollars have been spent on these supposed cures. Yet my friend just died from his heart medication, and they can't cure my diabetes. Something is amiss with our advancement."

Instead, they say, "Our medical knowledge and technology are the best in the world. We obviously don't have all the answers yet, but we are getting closer and closer, and if we just keep pouring money into the problem, we'll get there eventually. Look at all the progress we've made. We have endless drugs and medical procedures which weren't available one hundred or even fifty years ago."

Many people in this country work at dreary jobs for low wages. They struggle their whole lives just to get by, or to buy things that they hope will make their lives better: TVs, cell phones, designer shoes, and so on.

Yet they do not think, "I work all day at a job I don't like, trading away my life, and I barely get paid. I scrimp and save so I can buy junk, which half the time ends up at Goodwill or in the landfills. There are millions of people like me, and millions more who don't even have what I have. Why, if our society is so well-ordered, is it so hard to get ahead? And why are there so many people who cannot find jobs, or who have jobs but still cannot afford even the basic necessities? Something is wrong with our society."

Instead, they think either, "Wow, I wish I had a job so I could afford to buy things," or, "Wow, I'm lucky to have a job and to be able to eat tacos, hamburgers, or steak – whatever I want. I can watch TV, and I have indoor plumbing. I live in the most advanced society on the planet. We know so much and are able to do so many things. We've sent a man to the moon, we have earth-moving equipment, and we live in a democratic society where people have rights. Things could be worse: I could live in a country where they don't even have electricity, and where the government tramples on its own people. I choose to look at the bright side..."

But the bright side has a dark side, and this book looks at that dark side.

*   *   *

A few notes:
- I would like to be clear, since I mention Native

Americans repeatedly throughout the text, that I am not Native American, nor do I speak for Native Americans. I use their cultures (admittedly very generally) for comparison, solely because I am more familiar with them than with other indigenous cultures. But the examples I use, the points I make, and the damage done apply to indigenous peoples the world over.

• This book looks at our culture, and the word *culture* here encompasses our society, our lifestyle, our values and beliefs, our means of acquiring and accumulating knowledge, our education, and so on. We are very fond of discrediting other cultures because we think we are superior and hence can see their cultures more clearly than they do – we think we provide an objective view, so to speak. Every group of people we have encountered knows what it feels like to have every aspect of your culture examined, belittled, disregarded, and dishonored. Most people in our culture have never considered how this feels, but it is time we learned.

• I have made up and use the notation PEOC (Person of European-Originated Culture) throughout the book. The European and Euro-derived cultures are really all one culture, or what I refer to as culture in this book, with only stylistic differences. By PEOC, I mean to signify not only Europeans and their descendents, but also those living in their descendent colonies and countries the world over. For example, someone could be of African heritage and yet have been born and raised in the U.S., and hence be a PEOC.

By PEOC, I *also* mean to signify the *effects* of these people. Sadly, most of the world has been influenced to some extent by the actions of Europeans, and so, for example, the educational system

– or the government – of a country may also be PEOC. As another example, hospitals are PEOC. They were invented by Europeans and introduced into other cultures.

Though this definition may seem complex, I believe the meaning of PEOC will become very clear as you read.

• Often in my essays, I refer to actions taken by the people of the U.S.A., but my points refer to all PEOCs: Europeans, Canadians, Australians, etc. – they are all the same as U.S. citizens, even if their people think they aren't.

• People may think this book would be easier to read and more organized if I put everything related together: everything on education in one essay, everything on technology in another, and so on. But our education is not a separate entity, unrelated to all the other parts of our society, something that can be viewed separately – nor are our technology and religion and aggression. They tie together in real life, and so they tie together in this book.

• I have not given every example; I have not made every point; I have not answered every objection. However, I have painted my picture with enough detail, I believe, for the viewer to clearly see the subject.

In closing, please note that you have to read the entire book to get it, to see the whole, panoramic view. I ask my readers' indulgence in this way: Almost everyone who reads this book will probably, at some point, feel offended, not because I am trying to offend, but because this book challenges some fundamental beliefs of our culture. Some may feel defensive or want to throw the book aside as nonsense. But, perhaps, later in the book, that thing will be clarified and look less like nonsense. Or, though I have said something which is painful to hear, the reader will realize that it is at least just. I ask my readers to finish the book, to get the whole message and look at the whole picture, and, perhaps, to spend a few days pondering it. For some, I sincerely hope, this book will change the way you look – at everything.

Western Civilization*

Isn't it lucky for humans that we are the most developed, advanced species ever? Look at the food chain (developed by our culture) – humans are at the top of that. One quick glance at evolution (developed by our culture) will show you that we are the most highly evolved. The intelligence scale (developed by our culture) will tell you that we are the smartest species on the planet.

Humans are at the top of the species value scale (developed by our culture). It goes something like this: humans – mammals – birds – reptiles – amphibians – insects – trees – bushes – etc. Those we call the higher species are granted the ability to feel pain (a select few are even granted intelligence), but we believe it is okay to torture them and to dominate and control them for the betterment of humankind, for scientific experiments, and for the amusement and convenience of people. Those we call the lower animals are not even granted the ability to feel, let alone intelligence or emotion. And plants are barely alive on this scale.

And in Christianity (developed by our culture), the Earth was created by God specifically for humans.

---

* The term *Western Civilization* is based on the idea that Asia is the Far East, Europe is the West, and the rest of the world is inconsequential. (When the U.S. and Canada became consequential, they were added to the Western world.)

Clearly, humans are the most wonderful species ever – at least according to our culture.

And who are the most advanced and developed, most wonderful humans? Why, PEOCs,[†] of course. In the progress of civilization (defined by our culture), we are leading the way. (Other countries are just "developing" countries, trying to catch up to us.) Our culture, our government, our knowledge, our art, our health care, our values, our society, our religion, our military, our technology, our judgment, etc.: All are the best, according to us. Isn't it wonderful that we were born into the culture that is at the top; that, however you view it and whatever you view, PEOCs are at the peak? It's pretty amazing that one culture can outshine all others in *everything*. Though we may question the current state of affairs in this arena or that, we do not question the idea of the perpetual forward march of the human species, with PEOCs leading and lighting the way.

Our belief that we are more advanced and better than other peoples is not new. We were so sure we were more civilized than everyone else on the planet that Europeans felt (and PEOCs still feel) it was their duty to civilize the "heathens" and "savages" of the Americas, Africa, Australia, and islands the world over. Obviously, this was a pretty subjective call that we were more civilized, but clearly we believed we were (and still believe we are), which is the whole point, after all.

The invention of the wheel, the domestication of animals, the development of written language, industrialization – all these milestones of human development are milestones of PEOCs – and we are the ones defining them as milestones. (True, we

---

† For a definition of PEOC, see the Introduction.

did not invent written language, but we use it, and so it qualifies as a milestone, as opposed to, say, discovery of the vision quest, which many indigenous peoples use as a means of profound self-understanding and knowledge. We don't use that, so it's not a milestone. And though we didn't invent written language, I wouldn't be surprised if many schoolchildren believe we did. Either way, children are often taught that our written language is better than pictographic written languages, because we don't have to learn as many characters; hence, our way is superior.)

Indigenous peoples of the Americas did not domesticate animals, because they believed animals were brothers and sisters, not inferior species to be exploited in order to serve their needs. As equals, animals were not for humans to control and rule: They had their own self-governance rights, their own paths, their own selves. The PEOCs were not able to see this right in animals and were interested in their own convenience and comfort, without regard for the rights of animals. Lack of understanding of the natural world and its other inhabitants, lack of respect for those other inhabitants, and selfishness for comfort are not superior, higher traits. If you believe animals and plants have their own inalienable rights and place on Earth, then the domestication of animals was an atrocity, not a milestone in human development.

The wheel is thought to be a first step in the development of technology, and PEOCs worship their own technology and think themselves far superior in having developed it. Every new piece of technology is a giant step forward in the PEOC mind: electricity, automobiles, airplanes, computers, cellular telephones, televisions, MP3 players, machines to move the Earth and build skyscrapers, medical machines, machines to accelerate atoms, technology to collect data on the biodiversity of an ecosystem (supposedly without disrupting that ecosystem), satellites, GPS: It's a long, long list, and PEOCs chalk it all up on the plus side of superiority.

But PEOCs do not stop to think that indigenous peoples did not develop these kinds of things because they had no use for them. The wheel itself is very destructive to both the soil and plants, and hence to the whole planet. The clouds of dust raised by cars and bicycles driving on unpaved lands cause serious air pollution in some areas. Obviously, paving the land also devastates the Earth. If you love the Earth, you would not develop this technology. If you are of a culture which values nature, then all the roadways and buildings and dams and canals of PEOCs are not advancements. The development of machines to tear up the Earth more quickly and efficiently would only be thought superior, or advancement, by a culture which wants to tear up the Earth and thinks doing so is good. If you revere the Earth, why would you develop technology to destroy it more efficiently?

PEOCs think we are superior in erecting buildings, which we think of as permanent structures (as though we are unaware of the ruins at, say, Athens, which were undoubtedly thought permanent at that time) – as opposed to the temporary structures indigenous peoples used. Our buildings are not permanent; they must be constantly maintained and are constantly being torn down. But it does not occur to PEOCs that maybe this Earth is not made for permanent structures. So who's wiser?

It's funny, but when an indigenous culture *has* left ruins, which we think are signs of superiority, or at least of superior technology, many PEOCs like to speculate that the ruins are the influence of aliens from outer space, because surely the primitive indigenous peoples didn't have the technology and knowledge to create the structures. (We have no idea how they were created, and we're the self-appointed experts – so the obvious conclusion is that outer space aliens must have been responsible).

We have machines to pull the blood out of a person's body, clean it, and put it back. This is because we are unable to look at the situation in a clear way. We have determined that the person has a disease, that the disease cannot be cured, and that the only thing to do is to artificially clean the blood – so we develop a machine to do that. Now we have an awkward, I imagine painful, and technology-dependent process, for which we claim superiority. But the superior way would be to understand the situation, the world, and the person, and to end (or cure) the illness (which is what indigenous peoples would do).

You hear people asserting that stem cell research is the key to curing everything from Parkinson's disease to Alzheimer's. They complain that limiting stem cell research is keeping the U.S. from staying at the forefront of medical care. But stem cell research won't lead to any cures; just more drugs which have dangerous, sometimes lethal, side effects, which can be used to control the diseases. Stem cell research will also lead to more opportunities for scientists to show how brilliant they are in coming up with these dangerous drugs and to keep up the illusion that science leads to knowledge and that we're always having scientific breakthroughs.

Here's the point: Don't worry that we will no longer be at the forefront of medical care, because we are *not* at the forefront of medical care. This is just a lie we tell ourselves because we think we're superior. Our advanced, modern hospitals are a monstrosity in medical care. We have all heard horror stories: someone being admitted and getting the wrong operation; someone having a body part removed, only to find that the doctor had read the wrong x-ray; someone dying of an infection contracted in the hospital after a simple procedure; a doctor inducing labor because a woman is late delivering, only to find the doctor miscalculated the delivery date and just induced a premature birth…

Our advanced health care does more harm than good, despite the fact that its motto is, "First, do no harm." Doctors routinely prescribe drugs which they know cause negative side effects, which require more drugs, which cause more negative side effects. Tens of thousands of people die each year *because* they were in a hospital; hundreds of thousands die each year as a direct result of our superior health care system and medical industry.

Medical and pharmacy reps like to say, "Yeah, but how many people were *saved*?" But the real question is, how many more would be saved if we truly had superior health care? Our health care industry is, after all, business, interested first and foremost in making money, over and above saving lives. If some people have to die in the name of hospital efficiency or because the pharmaceutical companies are selling dangerous products, that's a trade-off the industry leaders are willing to make, because, they tell themselves, it's the best health care possible – not perfect, just the best.

Hospital apologists may say, "There are millions of stories where everything went right, and the patient was saved or had a successful treatment." But a successful visit, for example a successful operation – perhaps removing a uterus – isn't really a success; it's just what our medical industry calls a success. A true success would heal the person without putting them at risk for further complications, and *every* surgery (and *every* medication) puts the patient at risk; and the doctors know it, and they're willing to take that gamble with their patients' lives – because that's the best our medical system can provide. But just because sometimes the gamble seems to pay off, the fact still remains that the patient would have been better off if they had been healed without removing part of their body. And successes aside, there are far too many true horror stories to say our hospitals are good.

The medical industry doesn't involve any true knowledge, no profound understanding. It is about the medical procedures, not about healing. Our hospitals are piece by piece the product of people who had something to sell and convinced the hospital industry that *this* and *that* and *the other thing* would lead to superior care. The hospitals were happy to be convinced, because the markup they charge patients for each *this*, *that*, and *the other thing* is phenomenal. So you have people hooked up to all kinds of tubes and monitors and medications and computers, being subjected to all kinds of tests and pricks and pokes; if the person lives through this, it is a success. But the system does not save lives, and just because some people survive the system doesn't make it superior. The superior system wouldn't have these profit-motivated products and procedures. The superior system wouldn't have so much suffering and death.

It's interesting that when a shaman (or indigenous healer) helps someone to get better, they say outright that they can't heal anyone, only the Creator can do that; yet, when someone survives our medical system, we claim superior medical care. We say it's one more proof that capitalism is what makes this country great: People invent great things because they have an incentive to do so (the incentive being wealth). But what our great capitalist system actually leads to is a bunch of unnecessary, often harmful, treatments and procedures and medicines and practices, and barbaric medical care. And we, in our cultural blindness and arrogance, call it superior.

Look, too, at dentistry. Taking your mouth to a dentist is like taking your car to the shop: If you go to three different dentists, you will get three different opinions about what is wrong and how to fix it, and odds are expensive work will be strongly recommended. The only thing all will tell you is to use fluoride, because the fluoride industry has firmly entrenched in our dentists' minds the idea that this highly toxic chemical is good for teeth. I'm sure the dentists see confirmation of the beneficial effects of fluoride in their practices, because they see what they expect to see and ignore the rest, like in every other science.

All of our technology causes problems which need solutions, but the solutions always cause a whole new set of problems. The unhealthful conditions of water which make our superior indoor plumbing possible led to the solution of adding chlorine. Safe levels for humans – and anyone else who drinks the water, such as pets – were determined through tests on lab animals – and the PR of chlorine manufacturers, of course. The chlorine may dry out your skin each time you wash, but you can buy lotion (which my not end the dryness, but is full of questionable chemicals). And the internal health problems caused by a lifelong ingestion of chlorine are solved by denying that there are any problems – but the fact is that the average Native American in their seventies or eighties (pre-colonization) was much healthier than the average thirty-year-old in our society today. Electricity is the same way; its generation and use cause a boatload of harmful consequences, not only to humans, but to the entire planet...

Our modern cities require a massive infrastructure and present many safety hazards. We have lights that we leave on all night (street lights, porch lights, etc.) so that people will be safe, and yet people are not safe. Our cities are fire hazards, so we have to have fire departments and (leaky) fire hydrants and fire trucks and roads for the fire trucks. We need a massive system of (leaky) pipes to bring water to all the households, and a massive system of (leaky) pipes to carry away their waste. We need trash cans and trash bags and dumpsters and garbage trucks to cart off our massive amount of trash, and landfills to store it. We need street cleaners and shopping cart cleaners, but neither streets nor shopping carts are clean. We don't need but do have telephone lines and cable TV lines and television and radio broadcasting towers, all of it scarring the beauty of the Earth and sky. We see our cities as a sign of advancement and superiority and are awed by the fact that we have been able to create such an elaborate system. Many people in other cultures would be awed by the appalling and astounding drain on the Earth, which has not led to any benefit to the people in terms of higher knowledge, spirituality, better health, or even general well-being.

We think our lifestyle is superior because we live in houses with indoor plumbing and electricity, which are furnished with upholstered furniture. People in our culture prefer to sit on upholstered furniture, because we are lazy and self-indulgent, but this doesn't make it superior to sitting on the Earth. Only *we* would turn a cultural preference into "superiority," but just because we think our preferences are superior doesn't mean they actually are. Some people would actually rather sit on the Earth. We may think a 4000 sq ft house is the ultimate in luxury, but, to some, this would feel like a prison, so it's not really superior – it's just our self-indulgent cultural preference, and we've chosen to call it superior.

We're proud our culture has progressed so far that we can now produce massive quantities of goods, and we don't look at the fact that, in the production of these goods, we are harming the Earth, which is necessary to our survival. Nor do we look at the fact that we don't need all these goods – so it isn't really *progress*.

So indigenous peoples did not develop what we call technical marvels, but it wasn't because they weren't bright or advanced enough to do so. However, they were certainly wise enough *not* to do so if such a thought had occurred to them. They understood the world and how everything was part of everything else; they realized the interdependence of all things. We think we can generate tons of toxic waste and destroy millions of acres of natural environment without caring that there will be consequences; nor do we understand those consequences when they occur. Indigenous peoples could see the effects of an owl flying overhead or a pine tree shedding its needles. Our civilization has devastated the Earth, and the more technical marvels we create, the more devastation we cause. Is the superior culture the one that, in the last 100 years, has caused damage that the Earth will take thousands of years to repair, or the culture that lived for thousands and thousands of years doing no damage and not needing technical marvels?

The PEOC thinking goes, "But the Native Americans did not have all the knowledge that our technology makes available to us. We have paid a price for all our knowledge, true, but all this knowledge will eventually help us to fix those problems we have created." But our knowledge, the contribution of the natural and social sciences to our culture, is no knowledge at all. By the time the sciences were invented, western civilization had strayed so far from the path of truth that the development of the sciences was by people who were blinded; hence, they could not see that truth would never be gotten from science.

The blindness of our culture is cumulative; the knowledge is not. Our knowledge bounces like a funny ball. It is odd to hear scientists say, "What we now know to be true ..." and to smile indulgently at those less-advanced scientists of their past. I guess these scientists do not realize that in fifty (or twenty) years, "what we now know to be true" will also have been proven to be utter nonsense, and the scientists of the future will be smiling indulgently at them. Perhaps they think they are taking their place in a growing chain of cumulative knowledge, but that chain is full of broken links. Someone posits a theory, and everyone builds on it; but then, all of a sudden, they discover that the original theory was wrong, and everything built on it is a house of cards. So they either start the whole process all over with another faulty theory, or they move everything to the left two feet and just keep building. What people don't see is that science doesn't give us any real knowledge; it just strikes an authoritative pose and pretends to do so. In the end, the Native who lived on the land and who saw and experienced and understood how everything interrelated is the person who knew more than the scientist who collected reams of data about the biodiversity of the ecosystem and conducted experiments to create and test his theories.

Scientists are unable to look at what they are seeing, are culturally bound from understanding what they are seeing, so they cannot accurately say, "This is what happened ..." or "The reason for that is ..." This segment of our society, which we choose to label brilliant, actually has a very blind and limited mindset. For example (and this is purely fiction on my part, but it illustrates my point), perhaps indigenous peoples in some cultures used the appendix to channel the Earth's energy into their bodies for healing and stamina. In PEOC culture, we do not do this, and we do not know how to do this; based on this, scientists determine that the appendix doesn't really do anything and can be cut out of the body with no loss.

The point is that the scientists are starting with a blind spot which prevents them from realizing the purpose of the appendix.

Or here is another scenario: Imagine there are muscles in the human body which are absolutely critical to a natural way of life, but we don't use them in our lifestyle, so scientists determine that they are obsolete in modern society. They assume that what they call modern society is sustainable. Those muscles may very well be essential to human survival, and this society is what's obsolete, but they wouldn't see that. They think we have come so far, we will never go back – and why would we want to? The answer is that we were headed in the wrong direction the whole time.

Say you are in California, and you want to go to Alaska, but you're not sure how to get there, so you randomly start walking east. When you get to Kentucky and see you aren't any closer to Alaska, do you say, "Well, I'm headed in this direction, and I've come so far – I think I'll just keep going, and, hopefully, it'll work out. I'll continue walking east, and, hopefully, I'll stumble on Alaska eventually"? We think we will never go back, but the Earth may have other plans, and the Earth is more powerful than we are. Substitute *lost from reality* for the word *advanced* every time you hear someone talk about our culture, and you will get a truer picture of what they are saying. Even those who don't believe in the theory of evolution still view our culture as an evolution of the human species, a long forward progress full of milestones of development – but only because that's what our culture tells them about our culture.

The social scientists do not understand what they are looking at any more than natural scientists.

They are completely bound by their culture and cannot see that the social sciences are just another part of that culture, a product of that culture, not an objective field which can observe, modify, and improve the culture. They study a warped culture full of people who are indoctrinated into the culture (as they are) and think they can draw useful information from this study – but the culture long ago lost touch with truth; there is no truly useful information to be drawn from this culture. They can find plenty of fodder for useless theories, but they cannot find truth, because they cannot see what is not there.

They may call *human nature* the typical PEOC reaction to something, but the typical PEOC reaction should not be confused as the typical human reaction (though, in the PEOC mind, it usually is). Show me a circumstance where every single human on the planet would react identically before you call it human nature. If someone doesn't react that way, are they not human? How do we define "human"? How many people have to react that way for it to be "human nature"? These are questions for the great thinkers – I won't waste my time with them. Their contribution to our knowledge is nothing more than an intellectual exercise.

The notion of studying peoples and societies scientifically in order to better understand peoples and societies is flawed, in part because there is no such thing as human nature, and in part because there are no natural laws for the social sciences any more so than for the natural sciences. Whether in terms of a theory of gravity or in terms of a theory of the subconscious, the search for natural laws obviously won't lead to truth if, in reality, there are no natural laws. The only thing which supports the idea of there being natural laws is science. Life refutes the idea every day, but the scientists are too blind to notice. All of our natural laws are cultural beliefs, not reality.

Normal human development is a commonly used, meaningless phrase. The idea is that your child should be able to play with plastic blocks by a certain age and drink from a cup by a certain age and so on. The idea of what is normal human development is culturally bound and is intended to be actionable, but what are you going to do with it? Worry that your child is not developing normally? Try to interfere with *your child's* normal development? Give your child some experimental drugs to help them develop normally? Turn your child over to a psychologist, so the psychologist can try out the latest techniques? Maybe if everyone quit trying to interfere, normal human development (whatever that means) would be very different from what psychologists and sociologists have defined (i.e. invented). If your kids don't develop "normally," the problem is not with your kids: It's not your kids' job to develop according to anyone's schedule but their own, and it's not the parents' job to try to make them do so.

Psychologists have developed all kinds of tests to help you understand yourself better, or to help other people (a potential employer, your parole officer, etc.) understand you. As children grow, they are subjected to these tests from time to time. My response to the results of these tests was always, "That doesn't resemble me at all." But I wonder how many people hear the results of their tests and think they have found out something about themselves, and hence act like someone they're not because of their new knowledge.

If their theories are of such value, why have the social scientists done nothing to solve any of society's problems? For example, why are almost all therapies meant to reform rapists dismally unsuccessful? And why do we still have incest? –It is because the answers do not lie in the culture that spawned the problems, and the social scientists are a part of that culture. They will never solve the problems, because they do not and can not truly understand the problems – even though their culture tells them they do.

*   *   *

All of PEOC milestones and technology and knowledge are only advancement according to our culture, according to *us*. But PEOCs point to the way our society is ordered as another proof of our superiority. Let's look at that:

We have a constitution and laws, and we claim these make justice just, equally applicable to all. Moreover, we have it all in writing, so everyone knows the rules. We believe that power cannot be abused when the laws are written down and cannot be changed without going through a carefully developed process, which is also written down. Everyone gets equal treatment with these laws ruling the governance of the citizenry. We have checks and balances against the abuse of power, and, since everything is in writing, it has to be adhered to. Justice is not a powerful leader's whim: It is the same for everyone.

In the first place, it is apparent that PEOCs assume that, if a culture does not have written laws, it has no laws, or its laws are flexible and applied based on, perhaps, favoritism. This is an assumption based on PEOC culture: In our culture, if laws were not written, they would be applied sporadically and unequally, based on whim and favoritism. In fact, even though they are written, they *are* applied sporadically and unequally; justice certainly isn't equal and even-handed in this society. So I guess the solution of writing laws down didn't work to solve the problem of unequal justice. And just because there are laws against something, that doesn't keep people from doing it.

I believe indigenous peoples didn't have an unending supply of laws because they were not interested in controlling so very much of their people's lives. Of course, they didn't have all our crime. Plus, they counted on the wisdom of their elders, who were more interested in preserving their culture for the good of the whole people than in playing favorites. And does anyone actually think that they didn't know murder was wrong, if there were not a law forbidding it? Just because we need laws to tell us what is wrong doesn't mean everyone does; if it is part of your fundamental being that life is sacred, you do not have to have a law to keep you from murder.

We think our justice system, though not perfect, is the best that's ever been created. But the only way someone could think it superior is by growing up being told it was great, not perfect but the best human society has come up with so far, and by believing this. Anyone looking at it from outside the culture would be appalled. Truth has nothing to do with justice; often the goal is to intentionally obfuscate the truth, not to unveil or clarify it. Prosecutors want to convict someone (not necessarily the guilty party); defense attorneys want to get their clients off – unless they are overworked/underpaid public defenders, in which case they want their clients, guilty or not, to accept plea bargains. It is not about people sitting down with elders to determine the truth; it is about people needing lawyers who know how to manipulate the law and about sitting down in front of a judge who studied the same set of rules as the lawyers. As with our medical industry, it's about going through the motions and procedures and telling ourselves it works. It's all like a game show; and, for that matter, trials are often aired or reenacted on reality TV. For the right outcome to occur after a trial (i.e., a guilty person is found guilty) is a crap shoot; for the punishment to fit the crime is a miracle. Our justice system keeps the prison population brimming, but it doesn't perform any real service (except to keep itself and the prison industry in business, hence jobs). We think it's great because we cannot imagine a society in which people actually own up to their crimes, and where the idea of locking someone up as some sort of solution to crime is ridiculous. But how does it solve anything? The answer is that it doesn't solve anything; it's just what our culture determined long ago to be a brilliant course of action, and we went with it, without ever a look back. Our system does not reduce crime; it does not mete out punishment with a fair and even hand (for example, a rich person gets the charges dropped for something a poor person would serve 10 years for); it does not punish guilty people and let free those who are innocent (many innocent people end up in prison, and many guilty people are let free). If a corporation gets sued, say for making their customers ill, they are allowed to tie the matter up in court for decades.

And we have case law, wherein a judge is not supposed to react to the situation at hand but is supposed to reach a decision based on past cases.

We have countless pointless laws and codes. Often, laws are nothing more than rules to be gotten around. For example, we have numerous laws requiring truth in advertising, yet we still have deceptive advertising. Sometimes, too, the people who are supposed to be regulated by a law are the ones who write it, the goal not being to curb a certain practice, but to give the appearance that we are trying to curb that practice. If coal-burning companies write a law which allows them to increase toxic emissions, they don't have to get around that law, because it suits them fine as is – and the lawmakers can say we have a law regulating coal-burning plant emissions to safe levels, even though we don't. Who but PEOCs would think so much convolution and contortion is a *good* thing?

Some might say the complexity of our legal system is a necessity, a response to the complexity of our society – and people think the complexity of our society is a good thing, an indication of our sophistication, of our advancement, of our superiority. By that reasoning, an omelet that takes 20 steps to prepare is superior to one that can be prepared in 3 steps. If the omelet which was prepared in 3 steps tastes better and is better for your health, we don't care, because the other one is more sophisticated and advanced.

It is amazing, too, and you have to wonder why no one questions that our society is at the pinnacle – and the pinnacle is a society riddled with abused children, stray animals dying on the streets, hate, strife, abused elders... Those "backward" Natives, who are way down from the top of the pinnacle, didn't have all of these problems. People constantly complain about how our society is going to pot: bad manners, road rage, increasing crime, etc. In spite of all the faults about which they constantly complain, they say, "It's not perfect – but it's better than any other society which has ever developed." But they don't know about every other society that has ever developed, and, usually, they don't even know anything about *any* other society – except what their culture tells them about those societies, which is always inaccurate. So they are making a meaningless comparison. It's a little like I determined that the layout of my house is the best that's ever been invented without ever looking at the layout of any other house.

* * *

We invented capitalism, the greatest economic system ever (according to us) – it's what makes our great democracy possible – it's what makes our democracy great. Capitalism makes wealth available to anyone who is willing to work. In medieval Europe, some people were born into wealth, and the poor people were poor their whole lives, serving the needs of a rich class who thought they were superior...

Frankly, this description of medieval Europe sounds like a description of our capitalism. There are a few exceptions where someone is born poor and dies wealthy – but so were there exceptions in medieval Europe. The fact is that most people in our culture spend their entire lives in the same economic class (in our society = social class). Capitalist democracy serves the needs of the rich quite as well as feudalism did, and we only tell ourselves it's better because that's what we've been taught to believe.

We also believe our democracy to be a shining light of government of the people, by the people, and for the people. According to us, it is the greatest ever. We say we invented the form of government which most represents its citizens and gives them the opportunity to decide how they will be governed. Though we actually have a republic rather than a democracy (as in, "I pledge allegiance to the flag... and to the *republic* for which it stands"), people still think of it as a democracy.

Ignore the fact that millions of citizens eligible to vote are not even registered to vote, and that, of those who are registered, millions don't vote, and that political parties tamper with election results, and that voters are intimidated at the polls. Never mind that the candidates who win are usually the ones with the largest advertising budgets, and, hence, are the candidates who are *most* corrupt, since the advertising budgets come from people who want something for their money. Never mind the fact that it is virtually impossible for a candidate to win and hold any office without compromising their principles and betraying those who elected them to office. And don't ask, "If our democracy is such a great thing and such a model way to govern a country, why all of these problems?" Ignore all of this, because it's not the point.

In the pre-Columbian Americas, people could (and were expected to) do what they thought was right; they could go where they wanted (pretty much); they did not have the totalitarianism of majority rules ruling their lives. If they wanted to follow a different leader, they could. If they wanted to go off on their own, they could. That was *better* than democracy. Contrast that with our form of government, in which you can't and shan't do what is right; you should do what the majority wants to do, even if you believe it is morally reprehensible. You may argue or protest against something – for example a war – but you still support it, by supporting the government waging it, by supporting the culture, by paying the taxes used to wage the war, and by deriving the benefits of the war. You tell yourself you are not supporting it and are opposing it, but what you are really doing is supporting it and kidding yourself. How is this government superior?

Even if the U.S. weren't a form of plutocracy in the disguise of a democracy (which it is), and even if our elections were fair (which they aren't), our democracy is just what it is: a way to run and control a country, to enforce the culture on all of its citizens – whether they vote or not – to control its citizens. I mentioned earlier that in many indigenous societies, every life had their own way, their own path, their own rights; and indigenous forms of government reflected that. People weren't forced into the way of the majority. The governments weren't set up to control their citizens. Now *that* is freedom.

I read a story about the U.S. government's pursuit of the Nez Perce,‡ in which it was told how each Nez Perce had personal responsibility for their actions. In the context of this pursuit, each person had to decide whether to fight in each battle and how they would fight if they chose to do so. They weren't paid to fight. Each person had to decide whether this was a battle they believed in,

---

‡ *I Will Fight No More Forever*, selected bibliography.

if they were willing to fight, and what was acceptable to them to win. Conventional wisdom (of our culture) would say that such chaos in the ranks without firm leadership would be ineffective and would surely lead to losing the battles. Of course, this was inaccurate, because the Nez Perce won many battles against the regimented U.S. militias. (The fact that they eventually lost the war was not due to their lack of firm leadership, nor to the U.S. military's presence of firm leadership.)

Now look at our military. Many of the people in it are poor or disadvantaged, people who could see no other escape from the dreary lives they were destined to live in the land of the American dream than to join the military and hopefully get a better job than otherwise upon discharge. In our military, a soldier's job is to follow orders. Soldiers have no responsibility to know what the war is about and whether they believe it worth fighting; in fact, this is discouraged by the threat of imprisonment if they desert because they don't believe. They are told they are serving their country and that the war is just; if the war is actually about invading a country to set up a puppet government who will let our corporations come in and destroy the lives of the people, so be it – it isn't their job to know.

Personally, if someone told me to go take another person's life, I would insist on more than my government's assurance that this was a matter of national security before I would do it; if my punishment were imprisonment, at least it would not be the guilt of killing innocent people and helping to enslave others. To take another's life in war, I would have to be personally acquainted with the facts, with all sides of the facts, and with a certainty of there being no other option, a circumstance I could probably live my entire life without encountering. But for soldiers to take this kind of personal responsibility in the U.S. military would not serve the purposes of our corporations and their government. If our soldiers took that kind of responsibility, they would see that they are being asked to kill, not for national security, but for the profit of U.S. corporations, and they would refuse – or they would ask for more pay and work as well-paid mercenaries rather than low-paid hit men (yes, in our culture, some people are willing to kill for money). Just think: This country has been in more wars (many of them covert) than the number of years we have been a country. Which leads to another superiority PEOC culture claims: superior weapons (as if something is superior because it causes more destruction).

And we claim superiority because of the values we say our government exalts: equality, free speech (only a government which can conceive of censoring people's speech would have to include that, because, naturally, obviously, anyone can speak their mind), liberty, religious freedom, human rights, inalienable rights, the right to a fair and speedy trial, the right to bear arms... (This last is for civil defense against anyone who should try to attack us on our soil. It's easy to see why our government considered this critical after the way *we* colonized this country – heaven forbid anyone should try to do to us what we did to the Native Americans). Surely a government which has codified such high values is superior. Although we may not always succeed, the story goes, at least it is the goal of this country to meet these ideals. (By the way, most of this applies to European countries as well, although I may specifically refer to the U.S.) If that were true, and we were working toward these ideals – or the higher of these ideals – we might have something; not superiority, but something. But it is not true.

Some people feel that right now we are taking a misstep in our pursuit of high values, but that, even though in recent times we've been derailed from this pursuit, overall our country is striving to meet the loftiest ideals ever pursued by any government. A few people feel we've never stepped off the righteous path, but most say they are willing to acknowledge we've stumbled and strayed. But regardless of the fact that many liberals feel we stumble when conservatives control our government, and many conservatives feel we stumble when liberals take control, in retrospect it's all painted as progress. For example, early on in his administration, George W. Bush passed the Patriot Act, which many people believed dealt an "unprecedented" (their word) and devastating backwards blow to all those high ideals they believe our government promotes and pursues. But in reality, there was nothing unprecedented in Bush's act. This is an important point.

There have been many, many times when our government has blocked public access to its activities, and many, many times when it has curtailed the rights of its citizens. But every time it happens, those citizens who disagree feel that it is unprecedented, because they don't really know our history, because our schools don't really teach our history. In fifty years, if this country still exists, the Patriot Act isn't going to be studied in history classes as a backward step in our pursuit of high ideals any more so than any other presidential abuse of authority is.

Throughout our past, people have always thought that *during their lifetimes* we were taking missteps, stumbling and straying. People have believed this for as long as we've been a country (and before that, when we were a colony). But, in retrospect, the activities of our government are always portrayed as forward progress working toward our high ideals. When you study history, even on the rare occasions when you hear about a misstep in our history, it is always underplayed: It was a hiccup which did not detract from our overall forward progress; we learned from the experience and moved on; we improved. Our present missteps will also be historicized as part of the unfaltering progress of this country, working toward lofty ideals – even though they really aren't. What it boils down to is this: Everyone knows our country is working toward high ideals (even though we aren't really), and so our history all gets repainted as progress toward lofty ideals. We aren't actually working toward any high ideals; we're just telling ourselves we are.

People are constantly fighting censorship issues, and the fact that those who argue against censorship sometimes win seems proof of progress. But how is it progress if the issue is being continuously revisited; if it's never really settled; if we've never actually progressed beyond the issue; if the issue has to be re-fought constantly? Why do censorship issues exist if our Constitution and written laws and high ideals are so valuable, and we are striving to meet those ideals?

Look at the issue of equal rights for women. Women don't earn as much as men for equal work, nor have equal opportunity as men, yet those who believe in equal rights still consider the U.S. at the forefront of equality for women. And we act like we invented the concept of equality for women, when the truth is actually the opposite: We invented inequality for women. Most indigenous societies, pre-European influence, had equality for women: Women had equal access to the same opportunities as men. Ours is the backward culture that stripped women of equal rights, yet we are supposedly striving to meet that ideal. We never seem to actually reach the goals toward which we claim to be striving.

Some people (usually older people) go back into our history to date the downfall of all that used to be right with America; they don't think it is an entirely recent phenomenon. For example, some conservatives think everything got shot to hell with the New Deal, though many of these think we got back on track when George W. Bush was in office, and I'm sure most cash their social security checks when they hit retirement age, even though those checks are courtesy of the New Deal that they curse. And some liberals think, for example, that the development of the military-industrial complex started us downhill. But even these people, both liberals and conservatives, look to a time in the past when the U.S. was a great, just, and free nation – and they *still* think the U.S. is a great, just, and free nation, full of just and honorable people – we've just been derailed from our forward progress temporarily.

How problems like the New Deal or the development of a military-industrial complex (and so many others) were able to take seed in as great a nation as people imagine the U.S. to have been is a mystery. Some chalk it up to selfishness and the blindness of human nature on the part of the other political party. It's interesting that indigenous peoples, as humans, had human nature, yet managed to avoid these types of problems.

Some might credit the development of problems to our having an open society (in our belief). By this, they mean that we encourage plurality of opinion, in the hope that, by having access to many views, we will make better decisions as a people. Sometimes we fail; no one's perfect; but at least we don't have one person dictating for all.

But as to the plurality of opinion we claim, it is an illusion; we keep telling ourselves we have plurality of opinion, so we believe it, but it isn't really there. It looks like plurality because we argue and disagree so much about so many things, but there is no truly significant difference voiced in all these disputes. All are culturally in agreement, which is an important point. If, while listening to a debate, you feel like you've heard it all before, it's because you have. The only difference in all of our disputes arises from which article of our culture one wants to attack, or which article one chooses to use to support their point of view. And look at the way our debates and disputes are usually conducted: They rarely involve people presenting thoughtful opinions and then listening to others speak, but instead usually involve people presenting superficial or self-serving opinions, sometimes at the same time someone else is talking. And the concept of arguing something out and of one side winning the right to impose its will on others is completely cultural.

By saying we have an open society, people also mean that citizens are free to speak their minds and even disagree with authority: We are not a police state.

I have never heard of any indigenous society (pre-PEOC-interference) which in any remote way resembled a police state, but I can think of quite a few police-state-like traits and actions in the U.S., past and present:

Note (again) all the police-state-like provisions of the Patriot Act. Think about Guantanamo Bay, where thousands of people are imprisoned and tortured without any rights at all. Note the number of times the FBI and other government agencies have spied on, intimidated, and killed U.S. citizens. Recall the forced internment of Americans (of Japanese heritage) during WWII. Recall that, at various times in the history of the U.S., our government has forcibly sterilized various and multiple groups (ethnic groups, disabled people, etc.).

Look at the use of prayer in public schools, at various times in our history, instituted by those who feel we cannot leave it up to parents what and how they teach their children about spirituality. I realize some people claim that having prayer in public schools is actually an indication of how *open* our society is, the thinking (i.e., rationale) being that kids get to learn about different religious beliefs (as though all religions can be understood through this shallow treatment). But the *actuality* is that something that should be allowed to be a very private matter is turned into a public spectacle or a subject in school; that children with unpopular religious beliefs are often ridiculed; and that the whole process is typically another way for Christians to try to convert non-Christians or to force their religion on them. Moreover, if, in one child's faith, it is wrong to speak the name of the Creator, then, obviously, that child's religious beliefs aren't being respected when the class prays to God.

The police-state traits run uninterruptedly through all the way to the beginnings of this country. Remember the burning of witches in Salem. Recall that many settlements, back at the beginning of this great nation, had laws forbidding colonizers from running away to live with the Indians.§ Then consider the fact that we *have* police, and the propensity of some officers to assault those who disagree with them. Consider the fact of racial profiling. Consider the fact that we even have an FBI and secret government agencies. We have a government which regularly harms its own citizens and disregards their inalienable rights, but it's a good thing we're not a police state, isn't it?

When people say we are not a police state, they are comparing us to other PEOC countries or to countries which have suffered PEOC interference. They are not comparing us to indigenous cultures. In the latter comparison, the fact that we are a police state would be readily apparent.

Notice that, throughout the history of this open society, for the U.S. government and its citizens, it was not enough to confine the Native Americans to reservations and leave them alone to live there as they chose. We went far beyond that, taking it upon ourselves to enforce on them how they should govern themselves, to decide for them who is and who is not Native, to tell them how they must live on their land, and to take away their children to be educated in PEOC schools.**

---

§ *Lies My Teacher Told Me*, selected bibliography.
** *Kill the Indian, Save the Man*, selected bibliography.

44

The point of all of this was to eliminate plurality, not to encourage it. The plurality we encourage is actually very limited and only looks like plurality to people who are not used to hearing truly differing views.

When the founders of our country declared, "all men are created equal," they were declaring *their* equality to British royalty, not the equality of people they considered inferior. In other words, they wanted to be at the top of the social strata, not subjects of Great Britain's king. People of African heritage, Native Americans, and other non-whites weren't equal to *them*. Women weren't even included in their statement. And we may have passed laws since then to rectify the oversights or mistakes of our founding fathers, but the laws have not rectified the oversights, because people of African heritage and Native Americans and women are still not equal to men of European heritage.

We are not a country striving to live up to great ideals. We are a country which spouts lofty ideals so that we can pretend we are good or so we can feel like we are at least trying to be good – moving in the direction of good. As long as we are moving in the direction of good, the country is on track, and we don't actually have to get any better, because we will always tell ourselves we are getting better, regardless.

We also think our judgment is the highest and the wisest. We think we are so enlightened that we can pass judgment on all other cultures (though we don't take the trouble to understand them) and tell them the right way to live. If they don't want to live our way, we can't understand it and often label them "ignorant" or "religious fanatics" or "communists" (even if they've never heard of

communism). We are so sure we've got it right –
in spite of all our many, many problems – that we
feel free to impose our will on others without having any idea of or caring about the consequences
of our actions. It is a cavalier attitude, similar to
the way we feel about our technology. In spite of
the fact that our judgments are always self-
serving, we feel we have the right to pass judgment on the entire world, as if we are the arbiters
of what is good and bad.

But PEOC culture always thinks itself superior
in *every* way. Look at PEOC religion. The Christians, who dominated and controlled Europe,
thought their religion was right and other peoples'
religions were wrong. When they invaded the
Americas, didn't they find people who believed in
and worshipped the Creator and lived their lives
in reverence? What more could God want? Yet the
Christians believed that these people were worshipping God in the wrong way, that there is only
one right way, and that God had sent God's one
true religion only to them, of all the peoples on the
planet. If Jesus were the one true way, why didn't
God send Jesus to the Americas and to Africa and
Australia: throughout the world?

Many people even believe our languages are
superior, much more developed and sophisticated
than the languages of indigenous peoples. They
think indigenes were able to communicate only in
the crudest terms ("I saw many buffalo – that way
– walk for two days until you see a lone peak").
They imagine indigenous communication to be
only slightly more complex than they imagine bee
communication to be ("Pollen – that way"). Some
PEOCs think the languages of indigenous peoples
did not have means of communicating profound

thoughts. However, even though indigenous peoples didn't waste their time with all the abstract theories our culture is so fond of inventing, they surely understood honor, liberty, decency, etc. PEOCs picture indigenous peoples as being where we think we were tens of thousands of years ago, but we painted that picture based on the fantasy of our culture.

We even think our art is superior. Take a course in art history (= PEOC art history) if you don't know how superior we think our art is. It is presented as one forward step after another, a continual progression: the introduction of weight shift, the incorporation of science, shading, chiaroscuro, perspective... abstract art, non-representational art, photography as art, performance art, environmental art, computer art, etc. We think our art has taken leaps and bounds where other cultures' arts are left in our dust: crude, inadequate representations that we left behind long ago. And if you think art is just a superficial attempt to adequately represent the world, rather than a deep, spiritual representation of something, maybe you are right. But if you think art is more than a game of doing something new and different, though always in a way that fits into this culture, then we are not so superior. And we may have developed all kinds of technology to create art (and we love all of our technology), but that doesn't make it superior either. Just because we have 20 tools to carve a wooden sculpture, that doesn't make it a better sculpture than one which has been carved by hand, using stone tools that the sculptor understood.

We think a piece of art is remarkable, perhaps because of the detail and accuracy, often simply because it was created by a famous artist, but it is just an object that appeals to us superficially. If you look at the meanings behind PEOC artwork, you will find they are culturally bound. Art for us is not a means toward meaning, nor a representation beyond what our culture has defined as meaningful. Much of the art you study in art history is just what some rich patron could pay for, and even though the artist may have introduced some new technique in the portrayal, it's still just a piece a rich person wanted; the new technique is not superiority. Much PEOC artwork is a glorification of Christianity, as in the hundreds of pietas you see (these are also pieces a rich person paid for: the pope, or a cardinal...), but these, too, are interested in representation, not spiritual depth. The majority of PEOC artists were (and still are) part of movements, like the incredibly grandiose baroque (where did all that gold come from? – it is a fair question, because if we have to destroy in order to create art, then it isn't very superior, is it?).

Like everything else in our culture, we automatically make the connection that what we have done is superior. We do not understand the art of others, so it's a wild leap that ours is superior, but we have no trouble making that leap. An archaeologist may say, "This figure is supposed to represent a bear, and it was used in religious ceremonies," and people think they understand it now and that artists in our culture are capable of much better bear representations – and since we are very superficial, we think that superior. Or, if someone in our culture does an abstract representation of a bear, we think it superior, not because it looks more like a bear, but because the artist put something of himself or herself into the representation, thereby saying more than a simple representation would say. Either way, we endow our culture's artwork with more value. To us, their art gains its value as artifact, not as art.

So it goes with each step in the stairway which places PEOCs at the pinnacle of civilization as the most superior ever.

Pre-Columbian Native Americans, pre-colonization Africans, and other indigenous peoples did not have our superior health care system; they just had superior health. And they had a physical fitness and endurance that people today wouldn't believe possible and which would shame our Olympic gold medalists. Your body's not supposed to start failing in your 40's and go downhill from there – we just believe that, because it's how *our* health is. While it's true that many Native Americans and other indigenous people died from the many diseases PEOCs imported to them, this is because they had never lived in the kinds of unhealthful environments in which such diseases developed. The unnatural conditions of PEOC culture create physical as well as social diseases, and PEOCs were happy to pass them all along to other peoples.

The failings of pre-Columbian Native American and other indigenous cultures have been written up ad infinitum, only rarely on the bases of truth; usually in fictionalized versions meant to reinforce how superior the PEOC way of life is. The American Natives may not have been perfect (whatever that means), but they had a deep spirituality and reverence for life, so that they cannot remotely be compared to PEOCs in terms of destruction to the planet, devastation to its life and peoples, and straying from truth. We like to say that no culture is perfect because it allows us to tell ourselves that the atrocities we commit have been committed by every culture that ever was. But to say that their cultures were not perfect, either, and so our culture is basically equivalent to theirs, since there is no perfect in humanity, is exactly like excusing every atrocity we ever have, currently are, or will in the future commit. The level of our brutality and destruction was not possible in indigenous cultures, not even conceivable; and our brutality and destruction are not the results of our being more advanced. Sadly, we have done nothing to make the Earth a better place. More sadly, if we wanted to do so, we would not even know how.

If there were an alien life form observing our planet, they would undoubtedly have determined that the most advanced peoples on Earth had been destroyed by the most savage and barbaric. Our culture holds no actual superiority – the only thing to indicate superiority in PEOC culture is our own abstract thinking, born of a culture which thinks it is superior, telling itself that, in fact, it is. There is no real superiority, and a look at the actual cultures and their effects shows that indigenous cultures hold more of the qualities that we consider positive than we do. In other words, their cultures surpass ours even by our standards.

For example, in comparison to pre-Columbian Native Americans, those things that we consider negative are rampant in our society but were absent or rare in theirs. We say we deplore genocide, pedophilia, incest, domestic violence, greed, poverty, hunger, murder, theft, etc. Yet they are a daily part of life in our culture and were pretty much unheard of in theirs. But these problems are *caused* by our culture. For example, the Earth can easily provide enough food for every person on the planet. It is only because of PEOC culture that so many go hungry, because of our "improvements" to the Earth which destroy and pollute so much land and water, and because we have made food into a commodity which some people can own and others cannot afford to buy.

On the other side, we say we consider peacefulness, understanding of the physical world, honesty, integrity, generosity, wisdom, etc. to be positives, but they were much more prevalent and well-developed in the Native American cultures than in ours. For example, we say we love peace, yet somehow we manage to be constantly at war; until PEOCs came, Native Americans managed to be almost constantly at peace. For them, wars were very rare and not nearly as bloody and brutal as ours. Their wars were primarily non-lethal ways to settle disputes: They did not seek to destroy and crush their opponents. PEOCs, on the other hand, are not simply waging war when we wage war: We are not satisfied until the other side has been ground into a fine powder, until they agree to forsake their selves and become what we want them to be, until every ounce of self-respect and self-worth has been wiped from their hearts, until they are annihilated. We think this proves our power and superiority, but all it really shows is our brutality and contempt for others, our complete lack of respect, and our complete lack of understanding or compassion. For us, war is just a tool of domination. Thus, when George W. Bush started his war against Iraq by strategically destroying much of their country and slaughtering the people, he had the gall to call it a "shock and awe" campaign, rather than a "repulsive and repugnant" campaign which disregards all decency. And the people of the U.S. jumped right on board. That is the honor of PEOCs.

We say we value understanding of the natural world, yet we constantly develop technology which produces unintended and unforeseen negative consequences on this world. Native Americans, with their better understanding of the Earth and the interrelatedness of all things, would clearly have foreseen the consequences of our technology.

The pre-Columbian Natives (and other indigenous peoples of the world) rank higher by the standards we claim to embrace, yet we feel we are superior – and, interestingly, indigenous peoples didn't have that feeling of superiority we claim for ourselves. It's unfortunate that we place so much value in ourselves and in our culture, based on the belief that we are advanced and knowledgeable and superior. As you will see in the pages that follow, we are not as advanced and knowledgeable as we think we are. And maybe we were not so fortunate to have been born into this culture.

Knowledge

Science

Science is this culture's co-existing religion. Even those who disagree with some aspect of science (for example, the theory of evolution), still believe in the rest of it: chemistry, astronomy, physics, etc. And some who disagree with evolution have used science to prove creationism – thereby proving only science's hold over their thinking. Mainstream science may not approve of the scientific theory of creationism, but to me it's pretty irrelevant what they want to prove scientifically – a theory scientifically proven is still not truth. Science can be used to prove anything under the sun, and that is how science has been used over the years. The scientists of eugenics were able to brilliantly prove that Aryans were superior to Jews, people of African heritage, gypsies, and everyone else non-Aryan and that these people were sub-human.* This proof, in turn, was used to justify genocide during World War II (though, to be fair to science, anything will do to justify genocide for PEOC culture; they don't need a scientific basis to engage in the destruction of a people, and they were committing genocide long before science was invented).

Scientists claim for themselves the honor of being the searchers of truth and human knowledge. They imagine they are objective (whatever

---

* Though no longer accepted as "real science," at *that* time the field of eugenics was practiced by scientists in many PEOC countries.

that means) seekers; that they alone are moving, not just this culture, but all of humanity, closer and closer to ultimate knowledge of everything – and that this knowledge can be gotten only through science. Our culture considers them amongst the most brilliant people, and we develop I.Q. tests on which scientists will do well to prove they are smart. Obviously, this is circular reasoning (in a culture full of circular reasoning). The whole PEOC concept of intelligence is severely flawed; it is a meaningless measurement (in a culture full of meaningless measurements).

I had a teacher once who drew an inward-moving spiral to illustrate scientific knowledge, indicating that it is getting closer and closer to the truth, which lies at the center. A more accurate representation would have been a series of random points on a plane; meanwhile truth is out here in a third dimension. Science is not accumulative and does not lead to knowledge, and scientists are not brilliant thinkers leading humanity to truth.

The scientific method is: Step 1, Observe and describe; Step 2, Formulate hypothesis; Step 3, Use hypothesis to predict; Step 4, Perform tests to confirm predictions. The reasoning embodied by this method, the steps, and the results of science are all unsound. Let's look:

Scientists think they can isolate something and study just *that* thing to reach a theory or universal law about *that* thing – but they aren't taking into account all the other things or the entirety of *that* thing – or they are taking into account only what they consider relevant. But they do not understand and are culturally bound from understanding what is relevant. When they observe and describe, they are observing only what they consider pertinent, and when they perform scientific experiments, the point of their tests is to look at *that* thing, without the clutter of all the other things. Let's say a scientist performs an experiment, tweaks their hypothesis, and then performs a second experiment to confirm the findings of the first. –It is as though the scientist doesn't realize that time has passed between the first experiment and the second, with an infinite number of changes occurring in that time – as though the scientist doesn't realize that all those changes affect *that* thing, and hence the experiment. But all those changes do affect *that* thing, because *everything* is interrelated.

In other words, they think they are setting up carefully-controlled experiments, with all of the relevant factors carefully regulated, and they don't understand that this is an impossibility, because they can't control everything, and everything's relevant. Apparently they think the fact that no instant repeats itself is irrelevant – or do they even realize? They don't get it; they think you can isolate something to study it; but you cannot isolate something – not even if you study it in isolation. They say, "I'm just interested in *this* right now," but does *this* know that it's suddenly not supposed to be interrelated? "But," says the scientist, "that's the point. I'm interested in how *this* acts, regardless of what else is happening, regardless of other variables: That is how we discover our universal laws; that is how we discover the natural characteristics of a thing." But they are not discovering universal laws, natural characteristics, or anything else, because everything is interrelated, and they don't see it. They don't see that they aren't observing the same *that* or *this* in each of these experiments. They look at only what they consider relevant, rather than looking at everything. Indeed, scientists might say, "You can't measure *everything*" – they might as well say, "You can't measure *anything*," because it's all one.

Does anyone believe that indigenous people never observed a rock thrown into the air? That they never saw a rock thrown into the air fall back down? That they could not see that if a rock and a feather fall back down, they fall differently? That two rocks, if they come down, will fall differently? That one rock thrown twenty times will come back differently twenty times? A scientist might now be thinking, "So you're saying they were aware of gravity but were not advanced enough to come up with a theory to explain and predict the phenomenon. We scientists have been saying that all along." But this is not what I am saying.

Obviously, indigenous people knew that a rock thrown into the air may fall back to the ground, but they didn't feel the need to develop a theory about it, trying to detail each possible factor and contingency and then to name what they had just invented ("gravity"). They knew it in each instance, not as a theory. They just saw what was *there*, not a theory about what was there. This is one reason all scientific theories miss the truth and reality and keep needing to be adjusted or expanded: They are theories trying to universalize an instant to an eternal phenomenon. A theory can never detail everything – and everything is relevant, because it's all interrelated. Is seeing a sculpture of a child the same as seeing the child? The sculpture does not even fully reflect a moment, let alone the life of the child.

By trying to duplicate results and in expecting to duplicate results, you blind and deaden yourself to experiencing the reality. You think you already know what is going to happen, so you don't see it when the rock does not fall back down – which happens –or you fix the theory – but it's not fixed. And if the rock does fall, it is not because of gravity. People in our culture mistake the fact of the rock falling with the "fact" (= theory) of gravity, because this is how we are trained to view it, not because it's true.

I saw a magazine that had been littered on the ground, opened to an ad which called classic physics, "the user's guide to the universe." The arrogance here is self-evident, especially when you know that scientists realize their theories are full of holes. Sadly, classic physics is nothing more than a tired way of looking at the world, which will never lead to any truth. And some scientists who have realized this have developed what they consider to be a new paradigm, thinking that, for example, string theory or chaos theory or some other theory of the new paradigm (= the old paradigm) will get them closer to truth than classic physics, will plug some of those gaping holes which riddle their theories. What these scientists should take a moment to consider is this: The scientists of the past once held the same optimism about classic physics, once fervently believed that they were heir to a paradigm shift which would open for them every secret the universe had to offer.

Gravity and other natural laws are culture-specific phenomena, just like human nature; they are not universal laws. They apply only to those who do not see reality. Indigenous peoples of the world know this. They do and see things outside of our natural laws all the time. Shape shifting is a classic example. This is practiced by indigenous peoples I know of on two continents (and no doubt by many other cultures around the world). It is scientifically impossible according to the immutable laws of physics, and therefore cannot be done; and yet, people do it. Yet science holds that it does not happen because it is scientifically impossible. So people in our culture believe it does not happen – even though it *does* happen. PEOCs don't believe what is not a part of our culture, and shape shifting is not a part of our culture. If someone in our culture *does* hear about shape shifting, they assume it's just a myth, or that the people relating the story are too stupid to know what they saw, or someone fooled them, or they had a hallucination...

If I see a bird and say, "I am one entity, and that bird is a separate entity," then I am correct, and this culture can understand that. But if I see a bird and say, "I am the same entity as that bird," I am also correct, and this culture cannot understand. It is scientifically impossible, but it is reality.

Say you prepare a recipe that you have made many times before, and you expect it to taste the way it has always tasted. In this way, you do not see that every time – even every bite – it is a different taste. It's a way of training yourself not to taste (or, in the shape shifting example, not to see what is there), because you think you already know. It also serves to eliminate the possibilities of what could be: You may fail to realize that adding a little corn to this recipe will make it taste even better. (Or, in the shape shifting example, if you think it is humanly impossible for someone to change their form, you will never be able to do it – but that doesn't make it impossible.)

Someone may say, "But you cannot make the same recipe exactly the same way twice, and you'll never have exactly the same ingredients," which is true, but it is true in *everything*. You cannot duplicate results because you cannot duplicate events. And the scientist may say, "You may not be able to duplicate results exactly, but you can come pretty close and build theories on that," which, even if true (it's not, by the way), why would you want to? How is that helpful in finding reality? It isn't – it is helpful in building theories about reality.

"But we can create a theory which will give us the tools to react next time in a *similar* situation," the scientist might say. But if they tried to understand the next time – the situation, or event, or whatever – for what it is, they wouldn't need or want a theory clouding their vision. It's all just more circular reasoning in a culture which cannot escape circular reasoning, because you are starting from within the culture, and the rules are that you are not allowed to leave the culture to reach your destination; if it is outside the culture, you will never arrive. Science is very much a part of our culture. There's no such thing as "survival of the fittest," unless you define everything that survives as "the fittest," in which case you have said nothing; you have just jumped aboard the perpetually spinning wheel which is the circularity of PEOC logic.

"Sorry," someone says, "if I've got a kid trapped down a well, I'm going to want to know the best way to get him out, and that's going to include looking at past situations where we've had a kid down a well and the science to help in this particular situation." In the first place, a lot of the techniques that worked in the past don't work in this situation, and trying them just ends up wasting time. In the second place, if you don't try looking at the situation in a fresh light and without science, then it's easy to dismiss as impossible that which you've never tried. We are so indoctrinated into our culture that we cannot imagine someone who can react solely to a situation. We think all the baggage that science gives us helps us, but if we didn't have science clouding our vision, we would be better off. Here science is just acting as a crutch to hold on to, not a better way of getting the kid out of the well.

I heard someone say that humans *have* to pick and choose which data they process, that we would suffer sensory overload if we were aware of everything, that tunnel vision is a necessary part of living. But this is just our culture again telling our culture that the way we live is not only the natural way; it's the only possible way humans are capable of living.

Some may say I do not understand the complexities of science, but I understand them without the blindness of my culture. Albert Einstein was no more the greatest thinker of our time than my neighbor's kitchen table is. He may have taken science from one point on the plane to another, but he wasn't able to see the essential defects in science, which would have told him not to waste his time moving it around on a plane. (Short note, for those who don't already know, though it is old news: all of Einstein's theories, including his highly-acclaimed theory of relativity, have been discovered by scientists to be flawed and incomplete – no surprise there.) I understand the complexity of science. That is what science is: complex, abstract thought; not reality, nor a mirror, nor a description of reality. And why would you want to look at a mirror of reality or listen to a description of reality anyway, when you can just look at reality and skip the middle-man?

"But if science isn't real," a layman asks, "how can it give us technology?" The answer is, because you *can* look at something with tunnel vision, not to truly understand it, but to develop a theory. And then you can test that theory with tunnel vision. The theory doesn't have to be 100% accurate; it can be tweaked later, and you can ignore the aberrant data (science *always* has aberrant data). Voila, you now have a scientific fact to use in building technology. A bridge may collapse, or a foundation may crumble, but not always, and there's always some circular reasoning to explain these cases (and there are *many* cases, though not all are so obviously life-threatening). And if the bridge doesn't collapse, that doesn't mean that the science used to build it is true – science just takes that credit. I could, using the scientific method, invent my own series of scientific facts to use in building a bridge – just because it held, that would not prove my facts were true. The point here is that, though scientists would have you believe they are objectively analyzing evidence and reaching the only logical conclusion one can reach, this is not the case at all. The evidence could be interpreted in any number of ways logically – and all those ways would be wrong, because they are all interpretations, not reality. And since the facts used to build technology are derived using tunnel vision and ignoring the interrelatedness, there are *always* a myriad of unexpected, unintended, unforeseen consequences, which end up causing more harm than the technology was worth – but we don't see that, either, because we are conditioned to think: new technology = good. We ignore the negative consequences or build some new technology to deal with them and cause another whole new set of problems.

Moreover, what science and technology have given us is only good to live in this society and to someone indoctrinated into this culture. Technology which we consider good (never mind the negative consequences, for now), others would not even see a good side to. If you were to bring a Native American from 500 years ago into the present, I am sure he or she would not look around and say, "This is way better than the way we lived, wasting the land by just living on it, learning from it, and caring for it. What simpletons we were. With a little ingenuity, we could have erected giant buildings and paved the land; we could have damned the rivers and channeled the waters, taking those waters from the plants and animals who share our planet. We could have tamed electricity and had TVs to stare at for hours on end – what fools we were! We could have completely isolated ourselves from our Mother and our Father and spent our time living in artificial, dreary, dirty environments, indulging ourselves at the expense of the Earth and her children, blinding ourselves to reality. If we had only known..." Rather, they would say, with deep sadness, "They are destroying the planet in their selfishness for self-comfort. These people are blind and never look at where they are going or where they have been. They don't know where they are headed but are in a rush to get there... We are very lucky we did not have such an insane culture."

A car is only of value, "good," if your objective is to get from point A to point B as quickly as possible, with no interest in what lies between – such as for someone driving from their home to work and back, who just wants to get the commute over with. Without a society set up on the idea of hurrying from one place to another, this use becomes worse than meaningless; worse because, with the car comes the continuous need for gasoline and all the smog. I have so much pity for the plants, especially those living by major roadsides and freeways. If they are lucky, in the middle of the night they may have a few minutes without the constant noise and vibration of passing vehicles. And they are coated by each passing vehicle with a little more pollution. The rain and wind give the plants a chance to clean off a little, but the wind and rain are not able to clean the ever-increasing layers of smog covering our cities.

A microwave oven is only of value if your objective is to heat up food as quickly as possible, with no interest in the food itself, the quality of the food, nor the act of preparation. People are so far removed from this basic need that they only remotely realize that plants and animals gave their lives for our food. –Let alone do they think of thanking these plants and animals for another day of life. Most of the time, people don't really pay attention while they eat, anyway – they just wolf it down or eat while taking care of "real" matters.

Another problem with science is that scientists act like their field is holy and like anything they do will lead to more knowledge – hence progress, for the greater good of humankind – and so they will do anything, without conscience. Play with the genetic code (another fiction of science) – no problem, we're finding truth. Torture animals in laboratories – it's all for the greater good of humankind. Except it's not for the greater good of humankind; it's for the greater egos of the scientists and the greater wealth of those who control the science.

J. Robert Oppenheimer helped to develop the atom bomb and then decided that nuclear weapons development was a bad thing and that he should protest his own work – what typical scientific blindness. And do other scientists heed? –No, they also want to make their names in the field – then perhaps they will protest against the work they have done. If you think of Oppenheimer as a genius/martyr/hero, rethink of him as shortsighted, self-interested, and oblivious, and you will have a better picture.

Then look at the field of health, fed by the sciences of anatomy, biology, chemistry, and so on. With their knowledge, indigenous peoples were far healthier than PEOCs today, and the medicines and practices they used were far more effective and less harmful than PEOC medicines and practices. PEOC doctors take an authoritative stand, but, when something goes wrong, say, "Well, it's not exact." Why isn't it exact, since it has so many sciences backing it up? Could it be that anatomy, biology, and chemistry are not exact? Could it be that the cure for cancer is not waiting to be found; it is just waiting to be found scientifically? After forty-plus years of research and billions of dollars in donations, science still isn't able to do what many shamen can do.

Someone from a developing country told me of his friend with cancer. His friend went to a PEOC hospital, and they cut off part of his body. The cancer came back, he went to the hospital again, and they cut off some more. The cancer returned yet again, and another trip to the hospital led to the loss of more of his body, but not to an end to his cancer. The next time it returned, he went to a traditional healer in his country. The healer cured the cancer without cutting anything off, and that's the end of the story.

Science has categorized, this, that, and the other as spinal cord injuries, from which recovery is virtually impossible. What this means is that 99.9% of people living in a culture which long ago lost the knowledge to heal, when told they will never walk again, will never walk again. And that other .1% is the exception: miraculous. Here's the catch: If it weren't for that scientific fact that people cannot recover from spinal cord injuries and the blindness of our culture to other methods of healing, the ratios could be reversed.

Science believes it has to hurt or kill a thing to fully understand it. Take a species of plant, grow several under different conditions, cut off an arm, pull off some leaves, put it all under a microscope... Would someone understand you better if they cut off your arm and dissected it? (It's telling that the Native Americans were able to come up with so many plant remedies without ever dissecting anything.)

And then scientists have to categorize it – whatever "it" is. They categorize everything: rocks, animals, plants, the leaves on the plants, the parts of the leaves on the plants... They have to put things into categories to understand them; nothing can ever just be what it is. For every plant and animal, scientists feel a need to assign a "family," a "genus," a "species," an "order," and a "class"; plants also get a "division" and a "subclass"; animals also get a "phylum" and a "subphylum." Of course, this classification, taxonomy, is a hierarchical classification, and humans are at the top. We love hierarchies – they make us feel so superior, though they do nothing to aid in true understanding. There are no natural categories, and, by using them, scientists exclude information.

How many schoolchildren have had scientific categories – for plants, rocks, whatever – laid out for them and then been told to find some things to put into those categories, only to find that things have to be forced to fit?

Once they have categorized something, scientists attach an official, scientific name; if you're a lucky scientist who discovered a new species (kind of like Columbus discovered America, even though there were already millions of people living here), you get to name it after yourself – but scientifically, of course.

Yet for all their cutting and examining and sorting and naming, scientists do not understand the plants and the animals and the rocks. Scientists believe plants (and "lower" animals) cannot feel emotions, because, according to science, it is our brains which give us emotions: Plants do not have our brains; therefore, they cannot feel emotions. This is how poorly they understand the plants after cutting off their branches and tearing off their leaves. Their reasoning is faulty on multiple levels, but you can see that it is based on the same man-as-top-of-the-evolutionary-chain that controls all scientific thinking. More importantly, their fact is wrong, because plants can feel emotions. Not that it would matter to scientists if they suddenly realized that plants can feel physical pain and emotions. They have granted certain animals the ability to feel physical pain, and a select few the ability to feel emotions, but it doesn't stop them from torturing these animals in scientific experiments. The truth: Torturing an animal – or a plant – would not be okay, even if it did lead to truth or knowledge

– which it never does and *obviously* never can – but their tunnel vision prevents them from seeing the obvious.

Science leads up one blind alley after another, and that's the only place it can lead, because the very basis, the scientific method, is flawed. The scientific method assumes non-uniqueness, but each moment is unique. Here's an obvious example: Go stand somewhere for an hour, say on a busy street corner. The cars pass, but you'll never see them all in exactly the same position twice. Even if, miraculously, you did see them in the exact same position, the cars would have changed: Their odometers would have different readings; their tires would be a little more worn down. And the drivers would be different, having eaten or gone to the restroom, with their hair tousled or straightened... The plants on the street corner would not be the same; the air would not be the same; you would not be the same. And it's all interrelated. So the world is always changing; no moment is ever repeated.

If scientists actually looked at the world, they would realize this and realize that the scientific method is nonsense. They think it doesn't matter that some things are different because they think that some things are insignificant or are not relevant and don't affect their observations and findings, but that is their blindness, not reality. They're too busy in their minds – analyzing what they are observing and formulating hypotheses – to even pay attention to and truly look at what they're supposed to be observing anyway. It's odd, because you even hear some scientists say, "If a butterfly flaps its wings in China, it affects things on the other side of the world" – and still they don't get it. They are blinded into thinking science can give them answers, even when it is (or should be) obvious science can't. They think they can ignore the butterfly. To be fair, this blindness is not specific to science; it is how everything in our culture works: Locking people up in prisons doesn't fix the problem of crime, but we keep doing it. We refuse to see the obvious because we have a giant façade telling us we're doing things right, we're getting better and better – or closer and closer to truth – we are always advancing. –And any evidence to the contrary is disregarded. Science only thinks it's getting closer and closer to the truth because it tells itself it is.

If a scientist really wanted to understand, it would take many longs years of looking, to see that butterfly and its relationship to everything else; if the scientist actually undertook that kind of understanding, they'd drop out of science.

You can't observe and describe a phenomenon when you are culturally blinded as to what you are looking at – so the first step of the scientific method is like saying, "Start with a false foundation, and build upon it in steps two through four." The reasoning behind using a scientific method to understand is faulty; if scientists really could see that which they are attempting to observe and describe in step one, they would see that there is no next step. But they don't want to take that long journey: They got their degree; they know how it works, and they want to jump right in and make their names and make money. Besides, the field of science and their culture are telling them that they are pursuing knowledge in the right way, the only way true knowledge can be found.

Science starts with the premise, derived from PEOC culture, that humans are the highest species and that PEOC culture is superior to all others (and why wouldn't it be – it spawned science), and then it uses those bases to prove that humans are the highest species and that PEOC culture is superior. It's circular reasoning, but that's standard for all PEOC fields: philosophy, anthropology, mathematics, etc. Members of a field will call each other on *their* circularity and countless other reasoning faults, but they are all so arrogant as to think they can escape the same flaws, and they do not see that they cannot succeed. For example, someone figures out that mathematical proofs are fallacious – but instead of stopping there, he builds a whole new theory around his discovery. Go figure – think his theory is fallacious, maybe?

Science sees accumulation of knowledge as advancement towards truth but does not see it is not accumulative. This most intelligent segment of our society obviously is not taught the history of their field during their studies; and why would they be, since only the current thinking is relevant to build upon? A five-year-old science text is obsolete. And, more importantly, if they were taught the history of their field, some might realize that it has no progress or cumulative knowledge. These brilliant minds are entirely limited by their field, imagining themselves to be making great strides in human knowledge, while they are only groping in the dark, fumbling blindly, kind of like rats finding their way in a maze.

To summarize:

1. Science erroneously claims for itself and our culture a hegemony on knowledge. According to scientists, since indigenous cultures do not have

science, their knowledge is superstition. Truth is something only the super smart can seek to find and understand through science; scientists can then dummy it down for the rest of us so that we can "kind of" see.

2. Science believes it is getting closer and closer to some ultimate understanding as theories become more and more complex, but the complexity is actually just more and more clutter obscuring truth.

3. I could come up with alternate theories or facts for all our current scientific facts, and mine would be just as believable to people in this culture. My theories wouldn't be 100% accurate (no theories are): There is always aberrant data in science, which may cause scientists to patch their theory, or which scientists may choose to ignore (or which they may not even see). I could come up with alternate theories – but my theories would not be any more true than theirs are, so why would I want to waste all that time?

4. The nature of scientific questioning ("What would happen if I mixed this with that?") limits the mind of the scientist, closes off possibilities, and channels observation into a tunnel vision which excludes much of what there is to see.

5. What it all comes down to is that the natural laws of science are nothing, mean nothing. They do not exist except in the minds of those whose minds they occupy.

6. Scientists have certainly done their part in our culture to make this incredibly beautiful, marvelous, and limitless world we live in seem dull and mundane.

7. Finally, what science has to offer is what every other part of our culture has to offer: rationalization and support for the domination of others, through

our proven superiority (we are superior in part because we have science; our superiority allowed us to develop it) which lets us tell ourselves it is okay to dominate other peoples; and through the weapons of destruction developed by science, with which we subjugate others.

*   *   *

I do not give science credit as the cause of the problems with our culture. I think PEOC culture had already strayed very far from truth long before science came along, and this is why science was able to come along.

PEOCs, through science and technology, will surely not destroy the Earth, which is far more powerful than we realize. But we will make it unlivable for many of its inhabitants. How many are already dead because they could not survive in the world we've created? We are on a path which is destroying life – and what right do we have to do that to the plants and the sun and the moon and water and winds...? We may not know we're interrelated, but they do. Still yet, the Earth will survive, long after we have destroyed people and killed so many of Earth's other children.

Maybe you realize the destruction of our culture and of science and technology, but, paradoxically, at the same time, you think that science has given us a new awareness today of what we are doing to the planet. The problem is that this new awareness has been around for a long, long time, and it hasn't changed our course of destruction. The concept that we are destroying the planet is not new, and science hasn't helped and isn't helping to solve the problems we have created, nor is it capable of helping to solve the problems we have created. Science is a hindrance, because it causes destruction but, at the same time, makes people believe we understand and that something is being done, that the problems are being researched – but this research just causes further destruction. Whatever the problem being envisioned, a hole in the ozone layer or global warming, those who have faith in science look to the same kind of minds who got us into this mess to get us out.

Science is an anchor, keeping people tied to the culture. From within our culture, it *seems* to have given us so much knowledge, so much information about the workings of the universe, that people cling to it, because it *seems* to provide answers for so much, and we know of no substitute to give us those answers. But science is a part of the culture: It *keeps* us from looking at truth; it doesn't help us to see. It is part and parcel of our culture; as long as we cling to it, we are anchored to the culture which destroys.

The civilizations of indigenous peoples could perhaps have lasted for hundreds of thousands of years, but clearly PEOC civilization will burn itself out quite a bit sooner. Why do the abused plants and animals hold on? Are they comforting their Mother? Are they thinking of the time, in a few thousand years, when PEOC culture has culminated its destruction with self-destruction, and the Earth will take as much time as she needs to take to reclaim herself; to crumble the cities and pavements so she can breathe; to burst the dams so her blood can flow freely; to restore wisdom to life so she and her children can know peace; to clean the toxic pollution and all the devastation imposed by science and technology…?

PEOCs do not know their Mother.

Theories

Excerpt from a real theory (from Richard McKeon):

> The use of the common-places of creativity erects and fills the commonplace as a store-house of the familiar to provide materials for commonplaces [yawn] as instruments for the perception, creation, arrangement, and establishment of the new in existence, experience, discursive exploration, and inclusive organization [z z z z z].[†]

A lot of people read that and think it means something profound.

My version of a theory:

> Let us postulate that there is no such thing as order, only disorder.[1] Where does that take us?

> [1]By doing so, we rob the term of its polarization, but let us assume that it still has a

---

[†] From his essay, "Creativity and the Commonplace." See, e.g., *Rhetoric: Essays in Invention and Discovery*, Richard McKeon; Mark Backman, editor. Ox Box Press: Woodbridge, CT. 1987.

sense in that we can, for the moment, take it as a grounding (basis, foundation, ultimate beginning… whatever you will) for the universe [yawn] (inherent in this assumption is the possible conflict… which we will address presently [i.e., after 100 more pages of this drivel] by appropriately manipulating our language)… [z z z z z].
See, I can do it, too, but *I* know its b.s.

The way this game works is that someone comes out with an admittedly (at least, I admit it) nonsensical theory, which others in their field either find intriguing and build upon, or which they immediately attack and point out the flaws in, proffering their own theories in their turn. Either way, it always turns out that the original theory was flawed, though it may take them years or decades to realize it.

Day-in, day-out, scholars publish ideas, tracts, and treatises, "putting it out there" in the hopes that the academic community is learning something and PEOC society is becoming enriched. We have hundreds of periodicals whose only purpose is to print these theories. This is all done in the name of scholarly discussion, and the illusion is that it is leading to knowledge and to a better understanding in our fields of study. Nevertheless, they all dish out loads of criticism on each other, the point of this apparently being (similar to political campaigning) as much to show up the opponent as to make yourself look good (perhaps because they know their own theories won't hold water, either).

If you have the misfortune to read enough of this stuff, you'll find that many theories (in philosophy, rhetoric, sociology, and so on) have one idea in common: We do not know reality; we are shielded from knowing reality, by our language, by our mental constructs, by our lack of self knowledge, etc. For many, this is accompanied by the belief that we *cannot* know reality. Though in our culture this may be the case, the limits of our culture should not be mistaken for the limits of all cultures (though, by our culture, they usually are).

Our culture is so in love with its abstract thought and theories that it never even nudges reality. From this perspective, there is some irony: We think we are superior to other cultures because we engage in so much abstract thinking and have a massive body of abstract theories, but meanwhile these have been blinding us the whole time to the reality that they claim to be seeking and that other cultures are capable of seeing.

Sometimes people see a hole in the fabric, but instead of tearing away the material to see what's behind, they come up with another theory; they patch that hole with another piece of fabric. That is the way of our culture.

One point of all of our mental contortionism in abstract thinking is to reinforce the feeling of PEOC superiority (we don't just have language; we have theories about it, etc.). Since we have more theories than other cultures, we must have more knowledge than other cultures. The intellectuals and great minds who come up with the theories think they are on a higher quest, seeking human knowledge at all costs and in ways other cultures would never think of (which is true, because people of other cultures realize that these methods will never lead to true knowledge; our great minds don't see that).

We think that because we have more theories searching for knowledge, and we are ahead of all other cultures in this search, then anything we've done (or our culture or civilization has done), such as, say, commit genocide, is trivialized: Our great minds are engaged in the pursuit of knowledge, the highest pursuit of humankind. Hence, the world is a better place because of us (and our culture); our presence has a *net* positive effect on the world – and on all other cultures, who (after having been destroyed by us) can learn so much from the enlightened PEOCs.

Intelligence

In PEOC culture, we have the idea that the more evolved and advanced humans become, the more intellectual they become, the more they live in their minds, solving complex problems, rather than living in and as part of the world, with their thinking turned off. For example, we think we understand nature better than indigenous peoples because we think about it and collect data about it and build theories about it rather than simply live as part of it.

We believe those who spend much of their time in abstract thought about abstract concepts, creating more abstractions and inventing abstract theories about the abstractions, are the most brilliant, intelligent people, and we say this as a form of praise, as though it is valuable to be this way, something worth striving for. We think that the more time people spend thinking, the more advanced they are. In our culture, we see no value in turning off the thinking mind sometimes, *experiencing* the world, and letting reality inform our thought and give it a grounding, because we believe truth is to be found in abstract thought. This is what we believe, but all this belief is backwards; it's just the belief of our culture, not the truth. Since we are lost in our minds, out of touch with reality, and separated from nature, we think that humans are more advanced and evolved when they are lost in their minds, out of touch with reality, and separated from nature. We do not see that "intelligence" is just living in the mind, separated from truth, something we have come to praise only because it is a part of our culture rather than because of any real value.

Moreover, the whole idea of intelligence implies superiority (and, obviously, we give our culture credit as having the most intelligent people), because, if some people are smarter, that means some are stupider – and, hence, are inferior. No wonder our culture embraces this concept.

If you believe in God, consider: What Creator would create a world in which only some, those the Creator has gifted with intelligence, can seek to understand truth? Why would God want to keep some in the dark? It's true that in every indigenous culture I know of, some people were prized for their wisdom, but this wisdom was gained through years of seeking and learning and through a lifelong devotion to understanding the Creator's vision, not through some innate gift the Creator had decided to give to some people and to withhold from others.

There are some things you can't *think* yourself into understanding, that you can't *think* through, things you can only understand at a fundamental level that our culture would deride as superstition – but it's not superstition; it's truth. We have this idea that you should be able to prove something if it's true, but this is our culture's limitation on knowledge. You can prove anything you want, but you can't prove truth.

Thinking about living is not superior to living. Most people in our culture have a constant stream of thoughts running through their minds – while they are eating, while they are showering, while they are driving... – their own thoughts (what they have to do, what they wish they could be doing), the thoughts coming off the TV screen, their reaction to the thoughts they are reading off the page. Some can't quiet the stream long enough to listen to someone else; as soon as that other person starts talking, they start interpreting what that person is saying through their own thoughts. Some can't quiet the stream when they are trying to go to sleep. Most people have trouble turning the noise in their minds completely off. We have a whole culture of people who cannot react to the present, cannot even see it, because they are too busy living in their minds to connect with reality. And we think this is a sign of superiority, but it's just our thinking that tells us that.

Working on Solving a Problem...

...but never solving it.

In our culture, we like to think all the problems of society are complex and must be worked on by experts. And those who wish to address our society's problems and effect change start from what our culture says is square one: study and define. Studying and defining a problem have never lead to solving a problem, but anyone who wants to solve a problem in our culture automatically starts with "study" and "define," because that's what you must do to solve a problem in our culture's thinking. And then people can spend years and decades and centuries arguing about each others' definitions and criticizing each others' studies and theories, while the problem goes unsolved. It's amazing. (As though you cannot solve a problem without first nailing down the definition to the last hair's breadth of correct. Then you can move on.)

Every once in a while, the experts will throw out all the work that has been done in the past, because they will realize it had a faulty foundation; then they'll act like they are beginning something new, not working on a decades-old (or centuries-old) problem. They'll even say things such as, "We've only been doing research in this field for the past 10 years – it might take us a little longer than 10 years to solve a problem of this complexity." A problem may become an unpopular cause, so the experts lose funding for research. In 20 or 40 years, when the cause is considered important again, the experts, if they bother looking through the old research (if they're even aware of it), will discover that it is useless (for one reason or another) and will therefore "begin" studying this problem. These kinds of things happen all the time; they aren't exceptions. This is the way solving a problem works in our culture.

And it's so easy for these people to find holes and flaws in each others' work, in each others' studies and definitions, because there is *always* a hole: There is no ultimate theory, waiting to be created by a great mind, which will solve *any* problem. By their nature, definitions of a problem and theories about a problem are inherently flawed, because there is no truth to be found in abstract thought.

*　　*　　*

Look at the superstars of awards, the Nobel prizes: It's supposed to really mean something when you win one of these. One of the categories for Nobels is, interestingly, "peace": the Nobel peace prize is given to those who are working towards peace on a global level. It's sad, because this world is not becoming any more peaceful; we are obviously not *heading* towards peace in this world – and how are you working towards peace if you're never getting any closer? Actually, in our culture, that makes "sense." You can be working on a problem for centuries and not be any closer to an answer, yet you are still considered to be working towards a solution.

Our whole problem-solving process is just one more part of that slippery slope of sliding, untouchable truth in our society: Nothing ever gets nailed down. One day the problem with kids is mothers working outside the home, and another day it is mothers who build their whole lives around their kids because they are always home, and another day it is parents who don't spend enough quality time with their kids, and so on. Serial rapists have a chemical deficiency in their brains – except when they don't, in which case it is obviously their upbringing that caused them to become serial rapists – except when it isn't… And in the end, our solutions and our improved society don't really exist; they are as abstract as our thoughts.

Knowledge

It is very easy to manipulate our culture's knowledge, based, as it is, on the natural and social sciences. Look at toilet training. Experts warn that toilet training your child at too young an age may permanently damage your child; that this early toilet training could lead to problems with sleeping or cause bedwetting, which could, in turn, lead to emotional problems in adulthood... According to these experts, children should be at least two years old before you even start thinking about toilet training. But if you look at the pictures on packages of training pants, the children look like they are three or four years old. The reality is that you can toilet train your child as soon as your child can walk, with no harmful effects (many cultures do it even earlier than that), but this would not suit the companies who make diapers and training pants. They would lose millions – or billions – of dollars in profits if people taught their children to use the toilet as soon as they could walk. And so they prove, through the natural and social sciences, that it is bad to toilet train your child too young – and this proof is accepted into our culture as truth. This is one way knowledge is made in our culture, and it permeates every aspect of our society, not just child rearing.

We have nutrition facts, but "vitamin A" doesn't actually mean anything. Scientists have not (and cannot) determined the nutritional value to be gotten from food, but they like to pretend they have. Yet their nutrition advice changes yearly. And notice how we are urged to eat dairy products to get calcium (or to take calcium supplements); it never occurs to them how unnatural it is for *humans* to drink *cows'* milk, so they cannot see that their nutrition advice is skewed and is actually based on PEOC eating habits. But consider: How were indigenous peoples able to survive and live such healthy lives without concerning themselves with vitamins and without eating enriched and fortified foods? (And isn't it interesting that PEOCs have no issue with drinking cows' milk; yet we consider human milk to be gross? Figure that one out.)

We know that it's natural for siblings to quarrel, because, in our culture, siblings quarrel regularly. Psychologists have given us all kinds of knowledge about why it is natural. But in some cultures, siblings don't quarrel. This illustrates another way we know things: We generalize PEOC characteristics to all of humanity. We think we have many different cultures: German, French, Spanish, British, Dutch, Swiss, etc., and so we think we are looking at a cross-sampling of cultures when we draw our universal conclusions. But they are all one culture: They all have the same basis.

We think that since the French think their culture is the best, and U.S. citizens think their culture is the best, and Italians think their culture is the best (and so on), that all peoples of all cultures will think they are superior – but we are not really looking at a cross-sampling, are we? PEOCs think they all have different cultures, but the rest of the world doesn't see that. And regardless of any theory we may have that all cultures will tend to view themselves as superior, it is certain that not every culture dismisses or discounts others' cultures as lightly as we do; not every culture tries to impose itself on others because it thinks itself superior; not every culture destroys.

Someone told me about a study in which researchers gave foul, garbage-tasting formula to one set of infants and sweet-tasting formula to a second set of infants. This study was apparently meant to show how what we eat as children affects our food choices as we grow. *Apparently* the study added to our knowledge in this field, but *in reality* the study showed us something else entirely. This study showed us:

• Even though breastfeeding is in every way the best thing for babies, many mothers decide breastfeeding is not for them and rationalize a reason why it's best for them not to breastfeed – and so we have an infant formula industry. I realize that some women have doctors who advise against breastfeeding, but these women need to find new doctors. I realize, too, that some women are unable to breastfeed, perhaps because our brilliant medical doctors cut off their breasts, but these women are not enough to account for our booming infant formula industry. And ever hear of a wet nurse?

• Some parents are depraved enough to enlist their children in studies in which their children will be used as experimental subjects. Some parents are depraved enough to enlist their babies in studies in which they will be fed formula which tastes like garbage.

• Some person or group of people was/were depraved, selfish, and blind enough to conceive of a study in which babies, helpless infants, would be fed formula which tastes like garbage, this in order to add to the wide body of scholarly knowledge we have in this field. If researchers are willing to feed garbage-tasting formula (or any other formula, for that matter) to helpless human babies, you can imagine what they are willing to do to everyone and everything else, since, in our culture, humans are more important than everything else. Can you imagine how much tunnel vision it takes to conceive of such a study; how you have to be able to turn off every impulse of decency to conduct it? You have to be able to totally ignore the fact that these are living, breathing infants you are experimenting with. This is the kind of mentality necessary for the thousands of such studies which are being conducted in our great society everyday.

If you are on one of the weight- or diet-control programs that I imagine came out of this study, be grateful to those babies who were forced to eat garbage-tasting formula or eat nothing. If they grow up with eating disorders, at least it wasn't for nothing, was it? And if, in the end, no one is actually helped by these weight- or diet-control programs, at least we have added to our wide body of scholarly knowledge. If the programs don't work, it must be because we need to know more. Perhaps more studies are in order.

*   *   *

You can have one scientist (in the social or natural sciences) positively assert something with ultimate authority, and another scientist in the same field, who is also an expert, positively assert something which contradicts the first scientist. It's part of the whole "truth is flexible and belongs to the person who makes the most persuasive argument" mindset of our culture, mimicking what happens in courtrooms and religion and advertising and political campaigning. It's easy to see why truth is flexible in our society, why it is a matter of the most persuasive argument, or of scientific facts which are soon proven wrong: It is because none of it *is* truth. But it is on such truths that our knowledge is built.

Say you develop your knowledge of how languages develop based upon a faulty history of humans and their development, upon incorrect information as to which language led to which, and which language came first. That means that your knowledge of how languages develop is clearly not going to be correct.

Say people in one field discover they weren't quite right about a theory (for example, how humans developed). That doesn't mean all the corollaries (for example, how languages develop) are going to be changed. And even if the corollaries are changed, it's not really helpful, because the new knowledge in the first field (how humans developed) is still going to be wrong anyway.

PEOCs know the mind can heal, but they don't know *how*. So in our culture, using the mind to heal becomes, "Picture yourself healed" or "Have a positive attitude" or "Imagine it." Some people who use these techniques *do* recover, but many *don't*. And, let's face it – many people who have horrible attitudes recover, too; hypochondriacs are convinced that every cold or flu will kill them, yet they usually survive. But indigenous cultures had more understanding, with deeper and more effective ways of channeling the power of the mind (and of the Creator and Creation) into healing.

In our culture, using the mind to heal works only occasionally, as evidenced by the fact that so many people die of diseases or live with chronic illnesses or subject themselves to our painful medical care – obviously, if we knew how to use the mind to heal, we could help these people. In contrast, indigenous techniques of using the mind to heal usually worked. Plus, their medicines (made from plants, who work with us) were far more effective than ours.

In our society, a medicine can need to be taken for life, which is actually the preferable situation from the point of view of the pharmaceutical companies, because it insures sales throughout your lifetime. Or a medicine may just work on side-effects of an illness, without ever addressing the illness itself. Or it can be a hit-or-miss gamble ("This medication works sometimes" – meaning, "We don't really understand the illness or this medicine and what it'll do to your body, but a pharmaceutical company wanted to get something on the market, so try it"). And our pharmaceutical companies, in their great greed, are constantly inventing new illnesses and syndromes, and they are regularly inventing discoveries, such as, "X may *possibly* lead to high cholesterol, so you should take this medicine to treat X" (just on the off chance that they are right and that X actually may lead to high cholesterol). People will take a drug which may give them liver failure just on the chance that it *might* help them with chronic dryness of their skin. And we accept all this as the best that medicine can be at this time, the best medical care in the world, with the thought that in the future it'll be better. Through charities, people donate billions of dollars to drug companies to develop medicines, which those drug companies then charge people billions of dollars to purchase. It really doesn't make sense if you think about it, but we do not think about it.

Indigenous medicine was (and is) not like this. There's no profit in telling someone they have to take a medicine for the rest of their life if the medicine is a tea which the person could make simply by walking outside and pulling some leaves.

If a shaman said, "Well, let's try this for 6 months and see what happens – if it doesn't work, we'll try something else – and, by the way, you may have permanent liver damage at the end of the 6 months," it would discredit the shaman and end their career. But when a medical doctor says it, people think it's perfectly okay that there's no real knowledge, only guesswork. I have heard (at different times) of shamen healing everything from cancer to diabetes and have met people who have been cured. There's no such thing as an incurable disease; just inept medical care. Yet we claim superior knowledge of health care and how the body functions.

We think anatomy has given us a world of knowledge about the human body – yet anyone who has ever seen dogs play can see that they instinctively know the vulnerable parts of the body. And they instinctively know which plants they can eat. Some people are afraid of certain breeds – yet dogs instinctively know when a dog is friendly, even if it's a daunting Doberman. But the knowledge the dogs have, according to us, is "just" instinct. We consider it inferior: Even "lower" species have instinct. Though it's accurate more often than our knowledge, that is irrelevant to us. If something isn't derived from objective, abstract thought, it's not knowledge, according to us. Some people have experience with instincts and know to trust them; yet, we think they are not true knowledge. We believe we are now beyond such primitive methods of knowing: Instincts are great for animals, who don't have the higher reasoning capabilities of humans. In our culture, rather than being another source of information, instincts are labeled primitive and unreliable, below conscious thought (in another of our hierarchies).

The number of toxins we have in our society is astounding. Long ago, before we started improving (we think) the planet, there were poisonous plants and poisonous animals, and people pretty much knew which were which. Now we have toxins built into foods which should be healthy, and the majority of meat PEOCs consume is contaminated. We have chemicals permeating every part of our lives: toxic playground equipment and toxins in the toothpaste you use to clean your teeth, and the soap you use to clean your body, and the cleansers you use to clean your home. We have toxic chemicals that you can use to treat your olive trees so they won't develop fruit, the idea being that it's better to have toxic chemicals in your yard than olives (and that it's okay to poison and deform trees). We have the toxicity that came with our great invention of electricity, and the toxicity of electrical fires (if you ever encounter an electrical fire, try not to breathe – you'll wish you didn't have to, because the fumes are so foul and noxious).

We have toxins from all the artificial materials which make up all the things we feel we have to buy: plastic storage containers, nylon jackets, spandex pants, non-stick cookware, fiberglass cars, Naugahyde furniture... It's way too long a list, and I haven't even begun to scratch the surface: Most of the things in our lives are toxic. The air and water and ground are full of toxins, left there by our government and corporations, everything from chemicals and biological waste to nuclear waste. Our very lifestyle is toxic: living separated from our Mother. No wonder we are so unhealthy.

Cancer is a generic term, used to describe what scientists and the medical community consider (for their own convenience) to be similar but not identical illnesses. In other words, my liver cancer is different from your liver cancer, but the medical community feels they are similar enough to be treated as and called the same disease. Their tunnel vision keeps them from seeing what's really wrong with me, and their need to categorize makes them call it the same thing that's wrong with you. What it comes down to is they don't understand: not me, not you, not the illnesses, not the world.

A while back, scientists proved that smoking cigarettes causes cancer. This idea still holds for two reasons: First, after all the money that's been poured into the cancer research industry, they want to believe they've done *something* (and we all know that "something" isn't the prevention of cancer, or a reduction in the incidence of cancer, or an affordable cure for cancer, or a reliable cure for cancer). They have some toxic chemical concoctions they like to call progress towards a cure (the concoctions may kill you, the cancer may kill you, or you may survive – it's pretty much luck whether you live or die). Statistics can prove anything, even that we are winning in the war against cancer; but, in *reality*, cancer kills as many people today as it did 40 years ago.

The second reason the idea still holds is that the tobacco industry is a handy scapegoat. Blaming lung cancer on tobacco keeps you from looking at just how toxic our culture is, at all the toxins you live with every day of your life. You've got someone who quit smoking 20 years ago who develops lung cancer, and people point to the smoking as the cause – why quit?

Of course, there is a problem with their theory: Too many people who smoke are (culturally speaking) relatively healthy, and too many people who have never smoked develop smoking diseases (like lung cancer). This is how the whole secondhand smoke debacle came into being – to explain all those cases of cancer in which the person doesn't smoke. It's pretty idiotic but very convenient, because almost everyone has been exposed to secondhand smoke at some time.

Tobacco is supposedly so bad for you, that you know no one will discover that tobacco has medicinal value (even though it does). Tobacco has many virtues; it is just one of many plants we vilify in ignorance.

Of course, this isn't meant to encourage people to pick up smoking; in our culture, it's a habit, a dependence, an indulgence; there's nothing positive about tobacco the way we use it. Like all of our habits, it is unhealthy. But blaming everything on tobacco is just a screen to keep you from looking around. Never mind any scientific proof that secondhand smoke causes cancer, because science can be used to prove *anything* that someone wants to prove (not just in the health field). If scientists were to test an ideal mouse diet on their lab mice, the mice would still die in sufficient numbers for them to determine that seeds and grasses cause heart disease and liver failure in lab mice – because the conditions in which they breed and sell and test these lab animals are so cruel and barbaric that they are going to die, one way or the other, and when they do die, it doesn't prove anything more than that some people are selfish and blind enough to torture animals and ignore their pain.

Animal testing has absolutely no validity in terms of health or safety for humans, but many corporations have strong financial incentives to ensure its continued use, and all the money they make off the animal torture industry buys a lot of sway with lawmakers. So our culture's knowledge is that animal testing is not only legitimate, it is *necessary* – to find cures for diseases, to keep unsafe products off the market, etc. The fact that it does not serve these purposes is irrelevant to our knowledge. True, our cultural knowledge has been shifting on this front, very slowly, and mostly in terms of cosmetics; as far as medical testing, the question we ask is still, "What else would we use?" The real question is, "Why are we torturing animals?"

Perhaps one day, in the far distant future, we will no longer have experimentation on animals for our pharmaceuticals, cleaning products, cosmetics, and so on. But if that happens, people will have figured out other ways to make money off of torturing animals – we already have many other ways right now – and we will have invented new knowledge which makes torturing animals okay for those other purposes. PEOCs have been abusing domesticated animals for as long as there have been domesticated animals: beating them, overworking them, starving them… How do you think animals became domesticated?

Heaven forbid that someone should find a way to prevent cancer (like eliminating our toxic lifestyle);

that'd be the end of the multi-billion dollar industry of cancer research. What if smog were found to be the cause of lung cancer? The answer is that it will never be discovered to be the cause of cancer; it cannot be found to be the cause of lung cancer, because what would people do without cars? The oil industry would never go for it – and if you think that they don't have a say, you're sadly deluded. And so our knowledge is made.

People think our culture is highly advanced, enlightened, and knowledgeable – but they don't see that it's all a façade, an intricate lie, in which often even the liars don't know they are untruthful.

Technology

Look at the jobs of dreariness our technology has given us, jobs reserved for the majority of the workforce. For the benefit of these jobs, many live in poverty and squalor their whole lives or work to buy things. Even those who say they love their jobs come home after work and need hours to relax and unwind. Obviously, something is wrong with that picture.

I have known many people who work 60 plus hours a week, sometimes holding two or three jobs, yet barely making enough money to pay for rent, food, and water. These people frequently have to choose between paying the electric bill and having enough money to ride the bus to work. The charities (like the Salvation Army) that are supposedly set up to help these people often determine that they are not good risks for aid, since they are likely to need help repeatedly, and so they do not assist them.

I have known people who work 60 plus hours a week, skipping vacations and working weekends, all so that they can buy 3000-square-foot houses with HOAs, video games for their children, and SUVs with TV screens, as though it is more important for their kids to have material things than time with their parents. And I have known people who work 60 plus hours a week simply because they have nothing else in their lives: In a choice between sitting home alone or going to work, they choose work, because at least there, they're making money – and they can always find things to spend it on. And then we have the rich class (of course our society is not classless), a small group, some of whom work very little or not at all, but who reap the rewards of other people's work. They spend their lives searching out new ways to entertain themselves and new technology. All of these people, the poor and the rich, could live better lives.

* * *

Look at video games. They are a great reflection of our society and the progress of technology. They reflect our society in part through the values they promote and their content, often having themes of violence and aggression. Pitifully, I have also seen games such as "plan your dream wedding," geared, apparently, toward young girls. Many kids (and some adults) spend hours and hours a day playing these games, for years on end. Someone working in a college computer room told me that every semester he sees a whole new set of freshmen, who spend every night playing fantasy world games. Then they flunk out, and a new set takes their place the next semester. Imagine becoming so enmeshed in a fantasy world that it becomes like your reality, a "place" where you spend much or most of your time. The kids playing the games don't accomplish anything real. If they spent that kind of time and concentration, for so many years, in trying to understand nature, they would actually have something at the end of it all: a little wisdom, a little self-knowledge.

But people feel that video games are mostly harmless diversion; they give kids something to do with their time (because our society is all about spending time entertaining ourselves – and giving your kids video games is a lot easier than troubling yourself to raise them), and at least the kids become comfortable with computers, which is a plus. I once heard a criticism that too many computer games are geared toward boys, not girls – as though boys are lucky that they are more targeted to waste a majority of their young lives pursuing a pointless activity with no human value – all for the profit of the people who produce these games. So technology gives us something to buy with the money we make at our dreary jobs.

We believe technology gives us so many things that we depend on it – though through it we do not have better lives, better health, or more knowledge.

People go home after work to their houses which technology built, use technology to prepare food they bought (if they didn't pick up prepared food on the way home), and use technology to get through all the day's tasks. In some cultures, the manner of daily living is meaningful; every day is an opportunity to learn more about the world and yourself. But technology has reduced *our* lives to a series of redundant tasks to be got through.

We also have special occasion technology; for example, we can freeze sperm, eggs, and embryos, in order to allow infertile people to have babies. Won't it be sad when, in perhaps three or four generations, we find out that people conceived with this wonderful technology have something wrong, something not quite right? –Wouldn't it be horrible if it were discovered, after a few generations, that the descendents of test tube babies and babies conceived in Petri dishes couldn't have babies naturally? It would be right in keeping with our culture: Pass down all your problems to your children. Science doesn't know this won't happen; scientists never foresee the havoc they are wreaking. –And, sadly, when the problems, whatever they turn out to be, are found, won't it then be pathetic that our culture doesn't give up the wonderful technology, but instead looks to more technology for a solution?

People develop new technology to help students learn better – but students don't learn better (not that what is being taught is worth learning, anyway). They develop technology to ease traffic congestion – but traffic congestion gets worse each year. Some people would say the technology is not everything, but it's moving us in the right direction; things would be even worse without technology. Let's look at that: In an earthquake, the damage, injury, and death are most likely to come from falling structures – it's not the Earth that will kill you. So, obviously, technology plays a negative role, since it built the structures that cause harm. The great minds of our society are working on new technology, meant to predict earthquakes or lessen their effects, but this new technology, too, will cause problems which need more technology to solve. All of our brilliant advancements are just one step after another leading only toward destruction of the planet.

*   *   *

I hear some people say, "If you want something, you should be willing to work for it." But they do not work for it. Instead of, say, hunting for or growing food (working for it), they work for money to buy food. But working for money and then using it to buy food is not the same as working for food, though our culture would have you believe it is.

Indigenous ways of working for food had the advantages of providing healthy food (which applies to very little of what you buy in a store); of providing a healthy lifestyle (as opposed to driving to work, maybe sitting at a desk for 8-10 hours, and then driving home); and of keeping the people aware of what food is. You learn a certain appreciation, which is lacking in our society, when you truly understand that you rely entirely on the Earth and the plants and animals for your continued life, each and every day. You understand that plants and animals also have spirits and are not below humans. We don't get that. We think, pathetically, that we rely on our water systems and electricity and other technology for our continued existence, each and every day, and that we are *fortunate* to have these things. It's as though we don't realize we can live without these technologies, and live well. It is the Earth, which we are destroying when we create and use these technologies, that we can't live without. And, clearly, technology can't help us learn this lesson.

Written Language

This is one area (we think) in which we really shine in terms of superiority: We have written language, something only (according to us) the most advanced civilizations have developed. Though our culture may not have invented the concept of written language, we give ourselves credit for using it; we think having it makes us superior to cultures which don't have it.

Let's put aside the fact that millions of trees are cut down each year so that every U. S. resident with a mailbox can have that mailbox regularly stuffed with junk mail; and the fact that millions of tons of our advanced written language are dumped everyday into landfills, in the form of junk mail, newspapers, magazines, flyers, and so on. Let's put aside for now whether what is written has any merit; to the PEOC mind, the fact that we *have* written language is an indication of superiority, regardless of what we do with it.

But there's a catch, a flaw in our belief: Something your culture uses to further the goals of your culture is not superior unless it assists in achieving superior goals. Just because we use written language to further our terribly misguided cultural goals, it is not an indication of anything other than that we can use things to further our terribly misguided cultural goals. The fact of written language is not in itself superior. If a culture hasn't the need for written language – why develop it? Written language is just one more step in the PEOC culture, not a superior step; we just think it is superior because we think all our steps are superior. If you have a strong oral tradition and do not need written language, why develop it? It isn't like indigenous peoples who didn't have written language didn't have any language – they just didn't write it. Our culture may be such that we need written language to keep developing, but other cultures did just fine without it.

How has written language helped us to develop? It is fair to ask what we do with written language that makes it a sign of superiority rather than just a different path than other cultures have taken. In other words, what have we accomplished with written language, that cultures who do not use written language were/are not able to accomplish? Why is having written language superior – is it just our arrogance which makes us believe it superior? Let's look at what we have done with written language, and see what superior goals we were and are able to accomplish.

For starters, our culture uses written language for control, something the PEOC loves but is hardly worthy of praise. It allows those with power to determine what is remembered or thought of as truth in PEOC culture. We don't have to remember things, because we can write them down, and it is easy to forget when you don't have to remember. Thus, in our daily lives, we can make notes to ourselves to remember things (such as grocery lists), so we don't have to tax our brains. In terms of *truth* and *control*, similarly, we don't tax our brains to actually remember even recent history – and so it is quite easy for those in power to remind us, meanwhile rewriting the memory to suit themselves.

It's easy, too, to let your oral traditions become sloppy when you're relying on written language. PEOCs think that when something is passed down as an oral tradition, it is more likely to change than it would be if written, but that is based on our own culture, which we regularly universalize to apply to all peoples. In some cultures, oral traditions are passed carefully from generation to generation, but PEOCs cannot carry on an oral tradition, and so they think no one can. And how reliable are written histories? If someone made/makes a mistake copying, rewriting, or interpreting a manuscript, that mistake is the new truth. If someone simply doesn't like the true history, it's very easy to throw out the old one, rewrite it – and voila, history is changed. Even concerning recent events, most PEOCs will not remember what actually happened (assuming the people they rely on for information ever actually told them the truth about what was happening). After a generation, the past is obliterated from our memories. We rely on the written word to hold onto this information. And so our culture is overrun with history books that are complete fantasy, and we have no way of knowing, of sorting through the written lies, because they're piled so deep on top of one another.

Some families do have personal oral histories, passed down through the generations, but these are almost always tainted by personal interest ("My great grandfather was a hero in this battle..."). Indigenous oral histories helped the people understand important lessons which had been learned, rather than bragging about how great some ancestor was. Our written histories cannot make this claim, because they all make us sound like heroes and underplay any harm we have caused.

According to us, something has more authority if it is written. Obviously, since we rely on written language, we're going to give it that credit. And so, for example, Christians think their religion is *the* true religion in part because of the Bible, which they consider to be the written word of God. They think that somehow, because it's written down, it's true, as opposed to a religion which is not written; that the Bible is some kind of permanent record of God's will. I imagine some people think the Bible was written in modern-day English, but it wasn't. It has been translated and interpreted into English and all the other PEOC languages, translated into a large variety of versions, which often conflict with each other. Never mind the difficulties in translating languages and how much meaning changes; the fact that our culture has developed a science around translating ancient languages ensures that these translations are going to be wrong, because all science is.

It's funny that Christians claim more moral authority from a 2000-year-old text whose meaning has changed repeatedly and which has, at times, been deliberately revised to serve someone's purposes (such as King James) than they would grant to a religion in which each person has to directly make a connection with the Creator. Personally, I'd be more inclined to credit the first-hand knowledge; our culture wants it in writing.

Obviously, this book is written language. I chose this format for two reasons: First, I did not want to deal with all the anger I expect my words to inspire in the various hate groups which populate our society. In our culture, some people go beyond simply disagreeing, to targeting for physical harm or character assassination someone whose words they don't like.

The other reason I chose this format is because it seemed to me the best way to reach people in this culture. Most people in our society would not have the time, the patience, or the focus to *listen* to me say what this book says. In the middle of a sentence, they would start thinking about a project at work, how attractive that person is, or what they need to buy on the way home, because PEOCs have trouble turning off their stream of thoughts.

The point is, I did not need to write this: If we had a free and open society, I could just as easily have presented my view orally. Both of my reasons for presenting it in written form were cultural, and neither indicates cultural superiority.

Let's assume that some books *do* try to present material of a higher nature, perhaps books sharing the wisdom of other peoples. For many in our culture, though they may read these books, that wisdom is whitewashed into meaninglessness. For example, many people in our culture think they can learn from and honor the Native Americans of the past without caring about the Earth which taught them or about their descendants today, as though the Natives died out and are now just an historical footnote and some words in a book. But they did not die out. And those people who say they are concerned about the Earth usually think they can care for the planet, or at least do less damage than PEOCs typically cause, through better science. But science doesn't understand the Earth, and the Natives' lifestyles caused *no* damage – not "less."

If we lived in a culture which already had the wisdom these books provide; if our culture were not separated from our Mother and our Father, then we would not need these books – we would learn this wisdom as part of our upbringing. The fact that we do not have this wisdom and need to read books from other cultures is not an indication that we are superior in using written language. Indigenous peoples were able to learn from other cultures, too, and without the need for written language; they actually had to interact with and understand the people, and this helped to keep the meaning from being whitewashed into meaninglessness. This isn't an indication of inferiority on their part.

Some people might point to the greats, such as Shakespeare, as evidence of superior accomplishment. People celebrate Shakespeare for pondering the human condition without realizing that he pondered the PEOC condition. Some read Shakespeare simply for entertainment, which follows upon our cultural belief that we are living worthy lives by passively amusing ourselves. But some people study Shakespeare, reading or watching a play in order to better understand human behavior. The assumption here is that understanding human behavior is a matter of analysis and of understanding someone else's interpretation, rather than seeking information for yourself. It is the erroneous PEOC idea of studying other people's thoughts, of learning from the greats, because we do not all have the potential for insight.

There is no inherent need for written language, no inherent value in it; a culture is not inferior because the people don't use it. Indigenous peoples who had no written language were not all dying of boredom because they couldn't pick up a novel to pass the time; they were not spiritually vacant because they couldn't pick up a Bible; they didn't lack insight into the human condition because they could not study Shakespeare; they were not mentally unchallenged because they couldn't read up on the latest in string theory. We are very fond of finding ways to entertain ourselves, to pass the time, and to relax, but we are not superior because we have frivolous novels (and frivolous TV and frivolous magazines…) to fill our time, rather than using it for something both enjoyable *and* meaningful.

I once heard someone claim that written language allows us to develop more complex thoughts, because the writer doesn't need to keep the whole chain of thinking in their head. Again here we are generalizing PEOC failings to all peoples: The fact that PEOCs cannot keep thoughts straight in their heads becomes, in our minds, "no peoples can keep thoughts straight in their heads." Some of the speeches given by Native Americans during colonial times were written down by us. Without any cue cards or any kind of written language, these Native Americans managed to express themselves with the greatest eloquence and profundity; they managed to keep their thoughts straight in their heads.[‡] On the other hand, I have read many volumes of our culture's complex thoughts and would like to point out a couple of things. The first is that being able to write it down does not necessarily lead to being able to keep it all straight. Believe me, these great thinkers can forget where

---

[‡] See, e.g., *The Wisdom of the Native Americans*, Part 3, selected bibliography.

they started, get lost in their arguments, and contradict themselves, even if it is all on paper. The other thing I would like to call attention to is that these complex thoughts they need written language to keep track of are just wasted abstraction: meaningless theories, philosophies, and tracts that share in the fault of all that is PEOC, i.e., the failure to ever actually see reality or truth. Even if written language is required to develop these complex thoughts, their development is not a sign of superiority.

The Native Americans whom the colonizers encountered were not simple because of the lack of written language. They were clearly capable of deep reflection, of subtlety, of wisdom and understanding, of allusion, of simile and metaphor, etc. Thus, written language is not a prerequisite for deep or profound thinking, nor for deep and profound self-expression.

And think about all the treaties between Native Americans and colonizers that *we* wrote, never having any intention of honoring them. We could (and did) write anything we wanted into those treaties and verbally lie about their actual contents – how is that superior? And if those written treaties are so set in stone, why are we not honoring them, even to this day?

Written language is used for the texts with which we educate schoolchildren. I had a class in which they taught, incredibly, that written language is important because it is the only way to teach and pass on knowledge. Miraculously, many indigenous peoples the world over were able to teach their civilizations and histories to their children without the need for written language. But, after all, if children actually do something, and learn the meaning of that thing as they do it, and discover something about themselves as they do it, then they really learn, rather than if they just read something in a book. However, book learning does manage to pass on the meaning of this culture; hollow knowledge begets hollow knowledge. Children learn how knowledge is defined in this culture, but our definition wouldn't pass muster in a culture with true knowledge.

If there's a "problem" with a text book (for example, if a text describes marriage as "a union between two people"), no problem. Textbook publishers live for revisions, which entail selling another million books. They intentionally publish new editions every few years just to keep profits up. People can throw away all those old, incorrect texts, and the publishers can cut down thousands of trees in order to re-issue the book in its supposedly corrected form: marriage is "a union between one man and one woman" – that was worth the lives of thousands of trees, wasn't it? It's not like there is any other way to teach our children our beliefs about marriage.

And this is one of the great wonders of our written language: It's one more constant drain on the world: the killing of millions of trees, the use of chemicals in the production of paper, the manufacture of toxic inks, the use of pollutants in our recycling plants, the tons of contaminants which end up in the Earth, and the end result of millions of tons of trash left to litter our streets and fill our landfills. Guess it's not a sign of superiority if you look at that, is it?

A Note on Education

It's interesting that a successful teacher is one whose students do well on tests or go on to college, or, for a college instructor, one who publishes many scholarly articles, rather than one who leads students to a deeper understanding of themselves and the Earth.

Sometimes, when students in college (or high school or elementary school) study a subject, they think, "Man, this is bull" – but still they study it, learn it, and (perhaps unwittingly) internalize it so they can pass the class, graduate, and get a "good" job – which is, after all, the goal of education.

Often, when a student thinks something is bull, they assume they're not understanding yet, because it's this whole field, long and wide, and they are just (for example) an undergraduate. It will make sense later, they tell themselves. –And this is the real education: Don't question the field; question within the field; just absorb; become indoctrinated. And, sure enough, by the time later comes along, they have become so indoctrinated (brainwashed) into the field, that the warped reasoning has become second nature to them. They no longer even remember what was troubling them at first, or, if they do, they can now explain it away with some of that handy circular logic which is the hallmark of all of our fields of study.

And that is what we teach: fields of study, subjects. How many PEOC students are able to reintegrate those subjects into the reality of life? How many would even understand what I mean by that? PEOCs think that dividing up the world and knowledge into subjects allows for specialization and deeper research into different fields, but this is not the reality of the matter – its real utility is in fragmenting, controlling, and defining reality and in controlling and limiting people's minds.

By educating in subjects, which we do not integrate into all the other subjects and into life, we keep children from viewing a full picture of life. They get a bunch of puzzle pieces which don't fit together, because they are all distorted. It's hard to question the big picture when you don't even see it because you're too busy looking at "biology" and "history" and "physical education" and "communication"...

Old World New World &
Scholarship

A book called *1491*,§ which I have not read, was advertised as challenging our traditional beliefs about the pre-Columbian Americas, based on recent scholarship. ("Recent scholarship" is code for "a whole new set of inaccurate theories.") According to the advertisements, the author wanted to show that the American Natives conducted genetic experiments, which was supposed to prove that they were more advanced than previously thought – as though conducting genetic experiments proves that.

In the above book, the Americas are still considered to be the New World – and why wouldn't they be? All our scholarship proves the Americas are the New World, settled by people from Eurasia. We can't imagine that human life began in Africa *and* the Americas *and* Eurasia. One thing which is readily apparent from this kind of book is that PEOCs cannot believe the Native Americans as to their own histories that they originated here – we think their histories must be discovered (like the "New World") by far more intelligent and rigorous PEOC scholars/scholarship.

Here's my invented theory (all theories are invented): Humans originated on an island between

---

§ *1491*, Charles C. Mann. Random House: New York. (Vintage Books.) 2006.

Africa and the Americas. After 2,542 years had passed, some of the First People went East, and some went West. Many hundreds of thousands of years then passed, and the Descendents of the First People made homes all over Africa and North and South America. Some went to various islands the world over. The different groups or tribes developed different ways of speaking, but all remained true to the Earth.

However, there came a time when one tribe decided that they wanted to change their world in a way which did not suit the other peoples. It's not clear whether they were asked to leave or whether it was their own decision, but in the end they decided to find a new and empty land, where their changes would not affect the other Descendents (assuming that the first PEOCs still had decency back then).

In the New World (Europe), they began to implement their changes. Over time, as they got further and further from the Earth, they forgot their origins and developed stories about how they had actually originated there. And all the while, since they could not get along with each other because they all thought they were right and superior, they split into the many factions you see in Europe and the Middle East...

This is admittedly a completely fabricated theory, but it holds as much water as any other. If you say, "But this theory doesn't fit in with the current body of scientific knowledge," that is the point. The "whole body of scientific knowledge" is no knowledge, just a bunch of weak theories invented by people who, whether they realize it or not, have every reason to propound theories which perpetuate the idea of PEOC superiority.

There is no reason to believe that, with another 10,000 years of evolution, the Natives of the Americas would have become like we are today (at which time, 10,000 years in the future, we would have evolved far beyond our current state, so we would still be way ahead of them, of course). It is not about becoming like us, because we are not the advanced race we think we are. We think we are more modern; that the European colonizers were more modern than the Natives, but "modern" means "of the present time." The Natives were just as much of the present time (at that time) as the Europeans; if any of their cultures had/have survived colonization, they would still be modern. Our using this word simply implies they were behind us, less advanced, on their way out, obsolete. But they were not obsolete; their cultures had developed into *modern* spiritual cultures, whereas the European culture had developed into a modern materialistic and warring culture.

There is absolutely no reason to believe that Europe is an Old World and the Americas are a New World (in terms of human occupation, which is how PEOCs reckon old and new) other than that such theories fit into the whole PEOC superiority mindset and domination theme: These theories agree with PEOC religions and support our belief that the Americas were a new world waiting to be settled (= colonized) by Europeans. Native Americans, this thinking goes, were, in their own time, a force of invasion; this wasn't really their home, they just took it over, same as we did... (Do I need to point out all the flaws?) Of course, PEOCs can not give credence to Native American histories which say they originated here: PEOCs have determined that they have no real knowledge, only superstition.

The practice of calling the pre-Columbian Americas "ancient" follows this same mindset. The word *ancient* makes me think of things which are many thousands or tens of thousands of years old, not things less than 2000 (or 1000) years old. Yet PEOCs call many A.D. things of the Native Americans ancient, including, according to an L.A. County Museum of Art brochure, artifacts as recent as 1350 A.D. PEOCs do not typically refer to their own history from this period as ancient. We are using *ancient* as a relative term. It is as though, because (we believe) our culture is older, our *ancient* is older than theirs. (In other words, something your five-year-old did two years ago may be ancient history; whereas something you did two years ago is not.)

Obviously, we also like to call relatively recent events "ancient" because it removes the onus from Europe and its descendents for their genocide, the false implication here being that it's all ancient history, unfortunate events that have nothing to do with how we live today or who we are now. Another implication is that, since the Native cultures were ancient, they must have just died out naturally, as part of evolution, like the ancient European cultures; at least they were obsolete and on their way to dying out; they certainly weren't vital, healthy cultures which could have lasted hundreds of thousands of years more if they hadn't been cut down by invading Europeans.

Our scholarship regarding the pre-Columbian American peoples effectively says that we are superior to Natives in understanding and interpreting *their* history – the hubris of the PEOC mind is

116

unlimited. The fact that their artifacts are sitting in PEOC museums, where they can be examined and explained by PEOC scholars, who are utterly incapable of understanding them, is just added insult to Natives. (For example, if a PEOC sees a figurine which is half human and half animal, they may assume it is a god because, as far as PEOCs are concerned, shape shifting is impossible. But cultures around the world practice shape shifting, so the basis of their reasoning is faulty. Or perhaps a PEOC sees an armadillo figurine which was used in religious ceremonies and erroneously concludes that these people worshiped armadillos or this object represents an animal god. It may actually be a religious object used to worship the Creator, perhaps something for which to thank the Creator. Their reasoning in concluding the indigenes worshiped armadillos is kind of like concluding that Buddhists worship incense because they burn it in their temples.) We think any information indigenous peoples can provide about their cultures is necessarily subjective, as though their cultures keep them from seeing their cultures, but that *we* can (figuratively) examine their cultures under a microscope and come up with the objective truth. We don't see that *our* culture keeps *us* from being able to understand theirs.

Anyone who argues that it's important to study artifacts in an effort to understand history is either deluded, or foolish, or both. There is no effort in our culture to truly understand history. It is a false field, like every other field of study in this culture; a mental exercise, like a crossword puzzle – never leading to any truth or bearing in any way on reality: simply more abstract thought into the void which constitutes all the knowledge toward

117

which this culture strives. We think our field of history is so superior to what we call the myths of indigenous peoples, but our history is nothing more than invention, pure fantasy; their myths were passed down through the ages.

The insult against Natives embodied by the display of their artifacts is not unintentional – it is the essence of what European-originated culture is, a way to analyze and objectify them; another way to distance the Natives' truth from reality, as PEOC culture distances everything from reality.

It is also a way to subsume *their* artifacts and *their* history into *our* culture: Controlling and displaying their artifacts is like saying that these artifacts have now become a part of the grand and panoramic history of the PEOC culture, a part of our great cultural melting pot, into which everything is thrown and destroyed.

Spirituality

Christianity

I am not a Christian; I have never been one, in spite of the attempts by many people, over my lifetime, to convert me. I don't pretend to know what they feel and believe – all I know is what I see of their religion:

Most Christians are like everyone else in our culture in that they do not know their true history. They think Christianity has become corrupted and is no longer the good and virtuous religion it once was, but there never was a "once was"; it has never been the religion Christians claim it is supposed to be; never has it had the effect of spreading the values it exalts. "Peace on Earth" and "Do unto others" are not any part of the history of this religion, and I think many Christians would agree with me when I say they are not a part of Christianity today.

Christians began persecuting non-Christians at the beginning of their religion, and they continue to do so straight through to today, with nary a lag nor a hiccup in between. They do not call it persecution; yet, as one of the persecuted (a non-Christian), I can assure them that this is what it is. Christians began their history with forced conversions of Jews, Gypsies, pagans, witches, and others. Their message was often, "Convert to Christianity, or we will kill you." Thus, Christians began by killing thousands – and then tens of thousands

– and then hundreds of thousands – and then millions of people, because those people did not want to be Christians.

I have to take a moment to ask, how is *forcing* your religion on someone, sometimes under threat of death, a good thing? If someone agrees to convert under such circumstances, does anyone believe that they will have the same faith as one who converts willingly? Will they really have faith in the goodness of Jesus – will they really accept Him? If they don't truly accept Jesus as their Lord and Savior, if they only said that they accept Him to avoid being killed, are they "saved" or not? If they *are* saved; if the point is not to actually accept Jesus, but just to say that you do, then what kind of religion is that? And if they are *not* saved, then how was forcing them to "convert or die" a good thing for them?

I have to wonder, too, why did the Christians not try to convert people by living such exemplary lives and showing such an infinite level of spirituality and wisdom, that people would *voluntarily* want their religion? If they wanted to convert people, why didn't they (and why don't they) show those people how their religion made them *better* people, not worse people – is that too much trouble to go to? Because, as a non-Christian, I have to say that it is a religion I do not want. They do not have a deep and profound spirituality and wisdom which makes me say, "I want that." Christians say you have to experience it to understand, but when I look at and speak with those who understand, I do not see and hear people who have a profound relationship with God – I see people who are caught up in the PEOC way of life, like everyone else.

I see Christians who walk around with permanent, "I'm at peace with God" smiles on their faces. Leaving aside whether or not these smiles actually are genuine, let me grant to Christians what they say of their religion, that it gives them inner peace and strength – and, equally importantly, let them grant that to me. If Christians want to make the claim that their religion helps them in their daily lives, though I see no evidence of that in the way they live and the way they treat others, yet I will not dispute them; I can take them at their word. But I would like them to afford me the same courtesy. Why am I not afforded the same right and freedom to find peace and strength my own way? Why should I be told that I can find true peace and strength only through Christianity? Christianity does not give me a sense of either peace or strength – it gives me the same sense that every other aspect of PEOC culture gives me, a feeling of people who always believe they are right and superior, people who do not value others and who seek to dominate others.

Jesus said He is *the only way* to God: "I am the way, and the truth, and the life; no one comes to the Father but through Me." (John 14:6) Just by itself this statement is disturbing; inherent in it is the domination I sense in Christianity; and, beyond that, even vanity. Why did Jesus not say, "No one comes to the Father but through good and virtuous acts?" Many people live their whole lives by the values Christianity preaches, but, according to this statement, they cannot get to God if they have not taken Jesus as Lord. It is hard to explain to a Christian how disturbing this statement can be to someone non-Christian, but I can say that it *doesn't* make me want to convert; in fact, it has the opposite effect. If you look at this statement, it explains why many Christians will not grant validity to anyone else's spirituality – it is because *their* faith says that all other ways are false and will not lead to God. In Christianity, the only way to be good and to worship God is to believe in and follow Christ; there is no other way. Anything the Christians call sins can be forgiven, but refusing to take Christ as Savior cannot. In other words, if Hitler had "seen the light" right before he died, were he truly repentant and accepting of Christ in his last minutes of life, he would have gone to heaven – yet an indigenous person who has spent their whole life trying to understand how to serve God, and living in such a way as to revere God, but who rejects Christ (perhaps because they see how Christians *act*) would not go to heaven.

This statement also seems to be a statement of vanity, because being worshipped is of paramount importance to Jesus; it is more important than how you live. It seems the statement of One who is shallow, who favors form over function and dogma over spirituality. To me, this is not someone to worship. I could not worship a Lord who would bless a greedy or tyrannical person just because they had accepted Him, but who would reject the person who spends their whole life in reverence and awe of God's creations. And what Lord or God would?

This statement of Christ that you cannot get to the Father but through Him is like a scientist saying, "You cannot have true knowledge but through science": "You cannot know true spirituality but through Christ." Forever, Jesus is the intermediary, so you cannot make a connection directly with

God. I have known many Christians in my life, and I have known some who rarely mention God at all. They pray to Jesus; they thank Jesus for their food, and so on. Even if they were saying, "Thank you, God, and thank you, Jesus..." it might make sense – but God gets left out so often that it doesn't make sense. I don't understand this, but it is not what troubles me most about this religion.

"And Jesus came up and spoke to them, saying, 'All authority has been given to Me in heaven and on earth. Go therefore and make disciples of all the nations, baptizing them in the name of the Father and the Son and the Holy Spirit, teaching them to observe all that I commanded you; and lo, I am with you always, even to the end of the age.'" (Matthew 28:18-20) *That* is one of the things which troubles me most about Christianity, which makes me believe it is a false religion and a tool of domination, not a way to God or to an understanding of God's meaning. If you look at the definition Raphael Lemkin gave of genocide (and he is the man who coined the term), you will see that to destroy a people's religion and culture, and to impose yours on them, follows one of the definitions of genocide.* In other words, the Christian duty is to commit genocide by converting everyone to their religion, by replacing others' religions with

---

* As adopted into the Genocide Convention, Raphael Lemkin's definition changed quite a bit because of political pressures brought to bear by various parties who were actively engaging in the various forms he had defined as "genocide." Amongst these were Christians, who did not want to think of their tactics of destroying peoples as being on a par with, say, Hitler's tactics, though they *are*. But this is all another story. Lemkin coined the term, and I'll accept his definition; I think he made his point. For more, see *Kill the Indian, Save the Man*, selected bibliography.

Christianity. *That* is disturbing – and it doesn't make sense: Christianity is thus degenerated from a form of spirituality and a means of worshipping and serving God into a tool of domination and oppression, a tool of what many consider the most heinous crime humans are capable of committing. How can a religion say, "Do no harm to others," and, at the same time, "*destroy* others" (genocide obviously being a form of destruction)? And if you look at the *acts* of Christians, the way they have implemented this commandment from their Lord, you will see destruction and havoc throughout the ages. (And, sadly, if you look at a history of genocides, you will often see Christians initiating, committing, or abetting the devastation.)

The problem is not that Christians worship Christ – it's that they feel every last person on the planet must do so also, that only Christianity can save everyone's eternal soul, and that this salvation is of *paramount* importance. In other words, it doesn't matter what they have to do to save you, because, as long as they have saved you, anything they have done to accomplish this task is insignificant in comparison to the great good they have done.

Christians began saving people as soon as they heard and believed the message of Christ (and thus became Christians), and they continue to this day. As I mentioned earlier, they began in Eurasia, but, eventually, they found there was a whole world of people to convert.

Christianity is the religion taught to (= forced on) African slaves, so they could be saved, even as they were being sold. It was Christian missionary activities which facilitated the development of the slave trade, and it was Christians who conceived of and implemented African slavery. So Christians bought people who had been kidnapped from their families and their homes, and Christians transported them across the Atlantic Ocean in deplorable conditions, in which many died or were killed. Christians brought them to a strange land, to be treated like commodities, with no rights, to have their children stolen from them and to be beaten by their owners. Christians did all of this and yet claimed they cared about them and wanted to save their eternal souls.

The revisionist histories which say they didn't know it was wrong, or that African slaves were actually well-treated, because owners who did not treat their slaves well did not get work out of them, are nothing more than self-serving PR. Factory farm owners are using this same argument today: "We have to treat our animals well, or they will not produce." Go check out a factory farm, and see how well they treat their animals.

Christians thought lowly enough of the Africans to sell them, yet they claimed they cared. Which is it? –It can't be both. How did this fit into their religion? Were Africans the children of God or not? If they were, how was it okay to purchase them, to sell their children, and to kill them? Is this "do unto others"? And if Africans were not the children of God, because they were commodities, less than Europeans, then why try to convert them at all? I wonder, too, do Christians trouble themselves with such questions, or do they just follow in the rutted path of European-originated culture and tell themselves it is right because that is what they want to believe, without bothering to look at the truth?

I am not saying that Christians are the only people who are greedy, nor that they are the only people who engaged in the slave trade. But if all their religion does is allow them to act like everyone else, what good is it? They say it gives them strength in hard times. For example, a Christian may have sold a boatload of slaves, but, because the market was depressed, he or she did not make as much money as hoped, so he or she prays to Jesus to give them strength to get through the rough period. So the strength Christianity has to offer does not help Christians be good; it just makes them feel better about the bad things they do and the hardships they endure. This is a PEOC attitude, wrapped up in religion. PEOCs like to do whatever they want and to feel good about it. If things aren't going well, they want to believe a higher power is on their side and that some day things will be the way they want...

No, Christians are not the only greedy people in the world, but they act like they are holy and like their religion is justification for imposing their will on others, even though their religion clearly has not helped *them* be better. If they actually took the trouble to become better people, they would no longer seek to impose their will on others. They use their religion to indulge their greed and other sins. Clearly, in many of the instances I describe in this essay, saving people was not really of paramount importance – it was of no importance, and the actual goal was to make money. Yet Christians act like their religion is, by itself, justification for all of their actions, like nothing they do is truly bad because they are Christians and, thus, cannot be bad people.

I heard of an indigenous people (one of too many such stories) who lived in a rainforest. Because of the almost-constant rain, and hence the wetness of their environment, they lived naked and covered their skin with oil to stay dry. When Christians encountered them, they taught these people that nudity is evil and wrong and that they must accept Jesus and wear clothes to cover their bodies. The indigenous people ended up dying because the clothes got wet and stayed wet, and their healthy lifestyle was traded for a deadly lifestyle. The indigenes were not stupid or simple people who naively thought they had encountered superior people and followed them to improve themselves. Rather, they were lied to, coerced, and terrorized into following these people. To Christians, the important point is not that these people were destroyed and that all *their* spiritual wisdom is lost forever – it's that these people were saved before they were destroyed. Christians (seemingly) do not ask themselves, "How would God approve of this? How would God, the Creator, think it better for the Creator's children to be dead? Why create an environment where people would die off by wearing clothes if people are supposed to wear clothes? Why did God bother creating these people if God just wanted Christians to kill them all?"

The entire history, straight through to the present, of encounters between Christians and indigenous peoples is heartbreaking and tragic, and the indigenous peoples were *always* (and still are) harmed by these encounters, left worse off. I once read that the Catholic Church commissioned a study to determine why their activities were having a negative impact on peoples they were trying to "help." According to this account, the study concluded (not surprisingly, since it's all PEOC) that their *superiority* was the cause of all their destruction: In other words, the negative consequences of their missionary activities resulted from the fact that the target populations, being so inferior, were devastated upon encountering the greatness of such a superior culture; they were crushed upon realizing how paltry their own cultures and religions were in comparison. (I would think a truly superior religion would *uplift*, not *downcast*.) If the Church undertook this study, it shows that they are aware they are having a negative impact. By explaining away this impact with superiority, they assured that they would not have to curb or cease their activities.

I realize Christians tell themselves they *have* uplifted people, but a look at those people tells a different story. I've heard that many actually welcome Christians at first, because Christians preach what seem to be common values, such as "do no harm" and "love each other." And they find out after it is too late that the Christian idea of love is far different from what might be considered a common definition. Their love feels like hate.

Missionaries in Africa and the Americas worked their indigenous slaves to death but made sure to save their eternal souls. U.S. and Canadian citizens, through their governments, often using force and coercion, took Native American children from their parents, so they could be educated in PEOC residential schools, in the way of the Lord.[†] (It should be noted that taking children from their parents in this manner also follows one of the

---

[†] *Kill the Indian, Save the Man*, selected bibliography.

definitions of genocide.) The point, said the Christians, was that they were saving the children. Certainly the real point was to destroy native cultures, in part by not allowing the parents to pass on their cultures and their religions to their children. The point, for some, was that they were getting free labor out of the children; many people made a *lot* of money off this schooling system, which ran for close to a century. The point, for some, was that the schools enabled them to engage in child molestation without any significant interference. Undoubtedly it was about all of these things – but the Christians justified it all because, they told themselves, they were saving the children's eternal souls.

You may live a life of absolute misery, and your misery may be at the hands of Christians, but if you are saved, then you will go to heaven when you die and receive your reward for what you put up with in this life. (And if your people do not believe that you are supposed to endure a life of misery and wait for a reward in heaven, they need to change their thinking.) And the Christians who caused you all the misery will also go to heaven, because they are also saved. The children who were molested in the name of their salvation will be meeting their molesters again in the next life, because those child molesters are also saved: They have accepted Jesus Christ as their Lord and Savior, and all they need do is sincerely repent their sins, which I'm sure they do.

Christians attack other peoples' religions and ways of living and worshipping and say that, to worship the Creator properly, you must worship Jesus and live in *this* way (their way) – but *this* way does not seem to include any reverence, or even respect. Say you are of a nation of people who truly value life: the lives of other people, and the plants, and the animals, the waters, the rocks, the winds, the sun, the moon, the Earth. Your whole culture, deep and ancient, is a reverence of the wonderfulness of the life the Creator gave to all of Creation. And then you encounter Christians – and by the time you find out what they are really about, what their love really means, it is too late. Your people have been destroyed – killed or crushed by depravity and destruction. Often, drugs, alcohol, and suicide look like the only escapes.

I am sure many Christians have had the experience of something catastrophic happening – perhaps the loss of a child through kidnapping – or even a small catastrophe, something which disrupts your life, so that things that used to be enjoyable no longer are, at least for a time. You wonder if your life will ever return to normal, if those things will ever give you joy again. This is how many people feel once they have encountered Christianity. Christians may think, "If these people would just accept the truth we have given them and accept Christ as their Savior, He will help them get through it – we have given these people a tool to get through any hardship." –But Christ will not and can not help them get through it, because their (figurative) meeting with Christ was so horrible that Christ can never be to them what Christ is to Christians.

And these missionary activities which harm so many people are not history, a "regrettable error" of the past. They continue today. As just one example of this, there are Christian organizations which claim to help children around the world, running commercials on television asking for donations. They have reenacted the atrocious Indian Schools all over again, on a worldwide scale, and good Christians are still helping and supporting the genocide. It is as though Christians have convinced themselves that other parents don't love their children the way they do and do not mind having their children taken from them. It is as though Christians think that the molestation and abuse which occur in these Christian schools aren't really there if they pretend they aren't. Or, perhaps, it is just that they don't even consider these factors, don't even think about what their contributions mean, because all that matters is that these are Christian organizations; therefore, they must be doing good, so those who donate need not take time to consider the implications or effects of their actions.

Someone told me about a public television documentary which aired about past *and current* missionary activities. During one part of the documentary, missionaries were playing The Lord's Prayer, which had been recorded in indigenous tongues throughout the world. The narrator commented that these recordings are the last remnants we have of many now-dead languages. Apparently the missionaries felt they had done a service in preserving recordings of these languages before the languages had mysteriously vanished. But the point is that, between the time the missionaries showed up and the time the documentary was made, these peoples had lost their languages and their cultures – *because of* the missionaries' activities. It distresses me that these missionaries are not distressed at the loss of knowledge *these* peoples had gained over the thousands of years, at the loss of *their* contribution to spirituality. But Christians believe other cultures of the world have nothing to teach us about spirituality; they have only to learn from Christians. Christians think they are the only ones who can make a contribution to our spiritual understanding – because that's what their religion tells them.

Christians think no other peoples can contribute to human spirituality because Jesus is the *only* way, because Jesus said He is the only way. Everything you need for spirituality is in the Bible. Christians do not (for example) approach a people, thinking to themselves, "Let us first understand the spirituality they have now – if it takes thirty or even sixty years, so be it, because we have devoted our whole lives to God. Let us see what values their faith gives them and what spiritual lessons it teaches; then we will see if Christianity can add to that, to increasing their understanding of God. And perhaps this journey will also increase *our* understanding of God." Instead, they approach a people assuming they have no spirituality because it isn't dogmatized and codified into a religion like Christianity is, or that, if they do have a religion, they've got it all wrong, and it is their job, as Christians, to show them the *one* way.

Oddly, many Christians do not admit to this belief, denying it even as they practice it. The latest Christian gimmick is to meet with people for purposes of learning about their religious beliefs (they say) and for sharing religious beliefs. The real purpose, the *only* point of these meetings, is to convert the non-Christians, but the Christians cannot even be honest about it. What they truly want is to share *their* religious beliefs. While the other people talk about their spirituality, the information is processed in the Christian mind to determine how they can convince these people that Christianity shares their values but is better because they have Jesus, who walked among men. One reason for the sharing format of these meetings is to sidestep criticism of their missionary activities, but the point is definitely *not* to cease these same missionary activities. They just want to disguise them (i.e., to lie).

I understand that Christians may believe they *are* doing unto others when they introduce people to Christianity. They think to themselves, "If I did not know the glory of Christ, I would want someone to show me this glory. If I were not saved, I would want someone to show me the way to become saved." This *sounds* good, but, as is typical in PEOC culture, the view is skewed. Why don't Christians look at themselves, at how much their faith means to *them*, and understand how wrong it is to destroy a people's spirituality, how much a part of you your spirituality can be, how it can be the most important thing in your life, and how much it teaches you and gives you strength? They do not give other peoples the same credit with their faiths. It is as though they believe only Christians rely on their faith – every other people's faith is meaningless and can easily be replaced with Christianity. Why can they not understand that other people's spiritualities are as important to them as Christianity is to Christians? They do not look at this side of the matter, because our culture is not about looking – it is about being right and superior. For Christians, it is not important that people worship God – people must worship *their* God in *their* way (i.e., through Christ). They did/do not go throughout the world seeking to introduce people to God – these people all already know about God – they seek to introduce people to Christ.

Christians do not take the good in their religion and leave the bad. They do not say to themselves, "Perhaps *this* is allegorical, because it clearly says in the Bible not to harm others, and *this* would cause harm to others. Perhaps it does not mean literally what it seems, which contradicts the clear message of our Lord elsewhere in the Bible. Let's work on improving ourselves and understanding clearly the messages of God and of Christ, no matter how long it takes, until we are sure we understand the true meaning behind *this* – or until we can implement *this* and still maintain the imperative, stated elsewhere in the Bible, to not harm others. Let us be sure we understand the message of God before we go forth and, perhaps, mislead others and cause harm. Let us understand our religion fully before we try to teach it. Let's try to become what we *are* sure Christ wants us to be, to become people who do not harm others, and work towards a deeper understanding of God's message through Christ."

They do not want to take the time to be sure of Christ's message before spreading it throughout the world, because, for one thing, their Bible is written with a built-in sense of urgency, or this is how many choose to interpret their Bible. Soon, God will enact "His" Rapture,‡ and they must save as many souls as possible before then. (To some

---

‡ The "Rapture," as I understand it, is when God plucks those who have been "saved" from the Earth, to join God in heaven. Those who have not accepted Christ are left on Earth, and then begins the "Tribulation," which is when demons come to live on Earth with the non-believers.

non-Christians, this seems nonsensical: Why would God not give everyone on the planet plenty of time to hear about and choose to accept or reject Christ, if this is to be the deciding factor in whether or not people will enter heaven? Is God in a hurry? Or is God only focused on PEOCs in that "He" has decided that, since PEOCs are thoroughly corrupt, "He" is ready to enact "His" Rapture now – and tough luck for those non-PEOCs who've never heard of Christ?) For me, I would rather risk going to hell than risk becoming a genocidaire,[§] which I'm sure no true God would want.

Instead, Christians take the bad and throw out the good. They decide, for example, that it is much more important to save people than to maintain the imperative to do no harm, rationalizing, "If we have to harm them to save them, at least they will be saved." Christians also don't want to take the time to fully understand the message of God because, though they tell themselves they are selflessly spreading the word of their Lord, their *acts* are often motivated by what they call sins, such as greed, lust, sloth, pride, and vanity; not by piety.

Christianity seems to have none of the struggle or searching which are a part of many religions. Christians commit what their religion calls sins, and, apparently, don't try very hard to abstain from them – because, after all, they are only human. Jesus died for their sins, and so those sins can be forgiven. To me, indulging in these sins does not seem very respectful of Jesus, whom they believe died for these same sins. It seems like they

---

[§] I am using the term of Philip Gourevitch: See *We Wish to Inform You that Tomorrow We Will Be Killed with Our Families*, selected bibliography. I use the term to denote one who commits or has committed genocide.

would try *very, very* hard *not* to indulge in these sins under the circumstances – but that is obviously just how it seems to me and not to them. The only struggle in this religion seems to be to get through this trialsome life on Earth (and convert everyone you can while you're here); the only sacrifice, giving money to the church (because there's usually a financial side to anything Christian – which is, in itself, suspect). It's interesting that Native Americans thought of Earth as the paradise God had given them in which to live; even after passing to death, many return in spirit to this wondrous world. Their lives were "heavenly," not nearly as traumatic and stressful as the lives of Christians – at least, until the Christians came to save them. God gave the Christians paradise, too, and look what they have done with it. I don't understand why Christians seemingly feel no need to care for the Earth which God created, why they do so much to destroy it.

And consider how Christians pray. For Native Americans pre-PEOC, the entirety of daily life was a prayer of thanks and love for the Creator. They lived in a reverence which is beyond the ken of Christians. On the other hand, Christians are constantly praying *for* something. When they pray, they treat their God like a wish-granting genie. They may trouble themselves to thank "Him" if "He" grants one of their wishes; some may even trouble themselves to thank "Him" if "He" doesn't grant their wishes, but they all have that "grant me this" relationship with God, and they all have a long list of new wishes to request. It's pretty sad.

Christianity is, apparently, an effortless religion. Sure, there are scholars who study, for example, how many times this or that phrase is used in the Bible. But for the most part, once you have found Jesus, you have found the whole truth, so there is no need to search for God's meaning or seek enlightenment. You can hear about the Lord, be converted, and become saved all in the same day, and, by then, you're pretty much set. Thank Jesus for doing all the work for you and try not to indulge in sins.

To some of us who are not Christian, this can seem shallow. Did not God put us here for a reason? Though God may want us to accept Jesus Christ (according to Christianity), certainly that is not our only reason for being here. Didn't all the people who lived before Christ have a reason for being? In other words, it seems that, for many Christians, Christianity is not a means for fulfilling God's will, because, just by becoming Christian, you have fulfilled God's will, so you're done (except for converting non-Christians).

I have found, over time, that some Christians have trouble doing something good for its own sake, because they feel they would be remiss if they did not take the opportunity to exploit your gratitude and use it to convert you. Thus, for example, many Christian soup kitchens include a sermon with the meal. It's as though the point, for them, is not to feed hungry people – it's to convert people through a free meal. They may say the sermon is to thank God for the food, but the sermon then goes on to try to convert the listeners to the glory of Christ. (Did God make food cost money so that only some people can afford to eat? The perpetuation of Christianity – and all of PEOC culture – keeps soup kitchens in business, because it keeps hunger a reality.)

One day, some people handed me a flyer for a free concert. They didn't mention that it was a Christian band and that they intended to get people to show up for a free concert so that they could try to convert them. It doesn't occur to Christians that there is anything wrong with this type of behavior. They don't think there's something wrong in trying to trick people into joining their religion, nor (apparently) care that their trickery gives some people a very negative impression of their religion. They don't, apparently, wonder if there might be something wrong with a religion that you have to trick or mislead or frighten people to join. To some non-Christians, this looks like hypocrisy; to some Christians, it's business as usual.

It's strange to hear Christians complain about how immoral and decadent this country has become – because this is a primarily Christian country. (By the way, this is not a new lament – Christians have been making this same lament from the beginnings, but they always think it's new and that the past was good – same as all of PEOC culture.) The vast majority of people in this country identify themselves with Christianity; as Christians are so fond of pointing out, this country was settled (= colonized) by Christians and built by Christians (or the slaves of Christians and others over whom Christians held control), and it is run by Christians (as in every single U.S. president and most of the legislators and judges, as well). If this country is a mess, whom do they think is responsible?

Many Christians support leaders who are clearly immoral, who regularly engage in what their religion calls sins, solely because these leaders say they are good Christians and are against homosexuality and abortion (though, when one

140

has a mistress who gets pregnant, they are privately for abortion). Regardless of their views on abortion and homosexuality, most of these leaders are willing to engage in any immoral act which furthers their pursuit of wealth, power, and self-pleasure. Why don't Christians support leaders who are virtuous, who don't indulge in sin, who embody the precepts of Christianity? Is it because they do not have any such people in their religion? Again, if this country is a mess, who made a mess of it?

I have had Christians come to my door, trying to spread the word. After I tell them I am not interested and close the door, they stick a flyer in the doorjamb, because they cannot respect my decision. They will not respect me, but I should respect them.

When Christians tell me, "Have a blessed day," I want to (but don't) reply, "Have a cursed day" – because their greeting is not kindly meant; it is like saying, "I am going to put Christ in your life whether you want Him or not." It doesn't feel like a greeting; it feels like a slap in the face. What if you were a Christian living in a country where everyone wanted to convert you to Religion X, and everyone greeted each other with, "Greater glory through X" – the correct response being, "Greater glory through X." They know you are Christian and have no desire to convert, but they still greet you with, "Greater glory through X." What are you going to say? "Hi"? "Greater glory through Christ"? Either way, the greeting, "Greater glory through X," has already set an antagonistic stage for anyone non-Religion X. I realize that, in our culture, some people enjoy antagonizing others, and sometimes it seems Christians feel a duty to antagonize non-Christians, but think: Is saying something like this really going to convert *anyone*? Or is it just going to (possibly) cause resentment? Is it that hard to show some respect to non-Christians?

Not that Christians are necessarily more respectful of other Christians. They criticize each other because they are not Christian enough, or they are not the right type of Christian, or they do not worship correctly (and hence are damned even though they do worship Christ).

And, sometimes, it seems (to some non-Christians) that they do not even respect their own religion. They *advertise* their religion on TV and radio and billboards and put Jesus symbols and bumper stickers on their cars. I wonder if they realize that, to non-Christians, these bumper stickers make it seem that they hold their religion on a par with messages such as, "Get your burgers at Ben's," "I brake for clowns," and "I'd rather be golfing." And the messages on these bumper stickers are often unkind, even hateful. "Believe or be left" – honestly, that doesn't make me want to become a Christian or think more highly of their religion. You've got to feel sorry for these people, who worship the Creator, not out of reverence or awe or love, but out of fear, the fear of being left behind in case of "His" Rapture.

How else do Christians show their respect for God and Creation? They kill and maim millions of trees each December to celebrate the birth of Christ. Is this supposed to symbolize the sacrifice of a life? One tree for the nation might symbolize this (if that truly is the meaning); having trees in millions of households across the country seems to symbolize lack of respect, an utter disregard for these other entities, also God's creations. Isn't there

142

possibly something wrong in taking the life of an 80 foot tree (is it 100 years old? 200? – science doesn't know – nor do the Christians) to *decorate* Capitol Hill or Rockefeller Square for a month? And how much energy does it take to power the billions of bulbs used in Christmas decorations across the country? The Earth and other entities pay for all of this electricity – and we actually, *literally* kill people and destroy their lives to import energy from their lands to the U.S. Is this gross consumption really a way to *honor* God and the birth of Christ?

It seems Christians have no sense that the Creator gave other peoples ways to worship; nor that the Creator found a way to communicate with anyone other than PEOCs, and only through Christ; nor that the Creator loves *all* of Creation: people, animals, plants, rocks, winds, water...all of the Earth. They have no sense that right now, as you live, you live as part of the Creator and Creation; just because you die doesn't mean you will suddenly leave (or join) the Creator. To a non-Christian, hell and Rapture seem to be only concepts of fear, of control through fear, and of justification for domination. Christians do not think, "We are a part of God – if we want God to be good, we must be good," because, for them, God is a separate entity, not a part of them.

Maybe, someday, Mother Earth will rise up and say, "Enough" of those who are destroying her and her children. How ironic if she swept away those Christians who, in the name of their own salvation (and the accumulation of wealth), commit so much destruction; who, in the name of the Creator, destroy so much of Creation, if she swept away their empires and cities and churches, leaving only heathens behind to resume in the paradise God created.

Christians believe they will go to heaven when they die. It's "up," in the clouds; winged angels sing all day and fly around and play harps; there is only happiness and joy – none of the dreariness of this life. Everything is always good; there is no bad. All those who have accepted Christ as their Savior and only those who have accepted Christ as their Savior will inhabit heaven, the realm of pure good, eternally. (I guess once they are in heaven, Christians will finally find a way to get along with each other, because, here on Earth, they don't.) Sadly, some Christians feel it's important to baptize their babies ASAP, because, if their babies die before being baptized into Christianity, God will send them to hell (or this is what some Christians say, at any rate). So much of Christianity seems to be about fear, rather than reverence.

And non-Christians, the bad people, go to hell when they die. It is "down" (I guess towards China, if you live in the U.S. – and towards the U.S., if you live in China) and is inhabited by demons. Christians do not believe in karma, but what if the karmic retribution for being a Christian were to come back in the next life and be at the mercy of other Christians? Would that be so bad? Take a moment and think, not about the values Christians preach, but about the way they live and treat other peoples and the other entities of Creation.

I have heard Christians rationalize the maiming, torture, and abuse of millions of animals daily on the basis of their religious fact that animals do not have souls (a soul being the eternal part of your being). Ignoring the questions of whether they are right in the concept of a soul and who or what has one – how does an animal's not having a soul make it okay to cause it horrible pain and suffering? Is it because it will not be there in heaven to beat you up for what you did on Earth? (I realize that not all people who rationalize the maiming, torture, and abuse of animals are Christian – but those who are Christian have the attitude that they are holy, because of their religion, not because of how they act; that their religion makes their acts okay.)

Thus, for example, many Christians believe that factory farms are okay, because animals do not have souls. It is okay that animals are never allowed to move or to thrive or to have a single instant of happiness; it is okay they are cut to pieces while they are still alive and still screaming in pain; it is okay that their lives are unutterably miserable, indescribably torturous. Now ask yourself – would you want to be at the mercy of Christians?

I ask myself, why would the Creator send the one true religion only to PEOCs? Clearly they were (and still are) lost from true spirituality, from even understanding what true spirituality is – I can understand why God would think they needed spiritual help. But PEOCs corrupt everything: Surely God would have foreseen that PEOCs could not be trusted to carry the one true religion to all of the world in its pure form. Surely God could have chosen a people who would at least be able to agree on the most important points, on what was fundamental to the religion. Surely God could have found wiser and kinder messengers, if it were indeed God's *one* true religion. And surely God would have foreseen that Christianity could just be turned into another rationale for oppression; I cannot believe that God did not realize what PEOCs would do. And why, if He were God's son, would Christ say to go to all the lands and convert the peoples? Did Christ think everyone was like PEOCs? Was He not all-knowing? Did He not know that most indigenous peoples were *very* spiritual, and that this spirituality was a *part* of them: The idea of not thanking and respecting the Creator would never have occurred to them?

I can imagine a Christian picking up this book, reading this essay only, and condemning the whole book as an attack on Christianity (or, for that matter, a scientist reading only the essay on science, and condemning it on that) – but this is not a book about Christianity, nor science – nor is it intended as an attack. I am trying, as my title says, to get us to look at ourselves, our beliefs, our actions, our effects, and so on, because it all causes destruction to the Earth, to the peoples and other entities of the Earth, and to spirituality. We are all a part of our Mother and our Father, the spirit who works with our mother, and both are in all. By hurting each other, we hurt them.

People may say that the way Christians *act* is not what Christianity is supposed to be. All I know is what I see. For all I know, the whole Bible is allegory, and Christians have none of it right – I wouldn't dream of joining the ranks of Christians telling each other what their religion is *supposed* to be. All I see is what is.

The Meaning of Life

PEOCs spend so much time doing (or making money to pay someone else to do) so many meaningless, make-work tasks, it's astounding. No one stops to ask, "Does this task have to be done? *Should* it be done?" Someone invents something, so they create a need in consumers' minds in order to sell it. And so the PEOC lifestyle progresses.

It takes at least as much time to clean and maintain everything you own today (vehicles, home, yard, clothes, stuff) as people spent 50 or 100 years ago. Feel like you're always busy and never done? Just emptying your mailbox and shredding all the junk mail with your name and personal information plastered on it wastes time; same with sorting through and deleting junk e-mail. And if something happens, such as a car accident, at minimum you've got hours spent with the police, insurance companies, and car repair shops.

Look at your day, and take out all the time you spend doing tiresome, repetitive, meaningless tasks. Also take out the time spent at a tiresome, repetitive, meaningless job (or a job harming others) and time spent commuting (one of the daily tasks of life). Also take out time spent on mindless, empty entertainment (watching TV, playing video games, surfing the internet, going shopping, riding up and down your street fifty times on your motor scooter and driving your neighbors crazy with the noise) –

perhaps you need these diversions to unwind from your workday; perhaps these idle pursuits are what makes it all worthwhile for you – but take them out. Take out time spent on money-making schemes. How much of your day is spent doing something meaningful – and is it really meaningful? Many people, when they're done subtracting the meaningless, are left with nothing.

Contrast this with indigenous peoples, whose daily lives were meaningful; the idea of meaningless tasks was not a part of their lives. They didn't "kill time" and "waste time." Everything had value. If you were gathering food, you were also learning about the plants and the animals, and how your life interrelates with their lives. If you were preparing a fire to cook the food, you were also honoring the Creator and engaging in an act of Creation. We just pick up food at the store, bring it home, and turn the knob on the stove or punch some buttons on the microwave. Living, for them, was not simply tasks; there was meaning and learning behind each act. It's hard for people in our culture to conceive of how meaningful life can be, and I imagine many people think it would be a drag to spend so much time considering the meaning and import of your actions, when you can just go through life enjoying yourself thoughtlessly, and leave the Earth and other entities to pay the price and understand the meaning.

Most of us never get down to true meaning – we just spend our lives away. Collecting Pez dispensers – this is something that passes for meaning in our culture: hobbies, collections, fashion – not a deep expression of one's person (most people don't know themselves in any deep way anyway), but a superficial expression borrowed from someone else's vision. Most people define themselves in these externals, anyway – it is the only way they know themselves: the car they drive, the way they've decorated their home, the clothes they wear, the music they listen to, their hobbies, the shows they watch... And people put themselves into this meaning fully, having a meltdown if they miss an episode of their favorite show – or working 20 hours of overtime each week so they can afford payments for the "sexy car" (apparently some people have sex with cars) – or waiting in line for hours (or days) for a store's grand opening, so they can be first inside (some people actually do this).

For some, the meaning in their lives comes from causes. For example, maybe your cause is trying to save threatened and endangered animals. You think our culture has finally learned that it is wrong to make a species extinct and that, by contributing to this cause, you are helping to move our society to a point where we will stop endangering animals. Even though 100 years ago (and long before that) they also had the concept that it is wrong to make an animal extinct, and even though this belief didn't keep people from killing off animals, you hold fast to your cause. You are undaunted by the fact that, in spite of all the animal charities and the millions of dollars poured into them, we are endangering species more and more, not less and less. You are unfazed by the sad fact that the number of endangered and extinct animals isn't going down.

Nevertheless, there is a problem with your cause: As long as you are supporting the culture which is leading the way in the endangerment of animals, the culture which could conceive of hunting an animal to extinction or destroying its home (and the animal charities are a part of that culture), then you are supporting the extinction of animals, no matter how much money or time you give to "Save the Animals" causes. So the meaning in your life is meaningless.

It's true that a lot of endangered animals are in non-PEOC countries, but the endangerment comes as a direct result of PEOC and other Eurasian interference. The indigenous peoples of Africa (for example) did not have the problem of endangered animals before we came along. And while scientists dick around trying to determine why these animals have become endangered and how to save them (in a way which will not interfere with the activities of PEOCs), the animals die. These "Save the Animals" groups may not save a damn thing – and when one of these charities is looking for a CEO, they tend to want someone who can raise money, not someone who can save animals.

Apparently (but not actually), the bighorn sheep has been a protected species in California since sometime in the 1800s. Since then, the number of bighorn sheep in the state has been steadily declining. What kind of "protection" is that? I guess "protect" in this case means to actively and deliberately pursue activities which will destroy the homes of bighorn sheep and kill them off. (We like to abuse language this way in our culture; we are very fond of calling black "white.")

I am sure the "Save the Animals" charities would say they have a few success stories. But their success stories are often as sad as their failures. We think that saving some representative animals is the same as saving the species. We think that, even though we have devastated their natural habitat; even though their natural way of life is wiped out; even though *their* culture is destroyed – we have saved the species. No matter if their way of life is gone, because we still have some living representatives (it's kind of like the way we feel about the Native Americans whose cultures we destroyed). We do not look at the fact that there is more to it than just saving some living beings. These animals are a part of creation, they have their own purposes.

We think we are highly advanced because we run around spending our lives on meaningless tasks and because we have freed up our time to engage in meaningless entertainment, but it is not advancement to take the meaning out of life.

Spirituality and Everyday Life

The PR in PEOC culture (by those trying to sell things) is that this world is changing so rapidly that it's "a full time job just to keep up." –But life isn't changing any more rapidly today than it was yesterday. The idea of a frenetic pace leaves people thinking they've always got to be in a hurry, always catching up, and leaves them living their lives that way, not really paying attention because they are too busy. –But it's all a façade. If you have gotten along your whole life without having a personal computer, you can continue to do so – they don't do anything important. You don't need TV with cable and a five-room DVR to be able to relax and entertain yourself. From youth, we are trained to want things and to spend our lives working so we can buy them. When something becomes obsolete, we want the next thing, whether it's a pet keychain, a 32GB MP3 player, or a cell phone with all the latest apps. And since we are always playing catch-up, we don't really have to spend a minute (or have a minute to spend) wondering if we really want or need to catch up – wondering if all we need for joy and life and enjoyment and spirituality is already here, not being invented.

I have never had a mocha cappuccino – don't even know what one is beyond the fact that it has something to do with coffee – and yet I do not feel hollow and empty inside. I don't stroll through the mall just to see what's available for me to buy, nor wear designer shoes, nor seek to purchase an electronic phone book/scheduler/camera/music player/cell phone/GPS unit/ID card...

I take no prescription drugs (nor over-the-counter drugs, for that matter) but somehow manage to hang on to life. With not one of the myriad of small kitchen appliances available, I still miraculously am able to prepare food. I will not be re-decorating my home (ever) but yet can find something to do with my time. I will not be buying stain-resistant carpeting (which theoretically makes cleaning easier for you, but actually just imports into your home another boatload of toxic chemicals for your kids and pets to play on), and yet I am able to sleep uninterruptedly through the night. (If this essay doesn't seem to be much about spirituality, I'd say spirituality doesn't have much to do with our everyday lives – because this essay *is* about our everyday lives.) I will never restore a classic car, nor install speakers with 92dB sensitivity and 200W continuous power handling, nor take a 4-day-3-night cruise to the Bahamas, nor buy a home gym which will allow me to isolate my abs for a sculpted physique – and yet I can live a fulfilling life.

I want to live a real life, not go to my grave feeling like I never lived, like I missed it, like I was just rushing through and getting things done or catching up – or buying things in self-indulgence. I don't believe life is supposed to be about working so hard for a few moments of enjoyment now and again – nor about being exploited (by the company you work for, by companies who want your business) in order to take your turn (when you're lucky) at exploiting others. I have had these feelings many times in this society: I miss so much because I'm in too much of a hurry, or too busy planning in my head for later to enjoy what I am doing now – like I am missing the point.

And countless others in this society, feeling similar feelings, turn to their local bars (because, in our culture, numbing yourself to life is a time-honored way to deal with life), or to how-to books, or to spiritual retreats. And because of the complete spiritual void in our culture, people are eager to jump into what might be called pop spirituality. (The difference between pop psychology and pop spirituality is that real psychology can never lead to true knowledge, but real spirituality can.)

By *pop spirituality* I mean ungrounded spirituality. For example, we have people who treat their spirituality like it is part of the melting pot of our culture, borrowing other peoples' religions and destroying them by converting them to the PEOC world view. With this melting pot technique, other spiritualities are superficially learned and barely understood; spirituality is partially imported into our culture, without all the burden of the grounding, and it's all interpreted through our cultural haze. What you're left with pretty much has nothing to do with the original religion.

Some people try to incorporate as many different faiths as they can into their melting pot spirituality, as though this will give their spirituality a broader base; as though this way they will be able to learn *everything* that all those faiths can teach. This is another cultural blindness, a completely cultural approach to spirituality, which, as usual, leads nowhere. These people don't actually learn anything more than a few catch phrases or a few slightly-grasped ideas or beliefs, and so what they end up with is not the best of every faith; it is no faith at all. It is kind of a lazy way to go about being spiritual, a spirituality smorgasbord: Move on when you're challenged or when you tell yourself you've gotten everything you can out of this religion. No actual spirituality involved.

True spirituality is not a hodgepodge of misunderstood techniques and practices that people of our culture think we've improved. It's not a form without meaning, nor a veneer you paste over who you really are, nor a theory about life, nor a question of semantics. It's not something you learn overnight, nor something you acquire without effort or sacrifice.

Because of the complete spiritual void in our culture, people try to sell anything and everything as spirituality, from your daily exercise routine or bungee jumping off of bridges to actualizing your goals – but these are not spirituality either.

Yet in our culture, people actually act like *actualizing your goals* (for example) is a spiritual quest. They set goals and visualize themselves reaching those goals as though it is a religious experience. People give seminars to teach people how to live their lives this way. We have a goal-oriented society; we think we are supposed to have goals, that they are a positive force in our lives. Our culture has made a virtue of setting and going after goals; beyond that, people are encouraged to develop life plans, which are long-term goals that almost always revolve around acquiring wealth.

If someone doesn't have goals and a dream of where they will be in twenty years, and they are not spending away their life today for their dream of tomorrow, that person is a loser in our culture's thinking. We believe you should always have a goal you're working towards, so you can realize your life dream – when you achieve your goal (or give up), then you should set another goal. But this is a mistaken way to live, another cultural blindness, another idea we have backwards.

One problem with having a goal, as a general thing, is that it leads to tunnel vision, to not living in or reacting to the moment, but instead in living for the future. (It's worth noting that many spiritualities, such as Buddhism and many indigenous beliefs, emphasize the importance of living in the current moment, of being aware of the here and now. Interestingly, Christianity emphasizes overlooking the here and now in favor of looking forward to heaven.) Having a goal keeps you focused on anything but the (usually) dreary present, the here and now. It helps you cope with all the negative things about your life because you tell yourself you're changing those things, and thus it helps you avoid reality (which is not a good thing). And it fits right in with our hectic, don't-have-enough-time ('cause I've got somewhere to be) lifestyle. It's like a way not to live because you're spending your whole life pursuing what you wish your life would be. Usually, when or if someone reaches one of their goals, they have to set a new one, because attaining the first one did not give the happiness they expected, or because they've conditioned themselves to always want more. In fact, if you get to a place where you're satisfied and not trying to reach another goal, again you're a loser. The only people in our culture who are, perhaps, allowed to stop working towards something else are retired people, but even they still have goals. They may spend more time relaxing and enjoying what they've spent their lives acquiring, but they still pursue meaningless entertainment and self-indulgence.

It's a pathetic way to live, having desire as the primary motivation governing your life, but we think it laudable and praiseworthy. We act like someone without goals has given up, but that's our backwards thinking. It is the people who are constantly in pursuit of something else who have given up life.

*   *   *

Our culture has a plethora of churches and religions founded by people who claim to have unlocked the secrets of the universe. Like Christianity, these religions typically require money from their believers. Usually the founders are very rich, and you've got to wonder how that works: Are they spiritualistic people or materialistic people? Why do you need a 12,000 sq. ft. home filled with antiques or artifacts pilfered from indigenous peoples if you're at peace with yourself? And for those who join these religions: If you follow someone, aren't you relying on the clarity of their vision? Why do you have to have money to be able to afford spirituality? Might not the clarity of their vision be doubted if they prize the material – might it not be wealth, rather than your spiritual growth, that motivates them? Wealth is not a reward the universe has given them because they are so good. (If wealth is a reward for goodness and wisdom, then why are, for example, the major stockholders of the oil companies rich? –They're certainly not good or wise.) The universe doesn't work that way, and, if it did, it has much more valuable gifts than material wealth to bestow. Why do PEOC spiritualities almost always determine that the pursuit of wealth is virtuous and good?

I've read promos for books in which spiritual leaders talk about how you can incorporate faith into *whatever* you do (like destroying endangered animals' homes), or how science can be incorporated into your faith. That these spiritual leaders feel a need to try to incorporate science into faith shows they do realize that science is a religion in our culture. It also shows that they are not quite as enlightened as they claim. We are so far from truth in our culture, we don't even know what enlightenment is. These leaders are culturally bound and are unable to move past those boundaries. If science supports your religion, then your religion is culturally-bound. And if your spiritual understanding is limited by your culture, then it can go only as far as your culture allows. Spirituality, a relationship with the Creator and Creation, should go beyond the boundaries of any culture, or it does not have the infiniteness of a true spirituality.

* * *

People host spiritual retreats, the thinking being that if you go to a spiritual retreat for a week or a weekend, you can return to a life in this society with new meaning. PEOCs actually see that separation, wherein someone can spend most of their life doing tasks they just want to be done with, but have a meaningful life in a few minutes a day. Or they can have a job harming people or hurting the environment and still be a spiritual person, because it's just their job, and they need to make money. Maybe you go away for a weekend to learn a little Native American wisdom, and you think you can incorporate that wisdom into your life as a colonizer of today's Native Americans (because, though we do not acknowledge it, Native Americans have never ceased to be colonized peoples).

Are any of the people who voted for George W. Bush or who helped to manipulate Florida's 2000 election in order to give him the win bothered by conscience? (The results of this election were hotly disputed for a lot of reasons I'm not going to get into. I don't think anyone denies that Florida's election officials deliberately perpetrated a fraud on the people of Florida and of the United States. The Republicans didn't care, because this fraud helped Bush win the election, but let's be honest – if the Democrats had been the beneficiaries of a fraud, they wouldn't have cared either. Members of the U.S. Supreme Court voted on whether they would hear a case contesting the results of Florida's election, and the vote was split exactly on party lines. Maybe you were happy with their decision, maybe not, but does anyone still believe this highest court in the land is impartial?) Because Bush was given power, thousands of innocent Iraqis lost their lives, and this is besides thousands more people spread out all over the world. If you voted for Bush, if you helped Bush into power, then you're responsible for those deaths, whether you like it or not. (Some may say that Bush's war against the Iraqis was an unforeseeable consequence of his election. And if you change "un" to "easily-" in that last sentence, then you are right.) The point is, you can't just do something and then divorce yourself from the consequences – or be spiritually enlightened only when it's convenient.

And if you live in this society, it's impossible to *not* do *something* which is harmful and destructive. If you buy, for example, a compact disc, do you know how those who profit will use that money? – to destroy the Earth? – to collect exotic animals? If you pay rent in an apartment complex or purchase a condo, you are supporting all the landscaping the management uses. If they use toxic pesticides and herbicides which are accumulating in the soil, you are supporting that. If you live in an apartment, you are also supporting whatever the owner does with the profits. If the owner spends nights downloading child pornography, you are supporting those activities. Whatever you spend money on, you are supporting the activities of the person who profits. And however that person spends their money, another person makes a profit, and so on. We do not consider this type of support in our culture, because it would be very inconvenient to have to know what we are supporting with our constant consumption. Yet the support is there.

If you work for someone who cheats their customers, aren't you also cheating the customers? If no one would work for such a boss (or such a company), these bosses wouldn't be able to continue cheating people. But they can continue, because, in our culture, people need jobs. The people who work for the dishonest bosses and companies rationalize (i.e. lie to themselves) that it's not *them* cheating people – it's their bosses and their companies. And by the way, what does your boss do with all the profits from your labor? You're supporting that, too.

How does your bank invest the money in your savings account (if you are "lucky" enough to have one)? Bankers are looking for the highest return, aren't they? Do they invest in energy and pharmaceutical companies? Those businesses have high rates of return, but they also engage in morally questionable actions, which their investors support.

If you work to bring what we call advancement to what we call developing countries, you share guilt in the hunger and destruction which accompany our advancement. If you work as a pharmaceutical rep pushing pills, or as an actor in one of their ads, then the deaths and illnesses which result when people take these pharmaceuticals are your guilt. If the corporation you work for pollutes the environment, your work is supporting environmental pollution. People like to say, "He's just doing his job": The cop who harasses people for looking like "trouble-makers" or who persecutes minorities is "just doing his job"; the news reporter who reads one sensational and inaccurate story after another on the nightly news cast is "just doing her job"; the soldiers and CIA operatives who run Guantanamo Bay are "just doing their jobs" – maybe these people should get different jobs. If PEOCs didn't have this separation in their minds, wherein someone can do bad things all the time and yet be a good person and wherein spirituality is something disconnected from how you live, then suddenly we would not be a country of such good people.

Indigenous peoples are able to feel our Mother and our Father because they live with them – and, in our culture, we don't. There are some lessons in spirituality which cannot be taught, and if you are not living a lifestyle which opens those lessons to you, then you're obviously not going to learn those lessons. Spirituality is not something distinct from the way you live – we just like to think it is. Our culture corrupts spirituality like it corrupts everything else, makes it a discrete field, something apart from daily living (since our mode of daily living clearly will not admit spirituality) – but it's not separate, and our spirituality is not real spirituality; it's just business as usual with the label "spirituality" slapped on.

The Intention of New Age

Some people in our culture try to practice spirituality as attitude, using "positive thinking," "good intentions," or "looking at the bright side" as though they are spiritual practices. The problem with all of these is that they are in our heads, and there is an *actual* world outside of our heads. Though PEOCs love to live in the thoughts in our heads and there endow them with substance, this substance exists only in our heads.

The problem with looking at the bright side, for example, is that, to learn from life, you have to look at it without the blinders of looking for "the bright side." You have to look at the bright side *and* the dark side and every other side. The problem lies in *not* looking at the bad, in ignoring it and acting like it isn't there, and in instead focusing on the good. But just because we choose not to look at the dark side doesn't mean it isn't there. Those who are determined to look at the bright side avoid everything else. If necessary, they invent a bright side so they will have something to look at. (One could look at the bright side of trans-Atlantic slavery – but there isn't one.)

In our culture, looking at the bright side translates to finding something that you can call good in everything. If you think that there is at least one bright side to everything, i.e., "Well, at least we learned one of life's lessons," then you are just engaging in the usual PEOC self-delusion: PEOCs have shown again and again that they never really learn life's lessons, partly because they are so arrogant, and partly because of people who don't look at anything but what they decide to call the bright side.

Sadly, our bright side is often someone else's dark side. For example, our pioneers (= colonizers) thought it was a bright side every time we success- fully destroyed a Native American nation so that we could take over their land, but obviously the Native Americans didn't agree. Looking at the bright side is a way to put everything in a happy light, regardless of truth. It's absolutely consistent with our culture: The bright side is our spin on reality which makes us believe that, no matter how bad our acts and how much harm we do, there's always a good side, *something* positive. We do not want to reach a deep understanding – we'll just look at the bright side and keep happy thoughts. This does not reflect a chance for growth, nor a true spirituality; nor is it a truly positive force.

*   *   *

I am not a New Age follower; I know only what I have seen and heard from those who are: New Age spirituality is a mixture of indigenous cere- mony, quasi-Asian beliefs, science, psychology, and whatever the New Agers invent as they go. They believe very much in positive thinking, intui- tion, and good intentions, and they believe these things can take the place of any actual grounding or knowledge.

As part of your New Age education, you may, perhaps, attend a ceremony which is meant to teach you indigenous wisdom. The host of the ceremony may be someone who took a class from someone else who spent a year studying with indigenous people. According to New Age belief, this person has sufficient knowledge to host the ceremony, because it isn't really about understanding the ceremony or performing it correctly; it is just about the host's intentions. New Agers believe there isn't really a correct way; as long as the host's intentions are good, then everyone attending will benefit from the ceremony, or, at least, not be harmed. Let's look at that:

In traditional indigenous cultures, people had a certain grounding, an understanding of our connection to Mother Earth, to the Creator, and to all of the other entities of Creation. Children began gaining this understanding even before they were born. But even with this grounding, which was reinforced throughout childhood, once they began study in a field, the first year's learning was just an introduction to the beginnings. This first year might be spent sitting in fields and trees and in bringing water from the river. The meaning of all of this is that, if you don't have a deep and profound understanding of your connection to Earth, then any knowledge you gain in a field will never be understood. If you don't know how to honor the Creator, the Earth, and her children, then any knowledge you gain, you will never be able to properly implement. A year's training or studying certainly didn't qualify one to teach that field. The point here is that it's all interrelated, and there is no such thing as this or that "field" – that is just how *our* culture treats life, because we are unable to look at or see the whole.

I once asked an indigenous herb healer if she would teach me, and she told me to go learn her language. This makes sense, because there are some things which cannot be conveyed in English. But it also makes sense as respect for her and for the people who found this knowledge and carefully passed it down from generation to generation, adding to it along the way; as a demonstration of dedication; and as an acknowledgement of the commitment necessary, because to truly *understand* these things is a long process, not something you do overnight.

But New Agers are PEOCs and do not have a fundamental grounding. And so, because they do not understand the need for all the preliminary work which is meant to teach the student a deep awareness of the Earth, they skip it, and in its place they use *good intention* and *intuition* (which is not the same thing as ESP). *Intention* is a belief New Agers have wherein, before doing something, you inwardly declare (to yourself or to the universe) that you intend to do good by this act. And in the mind of the New Age believer, this is enough: If you do not understand something, your intuition will guide you – as long as you began by first setting your good intention, your intuition will guide you correctly. Even if you do no good, you will at least do no harm. A big problem with this thinking is that people in our culture always claim good intentions, yet they cause very real harm. Christian missionaries claim good intentions, yet that does not keep them from devastating indigenous peoples. New Agers may say to themselves, "We are trying to learn from indigenous peoples; we are not destroying them." But, since they have no grounding and don't really understand the Earth or her peoples, they wouldn't see their destruction. Their good intentions are all based on the same misguided cultural beliefs which guide all PEOCs.

New Agers like to use crystals, gems, and other precious stones in their healing, in their ceremonies, in their jewelry, and so on. They buy these stones and ignore the fact that Mother Earth is torn up and blasted to get them, that someone is breaking the bones of the Earth. They buy what they believe are special stones because not just any common rock is good enough to do whatever it is that they want to do. They have created, in their minds, a hierarchy of the value of stones, and they believe common rocks don't have as much energy or the same quality of energy as the stones they buy. But every rock has its own energy, and if they're feeling something specific in crystals, it's all in their minds: They don't actually feel and understand the stones, because they don't understand the Earth, and the rocks are a part of the Earth. Hence, though they could pick up a rock from the ground, which our Mother has yielded gladly and which is ready to be found and used, they prefer to choose one which has been torn from our Mother. (I realize, sadly, that many of the rocks lying on the ground in our cities were also blasted and torn from our Mother, to be used for landscaping, gravel, or concrete additives.)

Some New Agers find going to a hands-on mine an enriching experience, and there they destroy tons of rock to get to the "valuable" stones they hope to find inside. They don't realize that the rock they destroyed, looking for the precious stones, was just as valuable as the stones they sought. And they think it is okay to use stones which were torn from our Mother, because they have good intentions and because, they

believe, the stones are being used for good purposes, i.e., to heal people and to heal the Earth.
And they don't see the tragic irony in that. *They*
do not have the power to heal anyone, regardless
of what they tell themselves (which is another
reason that they need the grounding they by-
pass), but the Earth *does*, so, by destroying her,
they are destroying the healing power they try to
access. And if they want to heal the Earth, they
should stop harming her and give her a chance to
heal herself.

I realize that, when they speak of healing the
Earth, they are not really talking about healing the
Earth, which they don't really consider as worthy
of their attention; they are talking about healing
the *peoples* of the Earth. But the peoples of the
Earth are all connected to the Earth, even PEOCs,
though we don't realize or feel it with any depth –
so you cannot heal the peoples as a separate matter. Our well-being is directly tied to the Earth, not
in the shallow, survival-of-the-human-race manner elucidated by science, but in a much more profound way that scientists – and the other people in
our culture – cannot understand, because we think
of ourselves as separate from the Earth, chained to
it for oxygen and food, perhaps, but separate.
Interestingly, water, the Earth's blood, used to be
clean, and people's blood was clean. But now, water is dirty, and our blood, too, is dirty and diseased and polluted.

The New Agers who use stones attend rock and
mineral shows and go to crystal and gem shops.
They say they love, honor, and respect stones, yet
they are willing to buy and sell them, and they
clearly do not respect our Mother. And they ignore the stones they walk by, which are lying on

the ground. What they are doing is picking cool stones, and then, because they like them, deciding that they are supposed to have them – it's what the universe wants. If the universe wanted someone to have a stone, I think the universe would find a way to get it to them without the help of dynamite, earth-moving (= Earth-destroying) equipment, and the exchange of money. If the universe wanted someone to have that stone, it wouldn't be buried in a mountain, needing to be blasted or dug out, and it wouldn't be sitting in a store where Mother Earth is bought and sold. Perhaps the universe would leave that stone lying on the ground, where an aware person, one who actually *would* be able to work with it for good purposes, would spot it and pick it up.

These people don't question why the universe would want someone who has no wisdom and no knowledge of the stone to have it, at such a great cost to the Earth, because it does not occur to them that they have no wisdom or knowledge – they believe their intuition and good intentions will guide them in its use.

Many New Agers claim they can feel convergences of intense energies in certain locations, but they cannot even feel the Earth and the intense energy of the pain they cause – how can they think they feel these energies? They tell themselves they are doing good and that their good intentions keep them from doing harm. But they are harming the Earth and the rocks, plants, animals, and peoples whose lives are harmed by the mines, and they are harming the waters which are used in and polluted in the mines. Miners use toxic chemicals, which all end up in our Mother. And the people who love the stones use toxic chemicals to mount them in metal (also torn from our Mother) for jewelry and trinkets.

Whatever the end product of their studies – a store selling specialized New Age products, a healing clinic, or a school teaching others – the New Agers are exploiting the Earth and the peoples and entities of the Earth. It's very exploitive of Native Americans to borrow their wisdom without bothering to understand it, without showing respect to that wisdom, and without caring about today's Native Americans – except those who are willing to teach the New Agers. Perhaps the New Agers think they are carrying the torch, helping to keep the knowledge alive for future generations; perhaps they think they have added a little more knowledge to be passed along; perhaps they think they have improved on the indigenous wisdom, because PEOCs always think they improve things. But all this good is only in their minds.

What they tell themselves doesn't change the fact that there is a real truth outside of their minds, and the real truth is that their good intentions aren't helping, their acts are harming, and they aren't learning or approaching the truth in their spiritual search. New Agers have been sending out what they call "positive energy to heal the world" for quite a while now, but the world isn't healing, in spite of what they tell themselves in their self-deluded belief that they are having a positive effect. Someone told me he had looked at several institutions for his New Age studies, and all had warned about why the other institutions were not good choices. A few minutes later, he was saying that if everyone were into New Age, we'd be headed towards world peace.

They may truly believe truth is flexible, it is whatever you decide it is: Rock sellers invent characteristics and categories of stones, which they use as marketing tools to increase profits. Here is a fictional version of one of these characteristics: "A rock with a narrow tip is called an artist stone, a pen stone, or a paintbrush stone and is useful in treating people who feel they are creative." (I made this characteristic up, but the real ones are just as ridiculous.) New Age healers are fully aware that these characteristics are complete invention, but they run with it, thinking it doesn't matter anyway, because it's all about their intentions. They know nothing about the stones yet think it okay to say, "This will help" to their clients, because their intentions are good. Thus a marketing tool is truth. Why use stones – why not just use some bottle caps or plastic beads?

Even if it seems New Agers help some people to get well, that doesn't give their spirituality substance. Their healing industry is like our traditional medical industry: Just because some people come out of it healed, that doesn't mean it works. And like our traditional medical industry, just because some people are healed does not mean that it is a positive force or that it does no harm. They may not hurt their clients as much as our traditional health care does, because they don't pump them with toxic pharmaceuticals and slice them up, but healing with New Age techniques is hit-or-miss, just as much as with our traditional health care. A true healer shouldn't fail ¼-½ of the time. We just expect that, because healing standards are set so low in our culture.

*   *   *

New Agers think they are helping the universe to balance, adding positive energy to offset all the negative energy out there. They don't look at it on any deeper level than just "putting out positive energy," which can be as simple as sitting together, perhaps with a crystal to focus on, and thinking happy thoughts. Having a store where New Agers come to shop for paraphernalia also counts as putting out positive energy. They don't question whether their energy *really* is positive or whether putting out positive energy *really* helps anything, because, like all PEOCs, they do not actually look at the world.

Beyond that, on a fundamental level, they do not understand that the universe is already and perpetually balanced; that the universe does not need our help to balance things; that the universe does not *want* or *need* anything. They do not have a sense, nor do PEOCs in general, that the universe is always in balance. The only balance PEOCs seem capable of conceiving is that of science's natural laws (or, perhaps, God's Rapture).

We cannot conceive that the universe does not need our help to fix or improve it, or to restore the balance – as though the universe can't do it without PEOCs. We cannot see that the universe is *not* looking to PEOCs to save it, anymore than endangered animals or indigenous peoples look to us to save them. We are not motivated by good intentions when we cast ourselves in the role of savior; it is pure and unadulterated arrogance on our part to assume the role of helper or savior to everyone and everything, where no one else looks to us in these roles.

We feel like we are perpetually off balance, because of our culture, and so we *think* the universe must be so also, because we take our culture as the standard. We think the universe is off-balance because *everything* seems off-balance to us. But maybe we should try to see the balance rather than try to fix the universe, which doesn't need fixing.

PEOCs culturally think, because things aren't getting better, that we need to do *more* (or different) things – but that's just because we blindly assume we are in charge of making things better and that, eventually, we will succeed. It never occurs to us to leave things alone – but it did occur to indigenous people.

Many people have the feeling that they need to do *something*, like everything is falling apart, and anything is better than doing nothing. If it's not the best thing, they think, at least it's *something*. And this is the way our culture works, the reason we keep doing the wrong things. I have talked to many people promoting causes. When I point out the flaws in their programs, they respond, "Well, should we sit around and do nothing, then?" I am of my culture; I said from the start that I don't have the answers. Yet I know that championing or following a cause which is not properly considered and which will lead to new harm is not the answer to effecting change, to effecting a new course for our culture. It may make people *feel* like they are doing something good, but the reality is that they are just propelling our culture along the same course it has always taken: a blind path that the people of the future will protest against, as they, in their turn, blindly chart another course of destruction. Pursuing these causes just keeps people from looking at the fact that they're *not* helping, because they can tell themselves, "at least we're doing *something*."

We cannot look at ourselves and see that we are somehow the ones who are out of touch, that we are the ones who don't see what is there. We may feel disconnected, but, at the same time, we also tell ourselves that we, as a culture, are headed in the direction of being in touch, and that we are at least farther along to an understanding than other cultures. We are so sure we are the most advanced people on the planet that we cannot see that our whole concept of advancement is just something in our heads. Nor do we consider, "Perhaps we are simply creating acts which the universe balances, constantly. Since we are unaware of the balance, we create acts and make different choices in our acts than we would make if we were aware, if we were not *thinking* of ourselves as separate entities. Are our actions something separate, or is that just in our minds? Will the universe eventually balance the actions we are creating by causing the end of humans?" In our culture, we always think things are out of whack and that we need to fix them. Indigenous peoples see that everything is balanced, that they do not need to fix the world they live in, because it is already perfect.

All of this illustrates the need for a grounding to spirituality and the fact that good intentions are not a substitute for grounding. In fact, it is very hard, if not impossible, to have *truly* good intentions if you *don't* have a grounding: Your good intentions are just baseless, warm, fuzzy feelings, existing only in your mind, with no good effect. A truly good intention would involve some real sacrifice and an understanding of and reverence for the Creator and Creation.

New Agers have the same hierarchies as the rest of our culture, and people are at the top. In keeping with the rest of the culture, their hierarchies assume not only that some things hold more intrinsic value than others, but also that we, as a culture, have the knowledge and wisdom to determine and rank these intrinsic values. They think the rocks don't mind being mined; in fact, they are happy to be mined, because they know they are going to be used for a good purpose: to serve people. The plants, too, are happy to serve people. I heard a New Ager say the *Earth*, too, is happy to serve us, and I was offended, but the New Agers around me weren't fazed, because it is what they believe.

New Agers *do* speak of being grounded, but their idea of grounded comes straight from psychology, which is itself ungrounded, so their grounding is nonsensical. It is based on ideas such as, "Do you see the value of what you contribute to society?" Inherent in this question are the assumptions that you should contribute to our society and that every contribution is valid as long as the contributor feels it is. A hit man could answer, "Yes" to this question.

"Do you balance your time between helping others (such as assisting friends and donating your time to charities) and making personal time for yourself, to relax and indulge just for the fun of it?" Inherent in this question is the assumption that helping others and doing something for yourself are separate and exclusive activities. Also inherent are the assumptions that you should donate your time to charities and that you should indulge yourself just for fun. We like to think that everyone should spend some thoughtless time, concerning themselves only with self indulgence, disregarding how their actions are affecting the Earth and her children, almost like it is a responsibility on our part to be selfish. At any rate, a doctor who overcharges his/her patients and turns away those who cannot afford to pay could answer this question, "Yes."

"Do you enable the child within?" Meaning, "Do you make time for self-indulgent activities and buy self-indulgent 'toys,' without concern for how your actions are affecting the planet?" I think almost everyone in our culture can answer, "Yes" to this question – except for the poor. I've been poor, too broke to eat let alone indulge. I think many poor people would have to answer, "No" to this question – so I guess they aren't grounded.

"Do you feel validated in your relationships?" Even an abused wife could talk herself into answering, "Yes."

"Do you manage stress so it does not run your life?" I wonder if other cultures even have a word for stress. Our stresses come primarily from our lifestyle – if we didn't have this lifestyle, we wouldn't have these stresses. The whole concept of being stressed out is cultural, but then, our culture is very stressful (and only *we* would think that's a sign of *advancement*.) At any rate, all of those bosses who pass their stresses to their subordinates at work and to their spouses at home would be able to answer, "Yes" to this question.

The point is, these questions don't mean anything, and they have nothing to do with understanding oneself or the Creator and Creation. They have nothing to do with true grounding. They are just more cultural circularity; to someone outside of our culture, they wouldn't make any sense.

The PEOC idea of grounding is based on cultural ideas about how to view yourself and the world. It is something psychologists invented, based on studying people of our culture. Theirs are not by any means universal or even objective standards of being grounded. For PEOCs, grounding is about how you feel rather than about how you understand or how you act. You can lead a very destructive life (perhaps make business decisions which result in the endangerment of animals), and psychology can still make you feel good about yourself, so you can be grounded according to the New Age definition.

If you don't share the PEOC way of viewing the world, New Age spirituality won't make any sense to you. It's not about being in tune with the universe – it's about being in tune with the culture. This is the essence of attitude-based spiritualities: It's not about how you act; it's about how you feel about how you act. Develop yourself *within* the cultural boundaries. It's okay to be upset about water pollution, but you must channel that feeling into a "positive" outlet (i.e. one which won't actually help end water pollution) and not let the feeling overwhelm your life. *Be happy* – always – whether it's warranted or not! (If you need them, we've got drugs – or herbs – to help you.) If you actually should be having serious doubts about your life and what it means to the rest of the planet; if you should be *very* upset in our culture, they don't want you to be. Go through your life without any *fundamental* questioning – that's the first prerequisite to being grounded.

Our knowledge also plays a large part in making sure we remain ungrounded. Look at a field like astrology. Many indigenous people are able to read the stars meaningfully and very accurately. Once upon a time, PEOCs became exposed to this, and some decided they'd like to be able to read the stars, too. But they felt like they had to do it right, to improve it. A true grounding, that which allows indigenous people to read the stars accurately, was replaced by our form of knowledge. Astrologers approached the issue in the same way scientists approach things: They wanted to develop a methodology which would apply to all situations and which could be taught in a classroom-type setting. PEOCs think that if we can't formulate a process which anyone can apply, then something isn't valid. We think that if we cannot objectify something and pose theories which try to universalize it, which others can then build upon or attempt to rebut; if it is not something we can attempt to prove or disprove in the orderly fashion our culture has determined is the correct way; if the knowledge cannot be taught in the only way we know to pass on knowledge, then it isn't truth. So if you do not believe in universal laws which hold in all circumstances; if you believe, instead, that understanding is a matter of knowing the Earth and the infiniteness of the universe and of being connected to these, our culture will disregard your knowledge as superstition. Without this linchpin of the correct way, our knowledge, our truth, breaks apart and blows away in the wind, dissolving into nothingness. Making spirituality (such as astrology) into a field or a science, or into our version of knowledge, is one way to take any true spirituality out of play.

And so in astrology, we started with astrological signs and their categories (water sign, etc.). But there was a problem: Astrological signs do not accurately reflect people – they didn't work. So we decided we must also take into account the moon someone was born under. But astrology was still not accurate – so we decided that the house Jupiter is in must also be a factor. We're not quite there yet (but we're getting closer) – let's look at... Astrologers think that the more complex they make it, the more astrology reflects reality, but it doesn't. And what's missing is not the moon or the house; it's the grounding. Their field will never be accurate without this – and *with* this, they would not be constantly building on a faulty theory. For those who believe, astrology's a crutch; to those who don't, it's superstitious nonsense. The whole field casts doubt on indigenous star readers, who actually *are* accurate.

But PEOCs don't want to make the fundamental changes and sacrifices which would help us truly become grounded, in part because we don't even realize we're missing something, and in part because we love our self-indulgent lifestyle. New Agers are just as motivated by greed and desire for "the good life" as everyone else in our culture – just listen to them talk; you can't avoid hearing about making money.

Like almost everyone else in our culture, New Agers desire wealth and believe the universe approves of this desire. There is usually a financial side to anything New Age. They have a massive amount of paraphernalia you must buy if you want to do it right: stones, sacred and ceremonial objects, clothes, bells, scents, books, music, and so on. Plus, you must pay for your New Age ceremonies and classes, which are often taught by people who have something to sell. For example, a seminar in herbalism may be taught by someone who sells herbs, so that plenty of class time is spent talking about purchasing products, and the students learn that buying things is essential to their spirituality. A student in a New Age certificate program, during the course of their studies, is sure to hear about all the other certificate programs they should also take to enhance their skills. And so on.

Like other people in our culture, New Agers want quick results. They are not willing to invest years of study on things they can't use; they are not willing to invest the time it would take to truly learn. Someone can take a course, or a few courses, and be almost immediately ready to put what they have learned into practice. The spirituality has no actual depth. It's all about graduating or completing the course so that they can get down to business, just like it is for students in a university.

The indigenous peoples whom New Agers copy, whom they claim to honor, took care to pass knowledge down from generation to generation. They took time in teaching their people and in making sure that knowledge was not lost. Had they been more enlightened, like New Agers, they could have dispensed with this care and simply taught, "Use your intuition and go with what feels right. It's all in how you frame it, anyway." Why bother to pass on the knowledge of a ceremony, when anyone can invent their own ceremony, and it will be just as valid? Why bother to study indigenous ceremonies or practices at all, since New Agers believe they do not really need to learn them correctly and can just use their intuition to fill in the blanks? Why do indigenous peoples bother to pass down ancient knowledge if it's just a matter of having good intentions and using your intuition? The answer is that it isn't just a matter of good intentions and intuition.

True intuition comes to us from understanding our interrelatedness with everything and from the Creator and Creation, and, if you do not feel your connection, your intuition is just in your imagination. If the New Agers' intuition is so reliable, why does it not tell them to stop harming our Mother?

As far as good intentions, in most cases, it isn't about our declared intentions. (How do we manage to cause so much harm all around if our intentions are as good and honorable as we claim? How can good intentions lead to so much damage?). It's about our actions and their *effects*, and what are good intentions in our minds can have negative effects in the real world. We can (and do) call everything whatever we choose, but that doesn't make it reality, and that is the problem in substituting attitude for true spirituality.

I have received a couple of impromptu readings from New Agers in different fields, and both readings were way off the mark. However, if I believed, I suppose they would have made me doubt myself and have seemed like wondrous revelations. Someone might ask, "What's the harm of giving readings, even if they aren't accurate, if it makes people feel better about themselves?" While these readings may not cause as much physical harm as some of the drugs (legal and illegal) which people use to feel better about themselves, here's a better question: "What's the matter with helping these people understand the Earth and their connection to our Mother and our Father, so they will truly be able to understand and feel good about themselves, with a basis for that good feeling? What's wrong with their having actual grounds to feel good about themselves, rather than just something someone invented?"

You can have a lovely picture in your head about all the good you're doing (all of PEOC culture does), but that doesn't make it real. The idea that "it's all in how you interpret it and how you choose to view it" (i.e. there's no real truth) is cultural belief, not spirituality. It's true that everyone has their own point of view and different experiences, but your view is not a truly positive thing if it's pre-determined by our culture and your desire to keep happy thoughts.

How different is the New Age way of passing on knowledge from the process traditionally used by indigenous shamen? In the latter case, a wise shaman, knowing the characters of the young people, would choose the best person or people to whom to teach their knowledge, so as to make sure it was passed on correctly, for the good of the future people. The value of having a teacher who understands the essential need for a grounding is that the teacher can look at where you are, how well grounded, and decide it is time for you to go on to the next step *when you are ready* to understand it. This is as opposed to the New Age learning process, which is simply a matter of someone having money and wanting to take a certain class. To truly learn, I guess you have to learn the things you don't want to learn as well as those things you do.

New Agers think they have created a warm, positive enclave of people who really want to do good and who *are* doing good by pursuing a vision that no one else in our society sees, but it's actually the same vision the rest of our culture follows, with no understanding of true respect and no true knowledge of what is in play. If they really had good intentions, they would make the sacrifices necessary to realize them. They would have to sur-render their culturally-determined vision, to come to understand the world outside of our cultural blindness; they would have to surrender their be-liefs that we are well-intentioned and advanced. And they would have to relinquish all that our culture grasps, including wealth. True spirituality actually *does* require sacrifice.

Diseases of Society

(This is a partial list.) Government corruption; politicians and public officials for sale; pedophilia; adults raping children; children raping children; innumerable wars; innumerable military actions; innumerable CIA covert actions; violence by adults; violence by children; accidental shootings; vehicular accidents; prescription drugs that lead to kidney failure; prescription drugs that lead to liver failure; prescription drugs that are more likely to kill the patient than the disease being treated; prescription drugs that are tested on throwaway people; prescription drugs that are tested on throwaway animals; animals bred for no other purpose than to be tortured in labs their whole lives; animals tortured in factory farms their whole lives; animals mistreated by their owners; animals dumped because their owners no longer want them; stray animals who starve to death; animals put to sleep because they are unwanted; animals made to race or fight for their owners' profit and amusement; animals flayed and cut up alive; animals tortured by children; animals trained (tortured) to be in entertainment acts; animals "gone bad" after being tortured one too many times by their trainers – the animal is always the one blamed and punished; animals pent up in zoos for display; dogs forced to have litter after litter of puppies so their owners can sell them; dogs with ears and tails clipped so they will look the way their owners want them to look; animals hunted to be mounted on walls; animals whose homes are destroyed by the constant encroachment of people; animals left starving by the encroachment of people; extinct animals; endangered animals; steel traps to kill wild animals; bestiality; shoplifting; robbery; burglary; drug addiction; modern-day slavery; psychological experiments which permanently scar the experimental subjects; abuse of power; murder; mass murder; serial killers; gang rape; lack of public involvement; assault; mugging; car jacking; blood diamonds; McCarthyism; forced internment of Japanese Americans; loss of Native languages; destruction of Native cultures; invasions of other countries; feuds; sadism; masochism; cancer; diabetes; birth defects (the terminology of a culture which wants to control what is normal); water pollution; air pollution; noise pollution; toxic waste; visual pollution; companies that cause water pollution, air pollution, and noise pollution; custody battles over children in which children are the weapons and the victims; junk mail; telemarketing; criminals; police; police abuse; police racism; religious intolerance; racial intolerance; cultural intolerance; child drug use; parents who kill their own children; parents who yell at their children; incest; cults; suicide; mass suicides; unwanted children; exploited laborers; destruction of the environment; sprawl; homelessness; Guantanamo Bay; hunger; starvation; lack of health care; people with multiple jobs who cannot afford their water bill or the rent on the run-down place where they live; filth; censorship; infringement on civil liberties; corporate malfeasance; corporate monopolies; embezzlement; unmitigated greed;

sloth; vanity; pharmaceutical industry-invented syndromes and diseases; mental illnesses; child labor; homeless children; babies thrown away in dumpsters; dumped toxic waste; landfills; bad manners; absence of simple respect for others; massive consumption of the world's resources; hit and run; priests who have molested children being reassigned to churches in the poorer, ethnic areas; ghettos, barrios, reservations, slums; urban blight; people who make fun of those who are different; people who make fun of those who are what our society deems slow; the KKK; neo-Nazis; petty tyrants dominating their employees; incompetent bosses; incompetent customer service; people who yell at strangers because they are angry; lack of self-control; video game and internet addiction; obesity; nicotine addiction; phobias; elder abuse; old parents hit by their children; old people left to die in nursing homes; loneliness; helplessness; hopelessness; despair; boredom; domestic violence; police who commit domestic violence, whose spouses cannot call the police for "help"; police who lie under oath; stalking; road rage; vengeance; forced sterilization of people with "undesirable" traits (like ethnicity); genocide; colonization; slanted news coverage; sensationalized news; kidnapping; hijacking; carnival rides that fail and kill people; cars that fail and kill people; fraud; prostitution; teens and pre-teens forced into prostitution; prostitutes beat up by their pimps; men who have sex with teen and child prostitutes; sex slaves; beauty contests; child beauty contests; "disturbing the peace"; tax codes; legal codes; bureaucracy; government secrets; the FBI; the CIA; the NSA; secret government organizations; government spying on citizens; government murdering its citizens;

toxic household cleansers; toxins in foods; toxins which are illegal to use in the U.S. showing up in food we import from other countries; salmon farms; stocked lakes; oppression; credit card debt; guns; nuclear weapons and other weapons of mass destruction; agent orange; warheads made with spent plutonium left to litter other countries and harm the citizens we claim to be helping; swearing; deadbeat dads; women who don't know the father of their child; waste; prisons; lobotomies; illegal drugs; legal mood-altering drugs; people driving on drugs; gangs; mail-order brides; diets; smog alerts; hate crimes; cyber crimes; identity theft; lying; cheating; con artists; bombers; anthrax; conformity; dependence; lack of knowledge about how to live independently of society's institutions; people who die in a natural disaster or when lost in the wilderness because they cannot survive one week without having a place to go for water, food, and shelter; buildings which collapse in earthquakes; companies that weigh the anticipated cost of lawsuits from the deaths of their own customers vs. the cost of fixing their product; repetitive jobs; carpal-tunnel syndrome; birds swimming in unhealthful water because they cannot read this sign posted on a beach in Malibu: "WARNING Historical sampling data results gathered at this location indicate that bacterial levels exceed health standards. The County Health Official cautions that contact with ocean water at this location may increase risk of illness...," and a lack of concern, on everybody's part, for the birds who are swimming in the toxic water, because it's not like they are endangered species (yet); an ignored sign which the people of California *can* read: "$1000 fine for littering"; anorexia; bulimia;

torture; voter fraud; election fraud; antibiotics; antibiotic-resistant diseases; *millions* of prisoners; juvenile detention; hypocrisy; globalization; depression; cover-ups; the boy in the plastic bubble; prison rape; child pornography; children accidentally drowning in pools; children being cooked to death when accidentally left in hot cars; Child Protective Services; hit men; the mafia; necrophilia...

As I mentioned, this is a partial list. Just listing the diseases of our society could be a book on its own.

Many of these are old problems; priests have been molesting children since there were priests, and the church has known and covered it up since there was a church. Many are new problems, which have morphed out of old problems as our culture has supposedly advanced.

We have a problem with unwanted children. How do you not want a child? (I am not talking about abortion. How do you have a living, breathing child in front of you and not want that child? In many cultures, this would be impossible.)

I often hear people say, "There's too much. You can't think about it all the time or you'll go nuts; you need to take some time for yourself to relax and just not think about things." What does that say about our society, that there is so much misery and pain; that there are so many problems? What about a society where you have to intentionally deaden yourself to life and ignore the pain so you won't go nuts?

Ours is a sick society. If you want a cause to champion, there are plenty to choose from. The problem is that you cannot live in this society without being a part of (supporting) it, and these problems are all *integral* to the culture and society. Even if you are fighting against, say, air pollution (or any other cause) – at the same time you are supporting air pollution because your actions support the culture, and the culture is air pollution. Show me a society without air pollution and child abuse, and I'll show you a non-PEOC society. Maybe you will end one instance of child abuse, but, at the same time, you are part of a culture which will spawn the act again and again, so you're not helping end the problem. In many cases, we don't even really look to end a disease; we assume it is human nature and that the best we can do is to address instances. The pretense of fighting the diseases of society is a part of our culture which makes it look like we are trying to improve and makes people feel like they are making a difference. But they aren't, because our society isn't getting better.

Some people think that many of these diseases are a part of every society. They think that, though not all cultures are "advanced" enough to have identity theft, every culture has, for example, pedophilia and corruption. But this is a PEOC fantasy. They are comparing other societies to PEOC culture 300 years ago; back then, *we* still had these problems, but (they think) our society was too closed for anyone to admit it. They think we've progressed to where we can now admit the diseases so that we can find solutions, but that every culture has these problems, even those that don't admit to them. But their comparison is inaccurate. Jealousy may or may not be a part of every human society, but abuse of governmental power, domestic violence, and air pollution are not – though we *are* doing everything in our power to

189

introduce these problems into every other society on the planet.

We have the ever-popular advice, "You can't do everything; just do what you can: Recycle at home, take shorter showers, use your dishwasher only when it's full, change to energy-saving light bulbs, or combine errands into one trip. It all adds up." –Which it does; and what it all adds up to is a culture full of people who are too selfish and self-indulgent to make fundamental changes, so they just do "what they can"; and, as far as I know, it is not making a dent in our gross consumption, our waste, or our destruction. Some people seem to feel that doing what they can gives them a license to consume more: "It's okay that I order 10 catalogs and magazines a month, because I recycle them when I am done." How many people know (or care) that recycling methods also produce waste, and most involve toxic chemicals?

The list of problems doesn't shrink. PEOCs will study and fight a social problem or disease for decades into centuries but never end it. They'll never see the answer, which is that the problem is integral to our culture, i.e. our culture is the problem. They'll come up with theories and talk about how complex the problem is, but never get to the root because the theories are *part* of the problem because they are part of the culture. And any solutions end up leading to more problems and diseases without solving anything. We don't *end* problems; we solve them – and they don't end. PEOC culture had a serious crime problem, but instead of finding the cause, we solved it with police. Now PEOC culture has a serious crime problem and a serious police problem. We had a problem with abused children, and we solved it with Child Protective Services. Now PEOC culture has a child abuse problem and a Child Protective Services problem…

We are a sick society – and these social diseases were absent from pre-Columbian Native American societies and from pre-European-contact indigenous societies throughout the world. Before the Europeans came, indigenous societies did not have so much misery that people had to intentionally deaden themselves to life to avoid going nuts. And these social diseases are not signs of advancement, nor of a superior society.

Values

The American Dream

Anyone who is willing to work hard can get rich, own a home, buy a car, have health care, eat delicious food, and have money left over to buy things to relax and entertain themselves; with hard work, *anyone* can have the American dream. This familiar ideal seems absolutely fundamental to every citizen of America, the lofty goal of our founding fathers to make everyone equal. All you have to be willing to do is work hard, and you, too, can have it all.

Let's put aside for the moment the fact that, when our founding fathers arrived, there were already peoples living in America whose cultures allowed everyone to have a home and food and time to spend as they chose. And let's put aside for a moment the fact that many Americans and groups of Americans have found this dream in our society to be a lie. Let's put aside for now the fact that this society is a class society just as much as the feudal and royal societies of Europe, that those with wealth and power here hold onto that wealth and power just as tightly as did the nobles of Europe, and that a person born into a poor family here will most likely spend their entire life in poverty – and hard work has nothing to do with any of it, for the poor or the rich. These things simply show us that we brought all the failings of European society to the U.S. with us.

Let's look instead at what this great dream says about the United States and its founding pioneers (= colonizers). The American dream could have been to become the most peaceful nation on Earth and to help spread peace throughout the world, including to Europe, from whence these pioneers had come. The colonizers came from lands which had been embroiled in wars for time immemorial and were warring still. Just think, if peace had been the American dream, we would never have had slavery, nor committed genocide against the Natives, nor countless other horrible crimes which stain the history of this country.

The American dream could just as easily have been that anyone, as part of their natural path and search for truth, can come to fully understand and realize the beauty of the natural world and their oneness with all of life. Or it could have been for the country to become a nation able to live in perfect harmony with nature and its peoples to become guardians of the Earth.

But the American dream, the American goal, is to work hard to accumulate wealth and buy things, and many people live their whole lives for this empty goal (how our society is a reflection of this emptiness). The founders of this country were shackled by the culture from whence they had come from having any true vision: The PEOC way of life grasps the accumulation of wealth, and the colonizers came here (and were sent here by their governments) with hands grasping, as we can see from the way they treated the Natives. It would never have occurred to our founding pioneers to create an American dream of becoming peaceful, because they came from a warring culture and, without thought, they accepted war as a part of life. They were unable to see beyond their culture and its primary goal, and this is the dream they enshrined in what they called the New World, where capitalism claimed to make the lofty goal of accumulating wealth available to the masses, rather than just an elite few.

I was recently talking to a high school student, who said that, if he could afford it, he would go to college so that he could get a better job. As he said, "That's why people go to college." Education prepares people to spend their lives stuck in the rut of paid servitude and helps perpetuate itself, so that they encourage the same for their kids. No one questions education which is intended to help someone get a job rather than to, say, better understand him/herself and life. What is a better job? Of course it's one that pays more. The destruction that the job may entail and its value to life are not considerations. Someone told me his son works in the factory farm business. I thought it would be very painful to have a son working in such a cruel industry, but this man seemed to make no distinction between this or any other "decent-paying" job: They're all a part of this society and keep it running. In this thinking, if you're in the factory farm business, you're helping provide people with food, and the cruel conditions imposed on the animals aren't *your* fault – it's just the way business is done. Similarly, if you conduct torturous experiments on lab animals, that's also okay because, again, you are making good money, and your job contributes to society. It's good for the pharmaceutical companies because, even though the results are faulty (and they know it), when someone sues a pharmaceutical company for the death of a spouse caused by one of their medications, the

197

pharmaceutical company can say that the medication is not proven to be unsafe in lab animals – which still wouldn't mean anything even if you were married to a lab animal, because the experiments are meaningless.

If you work for an advertising agency and develop an ad campaign for a harmful product, it doesn't really count (you say) because *you* aren't manufacturing the product. If your job is to raise money for a cause, and you know that most of the donated money goes to buy houses and vacations for the people who run the charity, it's still a good job; you're still helping the cause. It doesn't really matter what you do as long as you're well paid – does anyone question whether such jobs are honorable? In our society, someone rich can expect to be nearly universally admired, and it doesn't matter how they became rich.

The U.S. society is set up around the dream of accumulating wealth, and the government facilitates the accumulation of wealth – though it facilitates a lot more for corporations and corporate owners than it does for average citizens. For example, car manufacturers came out with a product long ago (cars), but for people to buy them in any significant numbers, they had to have somewhere to drive them. So various governments (city, state, federal) paid to build all those roads we have (and they continue to do so). And if the government hadn't built so many roads, the car manufacturers wouldn't have sold and continue to sell so many cars. But the car manufacturers didn't build the roads.

The public airways – "public" meaning, supposedly, owned by every U.S. citizen – are used for the profit of corporations (ABC, CBS, NBC, etc.).

For the privilege of getting rich off of our airways, they are supposed to provide us with a public service. Stations make money primarily by selling advertising, and a huge portion of the profit stations make off of advertising comes from drug companies. So it's not unusual to hear a public service news story about new drugs which are now available to consumers, or about a new syndrome which has been discovered and which can be treated by a medicine which X company just developed. This is what passes for the public service they are required by our government to provide, though they also air public service announcements, such as "Don't do drugs" and "Don't smoke," which also don't do anything to help the public.

Of course, the market economy supports the accumulation of wealth. One needs money to sleep if they don't want to sleep on the streets – notice that our state and federal governments will not allow people to live on public lands (because if they could, they wouldn't work). People also need money to pay for gas or bus fare to get to work. To live in our society, you need a way to get money; hence, those who own companies and large corporations have a guaranteed supply of workers, because not everyone can be "lucky" and own their own business.

When wealthy people or their corporations are about to lose everything and fall into the pit of poverty in which the majority of U.S. citizens spend their lives (the majority of people in the U.S. are working class and poor – in spite of everything the government has done to define "poverty" more and more narrowly) – our government steps in to help them out. Look at our auto manufacturers, many of the major airlines, our banking industries, etc.

All of these have repeatedly been the beneficiaries of impressive amounts of money from the U.S. government. The thinking (i.e. one of the rationales used to justify giving tax money to the rich) is that these are large employers, and if they go out of business, a lot of people will lose their jobs. However, the problem of unemployed workers doesn't seem to factor in when one of these large corporations makes massive job cuts or sends massive numbers of jobs overseas. Saying "We have to help these corporations, or a lot of people will lose their jobs" is an argument against having people dependent on jobs, not a reason for corporate welfare.

It's amazing how many companies there are in the U.S. who pollute either nearby rivers, streams, and lakes, or the ground and groundwater – and the people of the community know this, and they and their children get sick – yet no one does anything to stop it, because too many people in the community are dependent on the company for their jobs. Think about how upside-down this is, how upside-down this culture is. This is one of the many problems of a society in which people need jobs. Needing a job also leads people to put up with sexual harassment and other abuse from their bosses. You can hear even black people complain about Mexicans coming to work in the U.S., because "they're taking our jobs" – this is the same complaint white males made (and still make) about letting black people – and women – into the workplace. It's sad that people are so desperate for jobs that they are willing to fight each other for the privilege of becoming indentured servants.

Then there are all the wars our government starts for the rich. For example, when the profits of the United Fruit Company were threatened in

Central America, our government was right there, fighting the scourge of communism – except that there was no scourge of communism, just a government that was trying to curtail the oppression of the United Fruit Company, and a threatened loss of profits for this corporation. But our government has created many, many wars for many, many U.S. companies; in fact, almost all of our wars have been for the profit of U.S. companies or/and wealthy U.S. citizens.

And you have political campaign contributions. These do a lot to buy influence in the government – if they are for significant amounts. The average citizen can't afford to donate $5,000 here and $8,000 there (yes, when you think about it, our elected public officials sell themselves pretty cheaply) – but large corporations and the wealthy *can* afford these contributions, so they are the ones who can afford to buy public policy. The neat thing (for them) is that they can use public policy to increase their wealth (thereby allowing them to continue making political contributions) and to keep the masses from getting a chance to gain some of that wealth (since they want to keep as much for themselves as they can).

And then you have education. Education, for which the government (hence you) pays, provides corporations with employees. Kids go to school and get used to following a schedule for hours on end, approximately eight hours a day, five days a week, virtually identical to a workweek. Whether or not the children learn to read, they are shown conclusively that "America is the best country in the world" – and that they should devote their lives to acquiring money. I doubt many graduates could find Madagascar on a map, but they sure know that "America is better than Madagascar" because America is the greatest country on Earth, ever. And they know the glories of capitalism. School also teaches kids to handle boredom for hours on end, another essential for most when they take their places in American jobs.

Schools also provide the value of other kids exerting peer pressure, to discourage independent thinking – and the teachers reinforce this, as does the authority of the school. Children spend each day being exposed to the PEOC cultural view; if they don't fit in, then the other students, the teachers, and the school administrators try to make them fit. Children who don't conform are taunted, disciplined, and sometimes asked to leave school. The effect of all of this is to encourage the children to think and act alike, rather than think for themselves. True, one child may be better at thinking through and solving a certain type of problem than another child, but neither will question whether thinking through a certain type of problem is a valuable way for some people to spend their time.

A secondary value of peer pressure is that, even at very young ages, children (or their parents, on their behalves) become consumers, so that they will fit in. They have to have the right kind of clothes and school supplies, or other kids will make fun of them or bully them.

Beyond that, many disruptive kids will be forced to take mood-altering drugs while in school. This is immediately profitable to the drug companies, as evidenced by the fact that they pay schools for each kid forced to take these drugs. There is also, clearly, a long-term profit for these drug companies, both through the child's continued use of the drug in question and through the fact that the drug will most likely have side effects which will lead to the need to take more drugs, likely manufactured by the same drug company. Additionally, the children as a whole are taught that order is more important than any child and that if you don't act how they want, then you are "disruptive." They also learn that drugs are acceptable, even beneficial, because the school they trust requires some children to take them and administers them to the kids.

Finally, by the time the kids graduate, most have learned well enough how to read, write, and especially "follow directions" to be of service in most of the jobs for which corporate America needs them, a conditioned workforce to join the ranks of workers, making those who own the corporations ever richer. The lucky students who get college educations will have even better jobs while they are enriching corporate America.

And so they go to work for 8-10-12 hours a day, to earn money – the great American dream, essentially trading their lives away for little, rectangular pieces of paper. Instead of enjoying life and being free to do what they want to do and use their time how they choose, they join the tired path of America. They land the best jobs they can, lie to get them if necessary, and then become chained to them: They sit in their cars in traffic for hours each day to get to work, do their jobs even when they don't like them or when they believe that what they are doing is morally wrong, spend hours more in traffic on the way home, and, if they are lucky, make enough to accumulate wealth and buy things.

And the parents are proud, especially if their kids make good money. If you are one of those unlucky parents who has unmotivated teens, there is help: companies advertise that they can help "unmotivated teens." It is sad that if your child doesn't show sufficient interest in making money, they are deemed a problem child. It is as though, if your son or daughter is not properly focused on making money (motivated), you can (and *should*) send them to be reprogrammed. I imagine that companies of this sort probably show kids the glories of what you can do with money (consume) and make the kids earn some money and spend it. No doubt there is also a punishment component, because our society always uses punishment if you are not of the mold, if you're "disruptive." I wouldn't be surprised to find employees in these companies who used to be unmotivated teens, who were brainwashed into the proper way of thought, and who now want to help other misguided teens.

* * *

Just think, if the American dream had been to live in harmony with nature, people wouldn't have to spend so much time working in order to have a little bit of time enjoying their lives: Their lives would be enjoyment. Instead of a society built on the pursuit of wealth and tough luck to those who can't make enough to live on, everyone would be able to have food, safe shelter, pleasure, and time to search to understand the world and their part in life.

It's sad how many people in this society never get down to living. They retire and still have to work because they don't know what to do with themselves, or because they weren't able to save enough money to live on in retirement. I would rather live than pursue money. Nothing I could buy is worth the cost of giving up my life.

As long as you are reaching for the American dream, as long as you are grasping for more, as long as your desire for wealth owns you, this culture has total control over your mind and actions – you can never be free.

The Market Economy

Even our subcultures, the people who consider themselves rebels, rejecting the dominate society, different and alternative, are a part of our culture: Alternative lifestyles aren't really alternative. Sadomasochists, conspiracy theorists, and Goths – all are smack dab in the middle of our culture. Bikers, criminals, and the mafia are not outside of our culture; they are an integral part of it, as are cynics, anarchists, and the heavily-armed survivalists. Atheists believe, just as much as Christians do, that humans are the center of creation, and they are as much a part of our culture as Christians are.

Thieves and con artists are not outside mainstream society. They are a part of the greed, grasping in their own way – and they do support our justice system, which in turn supports our prison system. Nor are murderers an aberrant part of our society – they fit right in: Look at how many murderers we *have* in our society. Whatever the reasons they kill people, they are all, or nearly all, cultural reasons, and murderers kill because they live in a society which says killing is an option. You may go to prison if you take this option, but it's still an option. (I am not saying that in indigenous societies no one ever killed, but it was *very* rare.) All of these criminals are like the leaders of our multi-national corporations, who are also thieves and con artists and murderers, motivated by greed, always grasping for something.

Some people think we do not have one culture in this country; we have many. But this is an illusion, like freedom of speech. For example, over the years I have known many people from other countries who have immigrated to the U.S., and sometimes, when there is a community of immigrants, people think they have a different culture. But these immigrants are people who think the U.S. is a great and free country; they want to make money and become rich; they want the American dream; they want to "make" something of their lives; they want to live like Americans; they believe in science and advancement; and they buy TVs if they can afford them. Sadly, sometimes they won't allow their children to speak their native languages because they want their kids to become fluent in English. These immigrants think making a better life for their children means working long hours for pieces of paper in order to buy stuff for their kids and send them to college, so their kids will be able to get better jobs and continue the cycle: They are very much a part of this culture. They do not see a different vision. At most these are subcultures, holding different traditions on marriage, thinking American children are rude, or preparing food differently; but all are subsumed in the roiling melting pot which is our society.

Perhaps the idea of a melting pot was that the best of various cultures would blend together to create the best possible society, or perhaps this was just what people said because it sounded good. But the reality is that everyone becomes a part of the dominant European-originated culture, though, obviously, not everyone has equal rights and opportunities. And just because they are part of our culture, this doesn't keep others who are also in the society from hating or having prejudices against them; but hate and prejudice, too, are a part of our culture.

Members of cults are not outside: Their vision is very much a part of our culture. They believe they are following someone holy who has taken human form, like Jesus, and they believe they are chosen and scorn or pity others who are not so fortunate, like Christians. Often, the leaders of cults rape the young girls or boys, which is also a part of our culture. The members do not look for truth in what they are being told; they look for faith. There is no actual grounding to their vision; they follow a different set of lies in one arena, but they are as content to look at the same façade hiding reality as everyone else in our culture.

Even the mostly-non-voluntary homeless subculture is a part of our culture. In our society, those who don't have enough money, those who barely get by (some of whom work *very* hard) lead very hard, oppressed lives. (It is a misery you cannot fathom if you have never lived through it.) This is a price rich people are willing to pay for their wealth. Capitalism requires a massive downtrodden class as much as feudalism or monarchy, and the homeless are at the bottom. They are victims of the market economy, and yet they support that economy: When they get money, they go to supermarkets and fast food joints, just like everyone else.

In our culture, meats come from cows, pigs, sheep, chickens, turkeys – because these meat sources can be controlled and owned. When someone says, "In this country, they eat guinea pigs," or, "In that other country, they eat dogs," people in our society react by saying, "Yuck!" as though we are so above that. At the founding of the United States, the colonizers were certainly not so picky about the meat they ate, even resorting to cannibalism, as did the Europeans during their innumerable famines. Obviously I'm not promoting cannibalism, and I realize that some people have religious beliefs about eating certain animals, but, for the most part, our meat snobbishness is nonsensical, nothing more than a way to make people dependent on money to buy meat, a snobbishness which developed so the ranchers could expand their industry.

Of course there are not nearly as many wild animals available now as there were before PEOCs invaded this country, because we've killed off so many of them, but if people could eat birds or squirrels or snakes and make a fire for cooking, it would be a blow to our food industry. If people knew which plants and which parts of plants are edible and how to prepare them, it would devastate our farm industry. Many plants we call weeds are edible and/or have medicinal value: dandelions, purslane, lamb's quarters, and many, many more. This is one reason people have been led to the same conclusion about plants as they have about meats, thinking only certain types are real food. Free food and medicine for the people is unthinkable in our culture (again, what does that say about us?). Of course it is in the best interests of the market economy to kill all that free food and medicine, to spray the plants with poisons, to label them "weeds." Just consider: Indigenous peoples lived by eating these things, and they were much more healthy and fit than we are. So why don't we eat them? The answer is, because they are readily available and free, not because they aren't as good for us or don't taste as good as wheat products and cheese. There are so many wonderful plants which are perfectly edible, healthy, and delicious – and yet people think they are not real food and we are not supposed to eat them because they are not lettuce and strawberries.

If just anyone could live off the land and never have to buy anything – never have to work except to gather food and make a shelter out of materials readily available from our Mother Earth – the whole PEOC way of life would be devastated, because it is built on the need to work to earn money for your survival, so that some can accumulate wealth. We are not taught any other way. And by the way, this is *not* a capitalist scourge: PEOC culture was a scourge built on the accumulation of wealth long before capitalism was invented.

I had a teacher who made the point that we could not all go back to living on the Earth (though obviously we all live on the Earth) by asking, "Who would make the toilet paper?" The circular reasoning here is that we have to live the way we have come to live, and we couldn't live this way if everyone went back to living on the Earth. Some better questions would be, "Do we really need this thing at all?" and "Why shouldn't we all learn to be creative and make our own supplies – why be okay just buying them and not knowing how to make them ourselves?" I assume this teacher was also making the point that someone needs to keep the economy going. But obviously, if we went back to the Earth, we would not need an economy, so this is just another piece of circular reasoning.

Think how much equality there would be in a society in which anyone could eat and there was no wealth to accumulate. It'd be kind of like what the Native Americans had before the Europeans came and imposed capitalist democracy, which is what we call our tyranny.

Life isn't supposed to be about working your whole life for a few years' enjoyment at the end (or the interminable heaven after you die). It's not about working your whole life to make someone else rich, nor about working hard to become rich, nor about having others work hard to make you rich. That view of life serves the market economy and helps some people accumulate wealth – nothing more. You really are supposed to enjoy your whole life. The process of living is not supposed to be *work*, separate from living itself. But the idea of working your life away to be able to live is firmly held in our culture, to the point that many people believe you have an ethical obligation to work (unless you are rich, in which case you have no ethical obligations).

Cultural blindness makes the wealthy think they have accomplished something – but pursuing wealth is actually a wasted life. People get rich by being greedy, destroying the Earth, and cheating others: their employees, their customers, each other... It's sad that our culture exalts those who love money so much that they will engage in this type of behavior. It's sad that some people want to make the meaning of their lives lie in acquiring large houses, fast cars, new furniture, and big-screen TVs; and that everyone must live the market economy life to make it possible. (Not that all the people at the bottom of the economic scale mind. That's the wonderful thing about our cultural

211

blinders: Some people actually believe that it's worth slaving their lives away, making someone else rich, so they can have their share of the American dream. And they can always admire the rich and dream about joining them.) And so the poor and homeless populations fuel the economy and enable some to accumulate wealth, plus they make great experimental subjects for drug companies, the government, and anyone else who has money and a use for them.

Ownership of Everything

People in our culture feel like Creation is about humans, like the world is all ours and we have the right to buy and sell anything and everything. We work diligently to find more and more things to own, and then we try to conceive of ways to own more and more. We want to own things which shouldn't be owned, because, regardless of what our culture tells us, they don't belong to any one person or group. And we treat things *as though* we own them if we can't find a way to *actually* own them.

Companies develop fruits with seeds that cannot grow, or they irradiate the fruits to destroy the seeds. This is a brilliant advancement the American Natives never would have thought of. You cannot buy a piece of fruit and plant the seeds (assuming they haven't been destroyed) in the U.S., or at least in some parts of the U.S., without breaking the law. And the same holds true around the world. If you want to grow something, you have to buy seeds, because some people own food and the right of reproduction.

Only PEOC society would have thought of granting certain people a monopoly on food; only such a society would want people to be dependent for food and have to pay for it: Not everyone is entitled to eat – you have to work for money to buy food. (The fact that many people end up starving with this system is not important.) Only those who contribute to society (= contribute to someone else's greater wealth) are entitled to eat. If you think this society is sick and diseased, and you don't want to contribute, you're out of luck, because this society isn't set up for that kind of an independent sense of honor.

We own other entities: the plants in our yards, rocks, pets, farm animals... They do not belong to themselves, in our minds; they belong to us. Our culture has always believed it's okay to own and buy and sell other living beings, including other human beings.

In our culture, people own knowledge. Granted, I don't give any credit to the authenticity of this knowledge: The fact that it can be owned is enough to make knowledge in this culture suspect, since there is an ulterior motive working in its discovery – that motive being profit, not truth. In indigenous cultures, if someone had knowledge which could benefit the people, it was their responsibility to share it for the good of all (and an honor to do so).

They're selling stars now, too, so I guess you can own a star. I wouldn't be surprised if you can also buy a planet and tell yourself you now own that planet, but perhaps our government wants to own all the planets for its own use.

Money itself is for sale. You can purchase something on credit and pay for the privilege of using money you don't have. And creditors set such high interest rates that, by the time the debt is paid off, often the borrower ends up paying three or four times the stated cost of the product – and the banks and lenders have a clear conscience, like this is a perfectly legitimate means to make money.

I guess it's easier to sell a TV if you say it costs $200 but then charge $700 over the lifetime of the loan than if you just put a $700 price tag on the TV.

In PEOC society, we have the idea of owning and selling land. This isn't a universal concept. The Earth belongs to everyone equally, as it belongs to the non-human entities. If you work your whole life to pay for what already belongs to you, that's your foolishness, or greed, or both. Instead, you should be telling your government it is an outrageous law that says someone can own land – change the law. The Natives did not have laws that required their people to pay for somewhere to live. But in our culture, we do not all have the right to have somewhere to sleep at night.

Water belongs to the world and all of its entities as well, but we have found several ways to sell it. Only we would think of dumping massive amounts of waste into the water: human waste, instead of feeding the bugs and the plants, goes into the water; chemical waste – into the water; nuclear waste – same place (only we would think of developing something as toxic as nuclear waste, period). When corporations dump these toxins into the water, they are acting like they *own* it (and then they disown it once it's polluted).

Similarly, companies who put satellites into orbit are assuming ownership of outer space. (I can't park my car in your driveway without your permission, can I?) We may say, "The satellites don't affect the Earth" – but we don't know. We never realize beforehand *what* the effects will be, because understanding the damage we will do (and we *always* do damage) is never as important to us as getting that technology going, as someone being able to make money off something. But just because we're too blind to realize how those satellites are affecting the Earth doesn't mean that, magically, they aren't affecting the Earth.

If someone could, they would find a way to sell air. And the way we are increasingly polluting it, fresh air may someday be a marketable commodity (we already have air purifiers for homes and businesses). How sad: pay to breath – right in keeping with the mentality of this society. But in our use of automobiles and energy industries such as coal-burning plants, we show the mentality that some people own the air to pollute – they pollute everyone's air, just as some people destroy everyone's Earth. If you had to take ownership of the pollution you create, and we could encapsulate your pollution to hang in a cloud over your head and leave everyone else's air clean, would you be so casual about polluting the air? By polluting everyone's air, people are taking ownership of that air.

How can people see what's coming (one quick look at L.A., with its ever-deepening haze of smog should be sufficient) and do nothing to avert it? When today's children grow up, will they blame their parents for having polluted the air to an extent that it is frequently unhealthful to go outdoors? No, their children will not blame them, because they will have grown up in a culture which says we are always progressing, smog is an acceptable side-effect of progress, and having days in which it is unsafe for your children to go outside is an acceptable price to pay for our lifestyle. (Sadly, many children don't go outside anyway; why go outside, after all, when they can stay indoors and play video games?) Do we blame our forefathers for having built the railroads, which killed off millions of animals, destroyed their lifestyle, and destroyed much of our natural world? Or do we think we are fortunate for having inherited this "progress"?

Today's children, when they grow up, won't even think twice about a world in which, on some days, the air is too polluted for them to go outside, because that is a part of their culture, and their culture is the best culture ever. No, when they grow up, their children will not blame them for the pollution; they will *thank* them for it.

Destruction for Money

Is there anything we will not destroy for money? Many products are sold which are labeled, "known to cause birth defects," and companies know that most people don't read the small print on the packaging which says, "known to cause birth defects" – so, obviously, birth defects are acceptable to make money. The same holds for "known to cause cancer in children," "may cause cancer in children," "can cause liver damage," and so on. Perhaps consumers assume that the U.S. government requires certain standards of safety before something can be sold; they assume that, if they're buying something in the U.S., it must be safe; but all the U.S. government actually requires is warnings, and it requires those only occasionally.

The bulbs people use to clean babies' stuffy noses have warnings about the serious health hazards they pose to babies, yet they are still used in hospitals and in homes. And there are thousands upon thousands of products out there with these warnings: check your garden hose, every electrical item you own, your artificial Christmas tree, your toothpaste – and everything else you buy. Of course, some states do not require warnings on the packaging, but the manufacturers still know their products may cause health problems, and still they sell the products. (You have to wonder about a society in which people would even conceive of

218

creating and manufacturing things which cause birth defects – or cancer, or brain damage...)

Scientists believe lead causes all manner of harmful health effects, and yet companies still produce and import dishes made with lead, for use on your kitchen table. I'm betting that those manufacturing, importing, and selling these dishes don't use them on *their* kitchen tables.

A few decades ago, Nestlé Corporation, knowing full well that breast milk is the best thing for a baby to eat, nevertheless launched a campaign in developing countries, to get women to use their baby formula. They knew that these women often did not even have potable water with which to mix the formula (thanks to PEOCs), and they knew that most of the women could not afford enough formula to keep their babies fed and would therefore over-dilute the formula to make it last longer. They knew babies were getting sick and dying because of their campaign, and they considered this acceptable for their own profit. Very simple to keep the baby away from the mother after birth, while they're in the hospital, or to give her a free sample, which would last just long enough for her milk to dry up and for the baby to get used to bottle feeding. Force the mother to use formula, or convince her that formula is better for her baby than breast milk, and you've got another customer and eventually millions (billions?) of dollars in profit, with only the cost of the deaths of thousands of babies. Nestlé was willing to pay that price.

When this wealth-creating scheme of Nestlé's became publicized in PEOC countries, people acted like they were outraged and organized a Nestlé boycott. But this was long, long ago, and, as far as

I know, Nestlé is still in business (and I wouldn't be at all surprised if they are still making money off their clever scheme), so I guess the people's outrage at the intentionally-caused deaths of children ended somewhere short of giving up Nestlé candy bars permanently.

We have automobile manufacturers who develop cars, discover that those cars have a design defect which could be fatal, and then weigh the anticipated costs of the lawsuits that will ensue (because of the deaths and injuries that will result from people driving their cars) vs. the costs of fixing the design defect. If they think it'll be cheaper to pay the lawsuits, they won't be fixing the defect; if some of their customers have to die for their profits, they can live with that. It's informative that George W. Bush sought to limit the dollar amount of punitive damages that can be paid in these kinds of "frivolous lawsuits" (his words) – meaning that lawsuits brought against companies which have knowingly caused death and illness are frivolous. Obviously these are the lawsuits he was referring to when he used the word "frivolous" – I never heard him mention "non-frivolous" lawsuits – and when he sought to limit punitive damages on what he called frivolous lawsuits, these types of lawsuits were included. He never sought to exclude non-frivolous lawsuits from the punitive damage limits.

So, if your child dies because a company knowingly sold a dangerous product, and you file a lawsuit against that company, know that George W. Bush thinks you are frivolous. I guess his legislation to limit the amount of punitive damages could have helped the corporations with their computations: 200 expected dead or injured times a maximum of $100,000 in damages = $20,000,000 in cost for lawsuits; repairing the defect = $25,000,000 in cost. To heck with repairing the defect.

And when it comes out during one of these frivolous lawsuits, brought by someone who lost a loved one for no reason other than corporate greed – when it comes out that the company knowingly sold a harmful product, is anyone indicted? Does the company go out of business because no one can conceive of doing business with such a company again? Do they go bankrupt paying off the lawsuits for the deaths they intentionally caused? The answers are no, no, and no. It's all acceptable.

Many of our wonderful goods contain (or simply are) hazardous industrial byproducts, which companies decide to sell as "goods" because they don't want to pay the immense cost required to dispose of the byproducts in an environmentally safe manner (like there is such a thing). For example, many fertilizers are loaded with industrial waste which is classified as too toxic for hazardous waste landfills – so they sell the toxic waste to you to put on your lawn – or to farmers to put on your food.

Bulldozing paradise is acceptable to make money. Greed is the guiding force behind all the destruction (they call it "construction") in sprawling areas throughout the U.S. Someone bulldozes an acre or ten of land and destroys thousands of lives – plants, insects, animals (all of which obviously affects humans, too) – just for money. Either they do not believe in God, or they believe God created all those lives to temporarily occupy the land until someone who wanted to make money off of it came along. I heard someone say, "They're throwing up buildings as fast as they can, so they can get some money out of this land" – like that was an obvious choice. But it's not an obvious choice – it's a cultural choice.

But what about someone building their own home – that isn't greed, is it? In the first place, most people consider their home an investment (so that greed is still playing a role). Beyond that, does their home have to be 3500 square feet? And does all the surrounding life have to be killed so the person can have grass for their comfort? People destroy life to create artificial environments and feel it's okay because they *can*.

All manner of destroying the Earth is acceptable to make money: polluting the waters, reshaping the Earth, blowing up mountains, digging mines, cutting down forests, changing the paths of the waters as they flow over the land.

We congratulate ourselves for our ingenuity in inventing ways to make money. (Many now call making money, "creating wealth." They are not actually creating wealth; they are not creating anything, but they are destroying a lot. The invention of the phrase "create wealth" shows us, among other things, that people deliberately try to make something which is negative sound positive.) Companies plan for their products to break down, usually right after the warranty expires – they actually spend time trying to create something that will break down on schedule. If it doesn't break down and need replacement, it needs maintenance. Everything needs maintenance: buildings, roads, landscaping (if no limbs need to be cut from the tree, the landscapers will find some to cut anyway, because having *something* to do each week is how they get paid). Ours is an idiotic system, conceivable only by people whose greed makes them always need to have something to sell and by people who feel that they always need to buy.

People invest to make their money work for them; if the company in which they invest kills kids, it doesn't really matter to them – it's not like *they*'re doing it. Investing is a shortcut to the American dream: "Anyone willing to work hard can become rich" thus becomes "Anyone can become rich – that is, if they have money to invest." It's the real American dream: just to get rich; forget the hard work.

The thing is, if money is being made, *someone* is doing the work and *something* is paying the price. The very act of creating wealth involves some destruction. Perhaps you hire workers and underpay them to keep your profits up – poor people don't count; why shouldn't you get paid for their work? If you're selling a product, the packaging costs trees their lives (paper) or causes environmental contamination (plastic); the transportation requires gasoline (smog, destruction of other countries so we can buy their oil); more trees lose their lives for the paper for advertising, etc. If you're selling fruit from your home, someone's driving there to buy it. And if you're using pesticides and insecticides and herbicides, the environment's paying, too. Plus there is the wildlife whose home you took.

If you're selling a service, the same holds. Someone or something always pays the price. If the service you sell is information – say on people's buying habits – those people whose buying habits you're tracking are paying a price in terms of personal privacy; trees are cut down for the advertisements which are sent out based on the information you provide; the advertisements which end up on TV cost electricity (which causes destruction of the environment), etc. Even if you think your service is wonderful, good for the environment, good for the people, good all around – if you're selling it, someone's paying you, and if someone's paying you, how do you think they made *their* money? And aren't you excluding from your wonderful, beneficial service all those who cannot afford it because they are poor? –But poor people don't count.

Those in the privileged class often say that poor people need to take personal responsibility for their situation, not only so that the onus is not on them to help, but also because they reason, conversely, that they deserve what they have. But when it comes to actually taking personal responsibility in the corporate world, from whence the privileged class derives its privilege, they are not so keen on the concept. Why do we have a (gutted) Superfund and Superfund sites? If a company destroyed, say, the groundwater for some region (the idiotic idea being that the groundwater contamination is contained to this site, as though water is a static entity), why is that company not required to take the millions they made in profits, and more, if necessary, to clean it up? And why are they not required to pay millions to the people who have been hurt by their pollution? (How much would a company have to give you to make up for your child being born defective [our culture's terminology] rather than healthy? If your healthy child developed leukemia, how much would a company have to pay to make that okay?) If it were not profitable for companies to cause all the destruction, they wouldn't do it.

Many things our corporations and government do, people predict will bring about the downfall of the U.S., which I mention not because they are accurate, but simply because people are apparently even willing to destroy their country for money. It's too bad their greed cannot destroy their greed, and the culture which spawned it. But who knows? –Perhaps it will.

Destruction for Thoughtlessness

Clearly, PEOCs are willing to commit any conceivable destruction (that is, any destruction they can conceive, and they spend a lot of time conceiving) for money, but is greed behind all the destruction caused by PEOCs? Actually, no – destruction is a part of our culture, so integral to our lives we don't even see it, do not even realize the harm we cause or the contempt we show for each other and all the other entities of Creation.

Pre-Columbian Native Americans had the highest reverence for the Creator and Creation, and every day their lives reflected this reverence. Their actions meant something: daily activities were lessons and involved thanking and honoring the Creator. They did not kill any life lightly; when it was necessary to take life for survival, they did so with thanks to the Creator and to the life they were taking. In ways we cannot conceive, spirituality was an integral part of every act; understanding how they could serve the wishes of the Creator and help the other entities of Creation was vital.

Now let's look at how PEOCs feel about the Creator and Creation, about the Earth and the people, animals, plants, rocks, water, and others with whom we share it. The answer is clear in our everyday actions, which reflect our feeling.

In our culture, people will throw litter anywhere without paying attention: lit cigarettes are thrown into living bushes (how would you like it if someone threw a lit cigarette onto you, and you couldn't move it, you could only let it burn your skin?). Glass bottles are broken where pets and children walk and play. Styrofoam, uneaten food, and spilled beer are all thrown onto the sidewalk and grass, into bushes, onto the Earth, with no pause. People leave plastics lying around, and these plastics can suffocate plants. Animals can inadvertently ingest them or become entangled in them, unable to escape. (What a great invention plastic was: toxic to manufacture, toxic to use, toxic to dispose of. Plastic litters the land and creates a hazard to all the other entities of the world; it's amazing that indigenous peoples didn't come up with this great invention. But, of course, we love it, because it allows us to buy more cheap stuff.)

Look at how we landscape. People landscape without any regard for how the plants will live there, crowded together without room to grow. A tree expected to reach 35' width at maturity is planted 10' from a building. And long before maturity, the trunk will outgrow the small hole in the concrete, in which it was planted. Someone will not think twice about planting a tree expected to reach 60' height at maturity under telephone lines that are 30' off the ground – but you know no one's going to be moving those phone lines. The idea we have is that it is okay to cut and maim these plants so they can serve our needs (= desires). Of course, in our society we have no patience for results, and the thought of waiting even ten years for landscaping to mature (let alone a hundred – by then the land will be in someone else's hands anyway, and they will want all new landscaping) is unthinkable. So we overfill it now, so that the ground will be covered, then once a month have someone mow the grass, shear the sides off the bushes, and cut limbs off trees. There is no point in all this. The trees and bushes and grasses have beautiful natural shapes; they are incredibly lovely to look at. Yet they are cut into our idea of what a tree or a bush or grass looks like. It's hard, too, to get away from the constant noise of lawnmowers, weed whackers, trimmers, blowers, chainsaws, edgers, and so on.

When people plant trees, many automatically stake them. Unless someone is planting during a windy season and they remove the stakes within a few months, they are hurting the trees with this practice. Trees are healthier when they are allowed to sway and bend as they grow. But in our culture, people do not take the trouble to understand what is best for the trees. We automatically stake them, often leaving the stakes in for years, as the trees grow and the stake wires cut deeper and deeper into the trees' skins. And when a strong wind comes, these trees are often uprooted, because they were never allowed to develop the strength to sway in the wind, or they break, because the wires left weak spots in their trunks. Or they die because the sap, their blood, was not allowed to flow freely.

People do all this landscaping without paying attention, without any recognition of what they are doing. Some have to do it for their HOAs (hence, there sometimes is a financial incentive). But for many, there is no HOA; it is a chore they hate; and yet they do it, because it's how things are done. Of course, there is a financial incentive for landscaping companies in this setup. It's also profitable for nurseries. Many mistreated plants die a lot sooner than those allowed to grow freely, so they end up being replaced. If a plant starts to die, often the landscapers will just rip it out and throw it away, leaving it to die amidst the sawed-off branches and filthy waste of our dumpsters and landfills – then they put in a new plant, as though nothing happened. (The idea that a living being can be physically harmed or killed without feeling pain is completely counter-intuitive and quite idiotic; it is the kind of thing one must rationalize themselves into believing.) And of course the oil companies benefit: The more gas-consuming devices we have, the better they like it. But there is no financial incentive, for those who pay, to over plant now and then spend month after month, year after year, cutting the plants back. Anyone who took the trouble could choose landscaping which did not require our brutal maintenance, but they don't care, so they don't take the trouble. Plants are just yard decorations to them, not living beings. It's sad, but most people in the U.S. don't even know what trees or bushes or grasses really look like. For the most part, people drive by these plants without really looking at them anyway.

PEOCs may realize that we could not live, in a physical sense, without the plants and animals, but I wonder if they realize they're a part of us and we're a part of them. I wonder if people in our culture realize the terrible emptiness of our *very beings* we would feel if we did not share the Earth with plants and animals – and I wonder if people in our culture would even feel that emptiness. It is as though we don't know how fortunate we are to share the world with the plants and the rocks and the winds and the animals, how they make our world wonderful.

I have seen adults sit around nonchalantly, watching as their children play nearby in what we call a vacant field, not caring as their kids pick up sticks and use them to hack away at the plants (not exactly vacant if there are plants and animals living there, is it?). And some parents buy BB guns for their kids, because they believe living birds and squirrels are acceptable for target practice, to kill and maim for fun. This is our reverence for life, our respect for the Creator and Creation.

I saw, in an expensive suburb, a sign designating "Nature Area," by the side of a major thoroughfare. The area was planted with trees and shrubs non-native to the desert in which they built the city. This is the pretend world we live in. (They would have been closer to the truth if they had posted that sign beside a "vacant" lot.) These plants do not grow naturally here. But the net effect is that even the plants are now dependent on society for their lives, because they must be artificially watered or die.

*   *   *

We have many contraptions and systems designed specifically for us to do things thoughtlessly. Look at sprinkler systems, which we can put on timers so as to water our lawns without a thought. It's much easier to do something destructive when you don't have to pay attention to what you are doing. It's easy to water a lawn which should not have been planted in the desert if you don't look at how much water is coming out of those sprinklers; and if you ignore the fact that rivers are dammed, and water is collected and channeled, and the desert's water features are destroyed, and that plants and animals die for that process of damming and collecting and channeling; if you don't see that people on reservations have no "wet water" to grow their crops (i.e., on paper it says they have water on the reservations, but there is no *actual* water on the reservations). If you don't have to pay attention, you can wait a month or two to fix that broken sprinkler head, which isn't even watering your lawn; it's just pouring water into the street. If you had to haul all that water, you'd waste a lot less. And, again, the fact that we have created so many systems which allow us to waste thoughtlessly and to cause so much destruction thoughtlessly is not a sign of advancement, nor of a society which has achieved superior ends.

Look at how selfishly people drive, another of our daily activities reflecting our reverence. While driving, people run red lights, speed in school zones and residential areas, yell, honk their horns, and flip each other off. Someone gets angry because they were cut off – then turns around and cuts off someone else. If a traffic light goes out, the intersection is supposed to (by law) become a 4-way stop, but one way (north- and south-bound traffic, or east- and west-bound traffic) gets on a roll and just keeps going. Drivers park their SUVs in spaces labeled "compact cars only," and leave the compact car drivers next to them no room to get back into their vehicles. People cut off bicyclists and leave them to swerve, and they cut off buses, leaving the bus drivers to slam on the brakes and the passengers to fly forward. On the highway, some tractor-trailer drivers decide they want to get over and immediately start moving over: if there is a car already beside them, then that driver can slam on their brakes or go over the cliff – their choice. Admittedly, not all of this is done with mal intent, but that is the point. During most of our lives, we *don't* think about what we are doing or how we are affecting others.

And coast to coast we kill thousands of animals daily with our cars. We hit bugs and birds with our windshields; we run over frogs, lizards, turtles, and snakes; and we slam into deer, skunks, raccoons, rabbits, badgers, armadillos, coyotes, and wild goats. Most people don't even stop to check on the animal, to see if it is still alive; they just continue driving, because they don't care: "They're just wild animals." They leave the animal lying in the road, in pain and terror. People in other cultures see this phenomenal arrogance in our culture, this astounding "They don't count" attitude, which we quickly learn in childhood and carry with us till death, and which we apply not only to animals and plants, but to people from other cultures, as well. This is the way people in our culture live, and then a lot of them go to church on Sundays to praise God and show their reverence for "Him" and all "He" has given – kind of another part of their lives, scheduled in for every Sunday morning or Sunday mornings once a month. Native Americans didn't have this separation, where, when you're dealing with the "real world," you can be morally ambiguous, because supposedly that's how life is in the "real world."

* * *

People get mad at their kids for interrupting their TV viewing, and they also set their kids in front of TVs to occupy them, so they don't have to take the trouble. They put their kids in cages (calling them "playpens") and use leashes on their kids when they're out walking so they don't really have to pay attention to them.

People put their kids into strollers and high-chairs, teaching their kids from the start to lean, not to sit up straight using the body's muscles; teaching them to have weak stomachs and bad posture (we have a whole society of kids as out-of-shape as the adults, who drive around reclining in their autos, then go home and recline on their sofas and overstuffed chairs).

People walk their dogs without any thought of a dog's nature, which is to stop and sniff for several minutes and then walk around, or perhaps run, until another scent catches them... They haul their dogs along at their pace, not their dog's pace. And some people simply take their dogs out to the neighbor's yard for their daily walk (we have a whole society of dogs who are as out-of-shape as we are) and leave the poop there for the neighbors to pick up. A lot of people don't bother walking their dogs; they throw them in the back yard and leave them to live their lives there.

Some like to get exotic pets. They'll go out and buy a komodo dragon, for example, without ever a thought that they have essentially sentenced that animal to a lifetime of solitary confinement, just so they can have a cool pet. The animal will be imprisoned in their house or a cage and will never get to associate with other komodo dragons and make babies and live the life of a komodo dragon. This solitary confinement is the punishment we place on our most degenerate criminals, and yet we don't think twice about imposing it on innocent animals.

People walk up to strangers and say, "Smile – it's not that bad." Perhaps the person to whom they are speaking lost a loved one in a car accident two days ago. Or perhaps that person was feeling perfectly happy before their rude comment – just because you're not smiling doesn't mean you're not happy – except to a shallow and superficial person. (What if they don't want to be happy?) People in our culture are so estranged from reality that, sadly, these people probably think they are being kind and caring. Similarly with those who tell strangers things like, "You look upset." If you don't know someone, you're hardly in a position to say they look upset, because you don't know what they look like when they're upset. Everyone has different facial expressions, and if someone has a natural tendency to turn down their mouth, or if their forehead has a pronounced wrinkle, it's pretty rude to walk up to them and say, "You look upset."

We have online chat rooms that people can log into in order to complain about all the things their fellow citizens do that drive them crazy – and no, not every culture has the problem of its citizens driving each other crazy. And we have pet peeves. Everyone has a pet peeve, because we all do so many things to annoy and anger each other. But many of the things we do are more than inconveniences: They cause real harm and show a total disregard for other people and the other entities sharing this Earth. The point is that we regularly, *daily* engage in destructive and selfish activities which have nothing to do with greed. Some of the things we do may seem like simple inconveniences or annoyances, but our underlying attitude reflects a fundamental lack of respect and consideration, a selfishness which is more than inconvenient or annoying. The same attitude which reflects itself in the annoyances also reflects itself in the destruction and harm. It is this underlying attitude which makes all the destruction we do for money seem okay to us. It is all based on our cultural way of viewing the world, in which others are less important than we are.

Partly, we do these things because it's the way of our culture, the way we were raised. For example, we don't think twice about putting our kids into strollers and chairs because, in our culture, people sit in chairs. Some of what we do is because of someone else's greed and our own self-indulgence: People have things they want to sell, and so they promote their products; PEOCs then buy their products, because, to the PEOC thinking, buying stuff all the time is a fun part of living.

But behind all the thoughtlessness and selfishness of our daily activities is the attitude and world view we have, which tells us that it is not important to pay attention to what you are doing or to consider how you are affecting other people, other entities, and the Earth, as you live your daily life. The things we do may have changed (for example, traffic has changed since the days of the horse and buggy), but the cultural world view behind the actions hasn't. At the beginnings of this country, people were doing things to anger and harm each other, too, regardless of what our enduring nostalgia tells us about our idealized past. This world view has always existed in our culture.

Indigenous peoples the world over had the highest reverence for the Creator and Creation, and, before they were devastated by contact with Europeans, their daily lives reflected this reverence. This essay is my snapshot of the actions of our daily lives which reflect our reverence and respect for the Creator and Creation.

Generosity

U.S. citizens love to talk about how generous they are: all those charities, all that foreign aid. Their government tells them, and they believe, that they are the most generous people on the planet. But hold on: The U.S. uses a fifth of the world's resources – it doesn't house 1/5 of the world's population or occupy 1/5 of the world's land – the math is wrong: we must be *taking* from other peoples. And it does not, by any super-powered stretch of the imagination, *give* 1/5 of the world's resources in its generosity.

I could hand you a basket of cherries and say that makes me generous – but if I just took away all your land with all its cherry trees, I'm not really generous, am I? Say you are Native American: If I killed your grandparents and claimed their land, I am not generous in giving you a pittance of what I gain from that land. (We delude ourselves with the thought that the land wasn't worth anything before we got our hands on it, and so any money gained from it rightfully belongs to us. We neglect to realize that the land gave these people every-thing they needed to live the way they wanted to live. We don't place a value on that.) We said we were generous because we gave the Native Ameri-cans reservations to live on after we had taken all of their land and devastated their lives. Who wants that kind of generosity? And now we say we are generous because we throw a little money at the "Native American problem" to supposedly make up for the shabby way we treat them – while conveniently ignoring the fact that they didn't used to need any money – and money can never replace what we take.

We live our lifestyle at the expense of all those people we claim to help with our charity, and I'm sure they would rather we just not take stuff from them to begin with, rather than help them after we've destroyed their lives. You can't really say you are generous for creating jobs in what we call a "Third-World" country so that people can work in a factory for slavish wages – after you destroyed their lifestyle in which they lived off of the land and didn't need jobs. Nevertheless, this is the form of our generosity. (I realize many PEOCs would like to deny that we are responsible for putting the world's indigenes into the dire situations in which many find themselves, and yet they were not in these dire situations before the intervention of PEOCs – they didn't do it to themselves.)

It's interesting that the Europeans have come up with their own system of reckoning, which has allowed some Europeans to determine that they, too, are the most generous people on the planet. They calculate generosity using percentage of Gross Domestic Product. Using this reckoning, they have determined that they, too, are incredibly generous, even though they, too, live their selfish and self-indulgent lifestyles at the expense of other peoples and the Earth. What's up with those Somalians – *they're* not generous.

I guess we PEOCs all want to be able to tell ourselves we are generous because we are all so blatantly selfish. Notice that no PEOCs calculate their generosity by how little damage they do. It's all a question of how much money and aid they give, even though they got this money at the expense of the peoples they are aiding. And, tellingly, the form of our aid always hurts the recipients, but manages to enrich us even more. (In other words, the only people we're *actually* aiding is ourselves.)

It may seem generous to ship food to a country full of "starving" people (important note: no one in the country need actually be starving for us to use this term), but it is not generous when your government's intent is to destroy the traditional farming in that country, to flood the market with a commodity and put thousands of small farmers out of business so they will have to go to work in factories, or to destroy the people's traditional eating patterns and diets and replace them with *our* eating patterns and diets, thereby making them dependent on us for food (a technique which worked so well for us against the Native Americans). When we do this, these are not accidental, unintended, or unforeseen consequences: These are deliberate, malicious acts on our part, whose outcomes are exactly in keeping with our intentions. We have wreaked havoc on their lives, made them dependent on us for food, and ensured an oversupply of workers for our slave factories. And yet we tell ourselves we have provided aid.

Some people in our culture proudly proclaim that they are supporting sustainable farming in the rainforests; that, because of us, indigenous peoples in the rainforests are using sustainable methods and planting a variety of crops; and that, therefore, we are helping to save the rainforests and the planet. We are also helping the people, we claim, because we found a way for them to make money off their land without razing it (because we are so ingenious at finding ways to make money). Science says the rainforests are critical to human survival, and that's the real point for these do-gooders; they believe they have helped to save the rainforests, and hence themselves. In other words, it is the saving themselves part that makes them feel such a sense of urgency to save the rainforests.

The first problem with our self-congratulations is that, we're so proud to have helped the people to develop a sustainable industry, we ignore the fact that, before we came along, they didn't need any industry, and they were better off. If they are living without the need for money, then we are not helping them by showing them a sustainable way to make money. But we are helping ourselves, because now we've got another set of people trading their lives away so they can export products to the U.S., for U.S. consumers to consume.

The second problem with our self-congratulations is that, just because we think something is sustainable, doesn't mean it is. This sustainable farming may be causing irreparable harm to the rainforests; we just don't see it yet (because we are so slow this way). We think we are, but we are not the world's arbiters of what is sustainable. Science has no idea of what is and is not sustainable, but the lifestyle the people were living before we "helped" was clearly sustainable, because it sustained their ancestors for thousands of years.

If we would stop destroying and polluting people's lands and making these lands unlivable; if we left people alone to live like their ancestors lived, then they would have sustainable lifestyles; they would have food, shelter, and enjoyment, without having to be our slaves. People in our culture may wonder why anyone would want to live like that, when they could be living in lumber and concrete homes, with running water and electricity. (Never mind that the homes, running water, and electricity we promise usually don't materialize anyway.) One reason someone would choose not to live like us is because our technology is harmful to the health; for example, our lumber is treated with toxic chemicals before it becomes a part of our homes. Another reason someone would not want to live like us is because our houses can feel like prisons to people who are used to spending most of their time outside, living on the Earth. Another reason is that our homes are too large, and we have to harm the Earth and destroy plants and animals to build them. There are many easily understandable reasons why people would not want to live like us. Perhaps beyond all others is this: Some people value knowledge, wisdom, and being in tune with nature, which is a part of us whether we want to acknowledge it or not. Some people value spirituality over materialism. But once someone adopts our lifestyle, spirituality is replaced by materialism.

The problem is that, as soon as we want something from some people, we take the choice away from them; we do everything in our power (and we have a lot of this kind of power) to destroy their lives and to make them have to work to survive. For us to say we helped is contemptible. (Would you rely on a criminal to describe the harm they caused their victim, or might they not minimize, in their own mind, the tragic effects of their actions; might not their point of view be skewed?)

The point of all of our aid is to further exploit non-PEOCs, and the point of calling it "aid" is to make ourselves feel generous, even as we act in our own self-interest. The point is not to be generous, it's to tell ourselves we are generous so we don't have to look at our selfishness. Obviously, no one wants our generosity – it is so costly, and if we *gave* less, I'm sure they'd be very happy – they just wish we wouldn't *take* so much.

Liberals & Conservatives & What They Share

In his book *Lies and the Lying Liars Who Tell Them*,[*] Al Franken asserts that liberals love the U.S. critically, like grown-ups, and conservatives love the U.S. uncritically, like children love their mummies. Regardless of how they love the U.S., the salient point here is that both liberals and conservatives love this country.

–So liberals and conservatives should be able to get along much better than they appear to. After all, what's a few million unborn babies compared to the *billions* of lives they've agreed to destroy in the name of spreading throughout the world the U.S. system of democracy and freedom. It's like two people who have agreed on the price for a car down to the last few hundred dollars. One side says, "We won't go any lower than $24,120," and the other side says, "We won't go any higher than $23,880." It is a meaningless squabble, but they are firmly entrenched in their positions, and the argument makes them feel they have freedom of speech, difference of opinion, diversity.

Meanwhile, on 99% of things they agree: They have the *same* cultural world view. For example, conservatives tend to prefer using terror tactics

---

[*] *Lies and the Lying Liars Who Tell Them*, Al Franken. Penguin Group (USA) Inc.: New York. (Dutton.) 2004.

(death squads, police actions, and so on) to control and keep other peoples in line; liberals want to dominate other peoples by helping them develop, thereby destroying their cultures and making them dependent on us. The point is that both want to change, dominate, and exploit other peoples. And both sides are more than willing to cross over and use the other side's techniques when it is convenient; they are just flip sides of the same technique, with the same goal, after all.

Our culture has decided to call our destruction of the Earth "development," and both liberals and conservatives agree with this designation. Conservatives want to develop as quickly as possible to make money, without regard to environmental destruction, which they think doesn't really exist. Or they figure that, if it does exist, it doesn't matter, because the world won't run out of oxygen during their lifetimes. Liberals want to make money through development as well, but they feel a different approach is advisable, called "sustainable development." In other words, they also want development, but they want to go about it in a different way, which they have decided to call "sustainable." (There is no sustainable way of destroying the Earth, and, for PEOCs, development always equals destruction.) Note that both want to make money through development of the Earth, and both want to change the face of the planet to match what PEOC culture says it should be.

Both liberals and conservatives believe the other entities of the Earth are resources to be exploited. Conservatives believe that if you use up one non-renewable resource, you can always find another one, so they prefer a no-limits approach. Liberals believe in exploiting resources at a slower pace, so those resources will have a chance to replenish themselves. For example, they don't have an objection to harvesting wild and exotic fish and coral for use in aquariums. They just want the aquarium and fish industries to slow the harvesting down, so that the fish and coral will have a (slim) chance to reproduce what PEOCs take, so that it will be a sustainable industry. Obviously, neither side suggests that we give up aquariums and let the aquarium and fish industries go out of business, because people need jobs and have the right to pursue the American dream. Tough luck for the fish.

Conservatives want to continue dependence on fossil fuel energy until it's all used up and they've made as much money out of it as they can, until they've destroyed all they can find to develop. Liberals do not think of eliminating dependence on energy – just on fossil fuel energy, which, after all, is bound to run out eventually – and they don't want to be stuck energy-less any more than the conservatives do. We have now developed plant-based energies, as though it is okay to grow and kill plants to power our cars and TV sets – so liberals are also willing to destroy in order to feed our insatiable desire for energy.

Liberals are not absolutely opposed to development in, for example, the Amazon, but they want it done in an environmentally sensitive way. (This assumes our culture is in any way whatsoever capable of behaving in an environmentally sensitive manner. If we truly wanted to be environmentally sensitive, we'd have to stay out: Notice that we've never left *anything* better off than it was before we got our hands on it.) The liberals also want the locals to benefit from the development – by, for example, having clinics built to treat the host of diseases we import to them. If U.S. corporations were to be what science calls environmentally sensitive and were to use the miniscule portion of their profits, which is paid to the locals for the right to destroy their land, to help those locals (by building hospitals, transportation systems, and plumbing), then all would be okay from the liberal point of view. Building those hospitals and transportation systems would suck them into our lifestyle, which liberals think is good for them. Typically, the hospitals and plumbing never actually materialize, but, from the liberal point of view, it would be a positive thing if they did. (Neither side questions why the U.S. corporations are in charge of how the pittance "paid" to the locals is spent, but I guess neither side considers leaving the question in the hands of the locals to be an option – it's not like they know what's best for themselves.)

Conservatives think it's acceptable if only the rich can afford to buy homes; liberals feel the poor should also be able to afford homes (at least, that's what they say – but they, too, invest in real estate in order to make money, thereby driving up prices so that the poor *cannot* afford to buy homes). But neither liberals nor conservatives question the concept of owning and selling land – nor of some people being rich.

They may differ in opinion on how to achieve it, but both liberals and conservatives want the U.S. to have a strong economy. And both have contributed to so many recessions. Also, both consume inordinate amounts of energy and goods.

So it goes: liberal/conservative – pail/bucket. And no matter how much those great principles upon which this country was founded are trampled and ignored, they believe this country gets better and better. How many of those conservatives complaining about moral decay in the private realm and liberals complaining about the public realm don't still believe that this is the greatest country on Earth ever (or, at the very least, that it is no worse than other countries)? Exactly: none. People will hail free speech (for example) as a strength of this country, no matter how much their speech is controlled.

I saw an article in the kids' section of a newspaper, soon after George W. Bush escalated his daddy's war against the Iraqi people, in which the author told of a man being arrested at a mall in New York for wearing a t-shirt which said, "Peace on Earth." The author then went on to ask kids which they think is more important in troubled times: A) Freedom of speech (meaning a t-shirt saying, "Peace on Earth" is a display of freedom of speech), *or* B) Supporting our leaders (meaning a t-shirt saying "Peace on Earth" does not support our leaders and our warring government). The point here is that this article led kids to get in on the interminable and meaningless squabble at a young age. And the argument is moot; no matter what is written in the constitution, this country does *not* support free speech. But both liberals and conservatives believe that it does.

Both liberals and conservatives would agree with the statement, "Look how far minorities have come," but conservatives feel the job of "giving" equality to minorities is done and that we've gone a little too far (affirmative action); liberals feel there's still a little more to do. But equality isn't going to happen in this country, so it's not really an argument. (However, it is worth contrasting racial relations in our culture to racial relations in the Native American cultures. Various Native nations took in, collectively, thousands of runaways – runaway slaves, runaway colonizers – and accepted them fully into *their* societies. They did not have to take 200+ years to make progress in the area of racial relations.)

I have heard white people claiming that the election of Barak Obama to president proves that discrimination is not a systemic problem in our culture. They claim that, though some people are racists, this election shows that our country as a whole is not. Those making this claim have very conveniently pushed from their minds our slums, reservations, and barrios; our use of racial profiling; the ethnic make up of our prisons; and the way our government and citizens treat Native Americans (among other things): All of these are indicative of systemic racism. Discrimination is an integral part of PEOC culture and is never going to disappear from our society built on that culture – and both liberals and conservatives believe fervently in the culture. They may disagree with this or that part of the culture, but the culture is a package deal, and the fight to change this part or that part is an illusion. As long as our culture is our culture, children are going to be born to parents who abuse them, minorities are not going to have equality, and there will be poor people...

Short history lesson: The term "compassionate conservative" is an oxymoron. It's like saying, "clean filth." Sometime during, if I remember correctly, the Reagan years, Republicans realized that they were losing voter points because conservatives were seen as not being compassionate (which they aren't) – and so they coined the term, "compassionate conservative." They did not change their attitudes; they did not make any attempt to incorporate any actual compassion into their empty, greedy souls and goals; they did not need to discover the meaning of the word "compassion" – they just added the adjective to their descriptor. Then voila, in the pliable U.S. citizen's mind, "compassionate" became associated with "conservative," and conservatives didn't have to leave behind one ounce of their greed and brutality. End of history lesson.

Liberals think they are better than conservatives because, they think, at least they try to have some compassion. For example, liberals say, at least they *want* minorities to have equality. But they are no more compassionate than conservatives: Their compassion is not real compassion; it is just what our culture calls compassion. Their problem is that they are completely bound by their culture and its views, beliefs, and values. They want minorities to have equality by being successful in school and having good jobs and being fully integrated into *this* culture. But that's not equality. Equality is the freedom to live how *you* choose, not to live how someone else chooses but with equal access to *their* opportunities, having equal rights under *their* terms.

Imagine that the colonizers had said to the Native Americans, when they first arrived, "You Natives can have equality in the new nation we are going to impose." Imagine that the colonizers had actually meant it and implemented it. This isn't equality. It's already not equal, because the net effect is still to take away their freedom and their right to live how they want. To have equality under this scenario, the Native Americans would have to give up their way of life and embrace ours – and so, they do not have equality. Put another way, the reason the colonizers were even able to gain a foothold here is because the Native Americans *did* have freedom, and they left the colonizers alone to live the way they chose. We want to "grant equality" by "allowing" people to live the way *we* choose, so it's not equality. Having people who think they are superior to you try to force you to live their way (or "allow" you to live their way) is not equality for you.

On another front, liberals think it is compassionate to go to a village in what we call a "developing" country to help them install plumbing – but it isn't, unless you believe it's best for those people to be like U.S. citizens. Plumbing is only good if you want to live in one of these dirt-, dust-, junk-collecting boxes we live in, isolating ourselves from the real world and destroying the natural flow of the water.

Liberals serve the "rah-rah U.S." cause *just as much* as the conservatives do. They believe, just as much as conservatives, that ours is the best culture, the best civilization, etc. They are just as ready to change other people's cultures as conservatives are, and imposing your culture on someone is genocide, whether you tell yourself you're being compassionate or not. Liberals end up destroying peoples the world over and spreading terror just as much as conservatives do, and their compassion is as arrogant and devastating as the conservatives' brutality.

Lying

You have to wonder, if our leaders' motives are so good and pure, then why do they lie? When George W. Bush decided to open up "protected" forests to U.S. corporations, why did he decide to call it the "Healthy Forests Initiative"? His Healthy Forests Initiative was nothing but a call for our corporations to systematically destroy forests. Why didn't he just say, "Look, our corporations can make a lot of money if they cut down these trees. What good are trees if we can't cut them down to make money?" Why didn't he have the honesty to call it the "Destroy the Forests Initiative"? I heard one person describe it as his "No Tree Left Behind Initiative" – why didn't he use that?

And when he decided to invade Iraq, why didn't he say, "Saddam Hussein doesn't want to roll over for our oil companies. We've been starving his people for a decade, and that hasn't brought him around. I'm going to start a war and take over the country, so that our great capitalist corporations can get a hold of the oil and make more money." Surely, given that capitalism is such a virtuous and good system, the people of the U.S. – no, people the world over – would have supported that. Why'd he lie and say they had weapons of mass destruction and were an imminent threat to the U.S. – even though he knew these were lies? Could it be that capitalism is not so inherently good that it justifies pretty much everything? (Notice that the U.S. people were not overly upset when Bush's lie was uncovered; it certainly didn't keep them from electing him to a second term of office.)

And when his daddy decided to invade Panama, why did *he* lie about Noriega being a threat to the U.S.? (And, I have to ask, why was the U.S. public thick enough to believe it? –Wait, we just invaded Iraq; in our selfishness, we've trained ourselves to believe anything we are told. –Never mind, I see why the U.S. public was thick enough to believe it.) Why didn't Bush Sr. just say that we wanted control of the Panama Canal and that he wanted U.S. corporations to win the lucrative contracts for the canal reconstruction needed at that time? Why didn't Bush say, "We are going to invade Panama, in spite of the treaty our government signed a decade ago, because that treaty is inconvenient for American corporations"? Surely his intentions were honorable; U.S. intentions are always honorable. So why did he lie about them?

I'm sure an apologist would say, "It's more complicated than that. You've taken a complex issue and made it seem like it was a simple A-B-C problem." In our culture, we like to pretend that issues are complicated, so that we can obscure the truth and make our selfish decisions seem justified. But these issues really *are* simple and straightforward, no matter how much garbage the politicians, CEOs, and apologists pile on top. PEOCs are easily deceived by this garbage, easily distracted from the truth, but the truth is still there and still visible, whether we look or not.

For example, after the Supreme Court ruled on our illegal detention and torture of suspected

terrorists, and declared we are to commit "no outrages upon human dignity," Bush asked, "What
does that mean?" after which he claimed that it's
"vague." If you have a respect for human dignity,
it's really not at all vague. The only way it becomes "vague" is if you want to commit outrages
on human dignity, and so you look for ways to
commit your outrages without admitting what
you're doing. That is when it becomes "complex";
but it really isn't complex. But most Americans
played along with Bush's assessment (and continue to play along, since we are still torturing
people), because, though they claim they are un-
easy with the torture that is going on, they actually do want our government to torture suspected
terrorists, *just in case* these people might possibly
be able to provide information. In other words,
they are completely willing to sacrifice some (as in
tens of thousands of) innocent people, just on the
off chance that it might increase their own personal safety.

That their leaders lie does not absolve the U.S.
citizenry of responsibility. For example, anyone
could have figured out that Bush was lying *before*
he started the war in Iraq – I did – and the fact that
they didn't bother themselves hardly makes them
good people; nor does it absolve them of slaughter. If they had troubled themselves at all, to at
least question whether Bush might possibly be lying, U.S. citizens could have averted this war (possibly) *before* going in and destroying the Iraqi people's lives. Of course, the "just in case" principle
was at work here, too, though: As soon as Bush
said the words that Iraq was a threat, we wanted
to invade *just in case* they might possibly be a
threat. For U.S. citizens, starting a war without

having all the facts doesn't really present us with a moral quandary. We do not look at the situation with the attitude that it is an incredibly horrendous step to invade a country, and that we have to take the time – however much time it takes to make sure we're not committing what our culture calls war crimes – before we invade. Invading another country is actually a pretty easy step for us, one we've taken many, many, many, many times.

Of course, even if U.S. citizens had not supported him, Bush would have tried to find a way to wage war against Iraq, but what is the name of the country that spawned and gave power to Bush?

No the liberal leaders are no better. They also lie regularly (Clinton is famous for lying), and the damage and destruction the U.S. government and U.S. corporations cause in other countries (and within the U.S.) doesn't suddenly stop when the liberals are in power, no matter what they claim to the contrary. Look at that bastion of liberalism, the Peace Corp. Do the volunteers realize (or care) that the populations we target for our "help" are chosen for strategic reasons? Why doesn't our government stop lying about why we are helping these people – and why don't these volunteers stop lying to themselves about their motives? Why not just say, "We are superior to these people; we have a superior lifestyle and technology. We know more than they do, and we are going to help these poor, ignorant people, whether they want it or not. Once we have restructured the way they live, modeling it after our own lifestyle, and have thus destroyed their culture (who needs war?), they will be dependent on us. In no time, the people will be wasting away their lives working at jobs. Perhaps they will be working in mines or factories, or perhaps they will be spending their days farming, trying to eke out a few dollars by exporting their food to the U.S. In this way, by helping them, we have also benefited ourselves." Why aren't these liberals honest about their motivations *and* the effects of their actions? They do not ask themselves, "Why should these people be wasting their lives growing *our* food?" because, to them, it is self-evident that people the world over should be trying to be like us and to develop strong economies. They lie to themselves that what is best for us is also what's best for them. Whatever holy thoughts they claim are motivating them, they are serving the U.S. – which is why the Peace Corps exists in this country.

Lying is a way of life for us: not just for our leaders, but for most U.S. citizens. Daily we listen to lies, and daily we tell them. We have a special category we call white lies, which are okay because they're just "little" lies. We have a whole vocabulary built around lying, from "perjury" and "deliberately misleading" to "omitting pertinent facts." Honesty is given little value in our society – it's just another option. We lie as individuals, and we lie as a country, and we expect it, and we accept it.

Look at our treaties; these supposedly enshrine, in writing, our vow as a country to behave in a certain way. We write everything down to show that "we really mean it." Sadly, as a rule, PEOC treaties mean absolutely nothing. We write them and force others to sign, and then violate them whenever we feel like it. In the great United States, we change presidents every four or eight years, and treaties a former president has signed are completely disregarded by the president in office. In fact, treaties the current president has signed are regularly disregarded. The signing of the treaty is supposed to be our promise, our word of honor as a country, but it is nothing more than our convenience, and the whole world knows that our solemn promise is a lie. And the same holds true for every other PEOC country.

I could continue for thousands of pages about our lying, because there is so much of it: It is what this culture supports. Why do politicians "evade the truth" and come out with idiotic slogans like "anti-violence"? Everyone who lives in this incredibly violent country is pro-violence. "Pro-family" – what does that mean? I haven't heard anyone own up to being "anti-family." Why is there such a thing as PR? Why are advertisements intentionally deceptive? Why do we have to have laws about lying?

Why do schools not teach the truth when, for example, they teach history? Why not just say, "We killed the Natives because we wanted their land. At every chance, we did everything we could to destroy them." If we are such a good country, why lie about our origins? If our motives were pure, why not out with them? Why not let our schoolchildren know that the father of our country, George Washington, was a genocidaire?

And for that matter, why did we lie again and again to the Native Americans, to get them to sign treaties which did *nothing* for them and did everything for us? (And no, the Natives did not break as many treaties as we did. Who has all the land now?) Why is our culture lost in such a quagmire of lies, if it is so honorable?

Freedom = Oppression

In this culture, nothing is free: not the Earth, nor the rocks; not the plants, nor the animals, nor the people.

The Earth is suffocated by roadways, sidewalks, and buildings. Barbed-wire fences line the highways and divide the country. You can't walk over the land, because it's all owned and posted, "No Trespassing." We have cut through mountains and covered the land between with pavement to create our highways. The Earth is bulldozed and blown up and leveled. Rocks are ground to dust; mixed into concrete; broken into pieces for yard mulch; taken from stream beds for landscaping; cut and polished to adorn someone's neck; and put on display in museums, like animals are put on display in zoos and circuses, and plants are put on display in arboretums and botanical gardens.

We've reduced plants to "landscaping" and "crops," because those are what they mean to us. We haul a 60-year-old cactus out of the desert to decorate someone's front yard; we keep plants in pots and sell plants and kill plants. We plant them so they are growing on top of each other and prune them and water them and own them. They suffocate under our litter, under discarded plastic bags, and under construction debris piled and thrown on them.

Nor do we respect the animals, nor grant them any freedom. We have animals locked in factory farms, in science labs, in dog pounds, in back yards, in petting zoos, and in water park attractions. We call animals "birdies," "doggies," "duckies," and "froggies," making them cute to our children, thereby robbing them of dignity, acting like they are just cuddly little toys. And we make cuddly little toys shaped like animals, to reinforce this insult.

We have the idea that animals just eat and sleep. If an animal is making its way around the forest, we conclude it must be looking for food, as though animals do not explore the world or take an interest in what is going on around them. We say we are doing them a favor by keeping them in zoos, because (we rationalize) there they are safe from poachers, or because this animal no longer exists in the wild, or because in zoos scientists can study them and learn about them (how does that work, you've got to wonder – but I guess they study people by going to prisons), or because of twenty other reasons, but who asked the animals if they want to live in zoos? We say we create natural environments for the zoo animals (at least for the supposedly lucky ones who aren't in 10-foot-square cages), but what we consider relevant to the animals' natural environment isn't what the animals consider relevant and natural, and lack of freedom certainly isn't their natural state. How does anyone think they can create a natural environment for an African elephant in a North American zoo? It's idiotic.

In some zoos and wildlife refuges, people walk right up to the animals, and we think that is an example of humans and animals living in harmony.

But it is actually an example of people requiring animals to give up the very essence of who they are – something which is hard for us to understand, because we do not know the essence of who we are, because we are imprisoned in the meaninglessness of our culture.

We put animals in entertainment shows; we import rare species to be pets, killing a thousand so that one can survive the journey from a foreign land, to be sold and imprisoned in someone's home. We deposit them in aquariums. We dissect them in biology class; we put them under microscopes to learn about them. We trap them in the wild and let them die slowly and very painfully. We gas them in our homes and spray them in our fields; we shoot them for sport (what kind of society kills for sport?) and force them to fight each other for our amusement.

When we call the United States the land of the free, the only thing we are considering is the freedom of the PEOCs who live here; the non-human entities don't count to us, nor does the Earth. The Native Americans do not count either. They pay the cost of our lifestyle. We've decided it's a trade we're willing to live with: their freedom to live as they choose for our freedom to go to the movies twice a month. And we make this decision every day. If you don't know the price of our superior lifestyle, it's just because you don't want to know.

And yet, if you look only at the PEOCs living in this country, you see they are not free, either. We have millions of people locked up in prisons; millions more locked up in mental institutions; millions more in juvenile detention. Even those who are not in the prisons and mental institutions are not free to live in just any way, but are chained to jobs so they can pay for food, shelter, and clean water, because food, shelter, and water are not free. If they want to sleep in public (an alley or a park), or to trespass, they get arrested and join the millions and millions locked up in jail. If they want to talk to trees, they are arrested and join the millions and millions locked up in mental institutions. When we talk about how free our country is, it's a very narrowly defined freedom; in fact, it isn't really freedom at all.

People are free to leave, but our culture is on a constant mission to destroy the freedom of every corner of the planet, so that, in order to move to many countries, you have to get an extended visa and prove you have sufficient income to live there. And we will not be satisfied until, in whatever country you live, you have to hold a job; until we have exported our "freedom" to every last person on the planet (and even then we won't be satisfied); until, wherever you are, you will live under the freedom (= oppression) of our culture.

People in this country like to quote General John Stark's words, "live free or die," and yet we do not believe in freedom. Next time you want to brag about how this country is "the land of the free," remember that, in this culture, nothing is truly free.

Control

I heard a sociology teacher say that it is human nature to try to control one's environment, but he did not realize he was talking about PEOC nature rather than a universal state of humans. If you want to realize that not all humans want to control their environments, look at how indigenous peoples lived in every diverse climate, from the coldest to the hottest and the wettest to the driest, all without re-designing anything. Obviously, those living in Alaska (for example) created houses which would allow them to live in the cold without freezing to death, but this isn't the same thing as controlling the environment.

PEOCs, on the other hand, would like to control everything and every part of the environment. To control water, we use concrete canals, dams, pipes, and faucets. Instead of letting water flow freely, as it used to move throughout the world, we try to capture it and direct its course. The natural water features which used to grace even the harshest deserts have all but vanished in PEOC countries (and countries we are forcing to develop).

Control was the point in domesticating animals. It was also the point of trying to wipe out the North American bison, an ever available food source for those uncontrolled Natives. (In other words, people in our culture were willing to make an animal extinct in order to gain control over other people. They killed millions of bison and left their bodies to rot on the plains.) The colonizers wanted to control Native Americans by making them dependent on us for food rather than letting them live in freedom.

Control is always the point of colonization – control of the people for control of their resources. And, since control of colonized peoples always involves destroying their cultures and imposing the culture of the colonizers, and imposing your culture on a "group" of people is a form of genocide, you can see that colonization is always a form of genocide. There's no way to colonize people *without* committing genocide.

In our mission to make everything fit the PEOC view of how the world should be, we seek to control every part of that world. We have animal husbandry, management of wildlife populations, and management of natural resources. We try to control which plants grow in our cities, putting in plants which would never grow there naturally, destroying those that do. We create artificial plants, which have pesticides and insecticides built in.

We've created millions of artificial indoor and outdoor environments. We want to control the contour of the Earth, leveling the land and paving over the uneven surface with asphalt. We wear shoes, and most people place a blanket or a chair before sitting on the ground.

People seek to control their children, rather than guide them. They also try to control their dogs, with leashes and choke collars. In many cities, we have laws requiring leashes, and some people control other people and their pets by calling animal control when someone is walking their dog without a leash, even if the dog is hurting no one.

Some people even try to control their dogs' odor and bad breath.

People buy or lease land so it will be under their control. Think about how small-minded that is. I would prefer the freedom to be able to make my home anywhere, to have all the Earth be my home and share it with everyone, rather than being chained to one plot of land, and to a job to pay for it. But PEOCs want their own plots, over which they exercise control. And they seek to control what their neighbors do with their plots, through HOAs.

The DeBeers family seeks to control the supply of diamonds in order to control their price. Diamonds are no so very uncommon and are not intrinsically worth any more than any other stones (people can say a diamond is forever, but it isn't; moreover, most of the stones lying on the ground will last far longer than any human being – you won't be here forever, so who cares if your ring is?); but by hoarding them, the DeBeers family controls the supply and, hence, the price – for those who belong to a culture which accepts this value.

Science is all about control, trying to give scientific names to everything and to classify all the species of the world. The whole notion of natural laws of the universe is all about control. Science thinks it controls the sum of human knowledge.

Our society wants to control how and what people think, and it seeks to create a melting pot, in which all diversity is subsumed in the dominate culture, thereby eliminating any *real* diversity or freedom. It seeks to control which news you hear and the way you view it.

It seeks to control minute details of people's lives; we have laws to tell you what you can and can't do in private. And corporations build giant databases to track personal details of your life in an attempt to control your future actions. There are businesses whose only business is to gather information about consumers. Next time you get a survey phone call – perhaps someone wanting you to participate in a health care survey, to improve medical care in the U.S. – you should realize that they aren't really calling to improve medical care in the U.S. (though they want to appear to care). The real reason for the call (or magazine survey) is to collect information about you, to add to the substantial amount of information they already have stored in their mega-databases. They collect this information in order to market it to people who want to sell you things. They don't want your opinion because they are concerned about improving your situation; they just want to know what kind of products you might be likely to buy. The goal of the companies who buy your information is not to explain something to you so you can make an informed decision; it is to send you ads which will make you believe you need (or desperately want) their products. You are a consumer, and if you don't do business with them, they have no interest in you. And since we allow our culture to control our thinking, these ads often succeed.

The history taught in our schools is controlled entirely by the culture and those who dominate, without any regard for truth or the well-being of the people. This applies not only to the constant revisionism we employ to re-paint ourselves as heroes, but also to what is considered worthwhile to relate about the past. Here's something you'll probably never read in a history book: "A great wind arose as they spoke, and leaves began to swirl into their faces." You may read it in a fictionalized history book, but in that case it will be made up, not based on what actually happened. You won't read it in a non-fiction history book (although, of course, all of our history books are fiction) because we don't consider the actions of the wind or any other entities relevant – only the actions of PEOCs. And when you read about "European settlers," rather than "European colonizers," it's because the word "colonizers" has a negative connotation. There were no European settlers who *weren't* colonizers; this wording is just an attempt to control how we view the beginnings of this country.

Christianity seeks to control the spiritual realm of every person on the planet. And when the Jews were in a position of power, they, too, sought to control and to force people to convert.

The PEOC mind would like a well-ordered universe: control. It has neither the strength, nor the understanding, to let every entity live and grow freely, and to take its place as a *part* of the whole – it wants only to dominate the whole. People cut parts off of plants to make them fit into the small areas they have assigned to them in their yards and never think twice about imposing this control on other entities – as though it is their right to enforce their will on others: people, cultures, animals, the Earth.

The only thing PEOCs don't seek to control is themselves. We do not control our addictions, our innumerable acts of self-indulgence, our selfishness and greed, our waste – all of it at the expense of those whom we do control. And though PEOCs have the idea that we have lordship over the entire world and all of its entities, we have no idea of responsibility. For those who do not believe in God, there is a sense that humans landed here as part of evolution, and since we evolved to be able to dominate, it is okay and natural that we do so. The planet is ours to shape and re-create as we see fit, kind of an ongoing process of evolution, and, after all, we are (we believe) improving it.

For those PEOCs who do believe in God, there is no sense that God wants them to take care of the Earth and her children. They believe God created the world for *their* sakes, for them to use and abuse. For them, lordship = control. God was just wasting "His" time in creating such a wondrous and splendidly beautiful world – but, fortunately, PEOCs have been and are continuing to correct God's defects. And thank God for the animals and plants and rocks and water God placed here for humans to exploit for God's Money.

Yes, a very devout Christian informs me, it's God's Money: Money is now holy, though I can't imagine why God needs Money. This Christian informs me that God blessed us with all the petty jobs people waste their lives doing as a gift to us, so we can earn "His" Money. One of the gifts of PEOC religion was certainly this tool to control people's minds, which allows the leaders of the church to convince people that they are being good by spending their lives in misery on Earth, and it is worth spending their lives this way because heaven awaits.

We love trying to control the world and greatly enjoy enforcing our will on others, but we are not actually in control; the world is not ours to control. What we don't see is that, sadly, what all our controlling behavior leaves is no wisdom, no respect, no room to grow, and no freedom:

no freedom for the controllers; no freedom for the controlled.

Racism

Obviously, there is much to say about racism in this country, enough to fill thousands of books. I am not even going to try to cover this issue, but I do want to ask a question. If you think the problem of racism is pretty much solved in the U.S., consider:

When someone non-white does something bad, PEOCs generalize their behavior to everyone of that race. But when someone white does something bad, PEOCs do not generalize their behavior to all whites. Whites commit more crimes, and more serious crimes, "on average," than people of any other race. But when a white person does something, it just reflects badly on him or her, on that one individual. If someone of, say, African heritage commits a crime, in the PEOC mind it reflects badly on all African-Americans. Why doesn't it just reflect badly on that one person, same as with whites? Notice that news reports almost always make it a point to state the race of the suspect who is non-white, but they mention race only occasionally when the suspect is white.

Although Muslims are not a race, most people in the United States act like they are. If they see someone who is Middle Eastern, they think that person is Muslim, and they don't want to get on an airplane with that person. After 9-11-01, a lot of people committed hate crimes against Muslims

(Middle Easterners). Those who committed these crimes rationalized that they were upset and angry over what had happened on 9-11, and they told themselves that their emotions justified their actions.

Now tell me: After the Oklahoma City bombing (committed by whites), how many people went out and killed white guys in their uncontrollable anguish?

Ethics

We have courses in business ethics, ethics in marketing, ethics in technical writing, ethics in religion, and on and on. Does this say that our culture is very concerned about ethics? Actually, it says that ethics are not an integral part of any area of our culture; they are separate from business as usual and are optional. What kind of society can conceive of something ethic-less? What kind of culture has to add ethics to every aspect of itself because the ethics aren't there already? That would be PEOC culture. And how sad is it that, often, the ethics taught in these courses have nothing to do with honor, justness, honesty, or any other truly ethical considerations?

Probably, some of the people who go into law enforcement think they will be good officers, that they will not be corrupt but will truly serve society. But once they are on the force, they find out that ethical means a whole different thing in police terms than what might be considered a general definition of the term. And this is true in many professions, because there is no one standard of ethical in our culture; it's a sliding concept, a flexible truth. If you are a prosecutor, your ethical duty is to follow the rules of the courtroom and try to get a conviction, whether the person is truly guilty or not. If you are a CEO of a corporation, your ethical duty is to maximize profits for your shareholders. There are no actual ethics involved in either situation; in both, your duty is to conform mindlessly to the rules of our society.

We have people, too, who think the right thing is simply dependent on what they want it to be. One driver thinks the right thing is for the other driver not to cut him off and make him slam on his brakes just because she doesn't want to slam hers. The other driver thinks the right thing is for the first driver to slam on his brakes and let her in, because that's where she wants to be.

Doing the right thing often gets the doer an award or a reward, in our society, because it's so easy for us to conceive of people *not* doing what our society calls the right thing. And often, children (and adults) assume that someone (or something, such as an organization) is good or ethical because they received an award. But anyone can give an award to anyone for anything; the whole process is quite meaningless. For example, I know of an organization that wanted to promote minority business development, so they decided to sponsor a minority business award. The man who won was a terrible boss whose employees hated him and whose business was very poorly run, but all of this was irrelevant to the organization sponsoring the award. They just wanted to give out a "Best Minority Entrepreneur" award.

In other words, just because someone or something wins an award, that doesn't necessarily mean anything. I'm sure many SS officers during WWII received awards and rewards which made children and adults proud of them, but they were not good or ethical. I wouldn't be surprised if some whacked-out business lobbies gave George W. Bush awards for his work on helping the environment, but that doesn't mean he didn't do everything in his power to destroy nature when he was in office. Awards and rewards have nothing to do with ethics (or reality, for that matter).

And we have our holidays – Mothers' Day, Secretary's Day, etc. These are our culture's way of honoring people, the one day when you are supposed to do right by the people who do right by you. Nice for the greeting card companies and florists, but why would a mother want her children to celebrate Mothers' Day? If your children love you, don't you know about it year-round, and doesn't a tacky card and bouquet of dead flowers trivialize that love? Do we have Mothers' Day because we know we do not honor our mothers the other 364 days a year? If we do, then why would we need Mothers' Day? If you were a horrible boss, would giving your secretary something on Secretary's Day make you a good one? If you were a good one, wouldn't you take the trouble to thank your secretary frequently, and not once a year?

How about our national holidays: Thanksgiving (not for Native Americans), Independence Day (not for Native Americans), Memorial Day and Veterans' Day (for all the many, many people who have fought in our endless wars), Christmas (let's admit it – it's a national holiday – but not for Native Americans), Columbus Day (that one's a treasure: honoring a brutal, ruthless man, who killed indigenous people for sport and worked them to death as slave laborers). I guess the society that can honor Christopher Columbus is the one that can conceive of something ethic-less.

War & Colonization

A Poor Measure of Wealth

In PEOC terms, the wealth or poverty of a country is measured by per capita income. "Per capita income" is an average. You take all the income earned by everyone in the country, divide it by the number of people in the country, and you get the per capita income for that country. So what PEOCs are looking at is how much money the people, on average, make. We are not interested in whether they have the things that people of our culture typically purchase with money, such as food and shelter; we base their wealth solely on income.

Someone from a developing country told me that the per capita income in his country is very low, but everyone has traditional homelands, so they do not have to go hungry or lack somewhere to live. And so, according to him, the low per capita income figure is misleading, because it does not give an accurate representation of the well-being of the people. –But it is more than misleading.

Using per capita income to measure average wealth or poverty around the world serves multiple purposes for PEOCs. In the first place, using per capita income to measure how well a country is doing implicitly assumes the need for income and begs the question, "Why do these people actually need *any* industry" (other than to supply PEOC insatiable desires)? The indigenous peoples of the world lived for countless thousands

275

of years without industry or income: They kept the land beautiful and unpolluted, and no one had to die of hunger or be in need of somewhere to live. The point is, there actually is no reason for the world's peoples to develop industries and raise their per capita incomes, except to serve the wants of PEOCs.

Another way we use per capita income is to confirm our superiority, as in "look how high our per capita income is." The fact that millions of people in PEOC countries go hungry and have nowhere to live doesn't matter, because our per capita income is high – *that's* what we're looking at. We use it to tell ourselves that the "average" people in our countries are better off than those in developing countries.

We also use per capita income to justify our activities, as in, "Look, these people have no income: They are very poor! Let's go help them" (meaning help ourselves). When we go into a country which has resources we want to exploit, we ask those in power to approve projects, such as putting roadways through their virgin forests (like we did to ours), damming their rivers, mining, drilling, logging, etc. We make it worth their while to approve these projects, and so a few people, those who are willing to work with us against the welfare of the common people, become rich. (By the way, if those in power will not approve the projects we want to implement, we overthrow their governments and replace them with people who *will* do what we want.)

The common people are now in debt to us because we did them the favor of destroying their land, and they will continue to be in debt to us for many years to come, probably for their whole lives.

If we have done it correctly, these people now need to get jobs, since they can no longer live off their land. Yet even though the common people in the region suffer heavily, the great increase in the wealth of those few at the top raises the per capita income in the country, and we proudly proclaim that we helped enrich that region, when in reality we definitely hurt the people.

We claim to be doing good, yet the average people, who did not want the development, often have to go to work in slave factories thanks to our help. (This also raises the per capita income, since they had no income when they were living off the land.) The PEOCs get a country in debt (a debt which they use to control and extort the country); control over the resources of the country (who is the main market for all the industries we want these peoples to develop?); and an unending stream of empty merchandise to fill our unending stores: electronics, clothes, decorations, shoes, furniture, toys, knick knacks, and all manner of stuff for us to buy, because the primary purpose of our culture is to consume.

People think they are doing such good, buying from some poor farmer in Ecuador or Guatemala. They tell themselves they are supporting the farming industry in Third-World countries – but never take a moment to question and consider: "Why should this poor guy in Guatemala have to spend his whole life growing food for Americans?" –And whether he's making what *we* have determined are decent wages is irrelevant.

U.S. Terrorism

It is devastating to see how drunk this country is on its own power, how ready to shove its will down the throats of other peoples who do not want to submit to this country's will (and they have that right). How quick we are to destroy a people if they stand in our way, meaning they want to continue to live the way they choose, and we want to destroy the way they live in order to exploit their resources. The people of this country are intoxicated with the power of this country and its supremacy in war, and it blinds them. Such power should come with a sense of responsibility to walk wisely and very carefully, but in this culture, it does not. We cannot walk wisely because there is no wisdom in this culture.

We like to tell ourselves that everyone in the world would like to be like us, but that is incorrect: Many people do not want to be anything like us (and they have that right). For example, there are still indigenous peoples in the world who don't want any part of our culture contaminating theirs, who don't want to become "advanced" so they will no longer know the Earth, who do not want to become like people who cannot even look to see their Mother and their Father. And there are non-Christians who do not want to be converted or to have anything to do with Christianity. We are not so perfect that we have the right to force others to follow in our footsteps.

We now say we invaded Iraq to help them establish democracy. If you look at the way the war has been going and what we have done to the people, you can imagine that there is a lot of anti-U.S. sentiment there. But if they wanted to democratically elect a religious zealot (our culture's word) or anyone else who hated the U.S., we'd never let it happen. So, the point is, we *don't* want a democracy in Iraq – what we want is control over the country. It's not about spreading freedom throughout the world; it's about subjugating peoples throughout the world and telling U.S. citizens we are spreading freedom.

I overheard a man telling pretty much anyone within earshot that the destruction of the environment is a Marxist conspiracy (talk about calling black, "white" – I guess this makes the U.S. and its corporations Marxist, since we are leading the way in environmental destruction). But the point is, "Marxist conspiracy" doesn't mean anything; it is just a convenient phrase, to have someone to blame for our actions (the Marxists made us do it); to rationalize our actions (the Marxists made us do it); and to predictably stir up public sentiment for some action or other which our government wants to take. There *never has been* a Marxist conspiracy – just a flood of people trying vainly, one after another, to escape the bloody terrorism and totalitarianism of the U.S. and other PEOC countries. Communism and capitalism (and socialism, which in practice is a form of capitalism) are not the only options for the economic system of a people. They are all constructs of the PEOC mind and are not really relevant to other peoples, but we like to interpret everything in our own terms, so we automatically call something communist if it is not capitalist.

After the 9-11-01 attacks, U.S. citizens were outraged that anyone could be so base as to purposely target civilians in an act of aggression, and we claimed we would never do that. But we were kidding ourselves, because we *do* wage war by purposely targeting civilians in acts of aggression – and U.S. citizens are not outraged; they are proud. In fact, if you study our PEOC history of war, you will find that attacking civilians was one of the forward steps in the progress of our culture. If you want to understand how people all over the world (most of them *non*-Muslim) cheered on the alleged perpetrators of 9-11-01, understand how U.S. citizens cheer on their government when it kills innocents, and understand how much resentment this causes throughout the world.

Our government has *always* used the tactic of targeting civilians, as did the Europeans before them. Who do U.S. citizens think we targeted in all the Indian wars? Who do U.S. citizens think we've killed in *all* of our wars? PEOCs perfected terrorism. We may claim we're making strategic strikes against important military targets, but that is just military doublespeak for "we're killing civilians."

After 9-11-01, some people heard some of the world's criticism of the U.S. and took a short moment to pause and think about the U.S.'s role in the world – or, more accurately, to defend in their own minds that we are a benign nation and a positive force in the world, and that U.S. citizens are good people. The fact that an overwhelming number of people in the world hate us does not faze them, because they believe all those people are just jealous (or are Marxists). The fact that an overwhelming number of people in the world supported the alleged 9-11-01 perpetrators doesn't faze them, either, probably because they never heard about most of this support through the U.S. press. However, they sucked up all the garbage our press reported which reinforced the idea that the U.S. is a benign nation. For example, many people were heartened by a Canadian editorial about how generous the U.S. is, and this editorial was spread far and wide: I heard people loving it and quoting its passages. (Note that Canada is probably not the best source of people to look critically and fairly at this country.) With the help of articles like this, everyone quickly went back to their self-induced stupor: "Rah-rah U.S.; we're the greatest country on Earth, we're such good people..."

If these people think they are blameless for all the death, torture, and oppression committed by their government and their corporations because they didn't know, it doesn't hold. It was their responsibility to know, and they could have known, even before 9-11. Their government calls black, "white," and U.S. citizens believe any outrageous or atrocious lie, but it is their responsibility to actually look at the color. If they don't look, they cannot claim, "We didn't know."

In *Lies My Teacher Told Me*,* James W. Loewen quotes Marine Corp Gen. Smedley D. Butler summarizing the wars he has fought for the U.S., all of them benefiting corporate interests: oil companies, fruit companies, banking companies, etc. This is what our many, many wars have been and still are about. If you say, "But helping these private corporate interests raises the standard of living for all Americans," you should understand something about yourself. If you think it is okay to kill and

---

* *Lies My Teacher Told Me*, selected bibliography.

enslave innocent people to raise *your* standard of living, or the American standard of living, then you are truly, completely morally bankrupt. And when our soldiers go off to war to "serve their country," they should know what they are doing, because these wars for corporations are not exceptions. Again – why do you think we're in Iraq?

Are our soldiers heroes? No: If your government puts a gun in your hand and tells you to shoot, it is *not* your moral responsibility to shoot – it is your responsibility to know the real reason you are being asked to kill, to assess the situation, and to determine if there is any way *not* to shoot. Since at least 99% of our wars have been wars of aggression (thinly disguised as wars of national security), in which there was not only a way but a moral reason *not* to shoot, the soldiers in at least 99% of our wars killed people unjustifiably. "Just following orders" did not work as justification for the Nazis, and it doesn't work for us. However, the "Follow your orders, soldier" mindset of our military is custom made for wars of aggression. It is no accident that, in our military, soldiers don't make their own decisions; someone else makes their decisions for them. And it has nothing to do with creating a better fighting force; our wars are very inefficient. We regularly kill our own soldiers and our allies (friendly fire); we poison our own soldiers (Agent Orange, etc.); we kill civilians (though this is intentional on our part); we waste supplies; we spend money which goes straight into some rich person's pocket; and so on. Sadly, what the "Follow your orders" mindset tells other peoples is that, for PEOCs, going to war and killing people are not momentous enough that PEOCs feel like they really have to understand why they're doing it; they are willing to kill based on orders.

Soldiers tell themselves, "I am serving my country," but that is a meaningless phrase. Unless you believe that our leaders have never lied to us, in all the history of this colony/country, and that we have never acted unjustly or in error, then it is your responsibility to determine each time and every time whether this war (or "military action") is justified – and that means not just listening to those promoting war and looking at their evidence, but listening to other sides as well.

The American people acted restless with the war against Iraq and none too happy when they discovered that Bush had manufactured the evidence which proved that the Iraqis were an imminent threat to this country – and that, in fact, Iraq had had nothing to do with the attacks on 9-11-01. As I mentioned before, this didn't keep them from electing Bush to a second term, so they weren't *too* upset about it, but some people acted like they had been betrayed. But wasn't it their responsibility to verify all the information *before* they supported the invasion and before we started the war; before we went in and destroyed the Iraqis' country; before we took the lives of thousands and thousands of innocent people; before we destroyed their homes, food, and water; before we left their country littered with more of our nuclear waste?

Why do we think it is okay to act before we are sure of our facts? –Because we are selfish: Even the chance that there might be danger to us is more important in our thinking than the destruction of others. We really have no idea of the actual consequences for others of our actions, of what it feels like to be attacked by people who have no mercy, no empathy, no compassion, and no respect for those they attack. We don't understand how we affect others because we have not suffered their fate – and because we really and truly don't care. In terms of Iraq, we're still lying to ourselves and telling ourselves that our brutal war is a good thing, because, we say, "at least" we are bringing democracy to that country.

No, our soldiers are not heroes – and neither are the U.S. citizens, even though we like to tell ourselves we are. We are terrorists.

Modern-Day Colonization in the Amazon

Some people still hold the delusion that the colonizers of what we call the United States tried to bring the native peoples who already lived here up to their level (which would be the level of some of the most brutish, selfish, brutal, greedy, cruel, genocidal, intolerant, racist people in the world). Most people these days, just like the people of our past, are actually blind enough to believe that a culture embracing murder, rape, pedophilia, slavery, hate, intolerance, and oppression has something to teach other cultures. But the truth is that the driving force behind any colonization, including the colonization of this country, is unmitigated greed for what belongs to someone else.

Sadly, we are still "raising up" unfortunate peoples. Lately some Amazonian Natives have had the misfortune of becoming the recipients of our aid. Private organizations and private investors are helping to create sustainable industries in their lands "so that they can retain their cultures." (Obviously, if their cultures do not include industries, they will not actually be retaining their cultures.) These private organizations and investors explain (= rationalize) that large corporations want to get hold of the Natives' resources, so they have to develop sustainable industries as an alternative. They rationalize, furthermore, that the Natives obviously need income, because they have to fight legal battles with those large corporations who want their land. Their rationales are just more of the circular reasoning which seems to be the only kind of reasoning of which PEOCs are capable. (We have to help them develop industries so that the large corporations don't help them develop industries.)

If these private investors really wanted to help, perhaps they'd use their investment money to fight those legal battles against the PEOC corporations who are trying to go in and take over the land. They'd leave the Amazonians alone, so that they truly *could* retain their cultures: As soon as we've made them join our cash economy, their cultures are destroyed – we've digested them (but the private investors, who used them to create industries, will have made a ton of money, which is really the point).

The people responsible for this latest havoc couch their intentions – to themselves, to the Natives, to the world at large – in terms of the highest ideals and the most compassionate motives, but they are just doing what PEOCs have always done: destroying the traditions and cultures of peoples we claim to be helping, and benefiting in the process.

Maybe they think they are trying to learn spirituality from the Amazonian Natives while helping them to modernize and update their daily way of life to "today's" world, sort of a payment-in-kind. What they don't see is that the Amazonians' daily way of life is a part of their spirituality, not something distinct. We like to imagine this distinction because we like to imagine that *we* can be spiritual in our daily materialistic, self-indulgent way of life.

We like the idea that you can work to accumulate wealth and have all the luxury and extravagance of the PEOC lifestyle and still be a spiritual person. –But this is just what we believe because it is what we want, not because it is reality. For the Natives we claim to be helping, their daily acts and their daily way of life are connected to their spirituality: They are more than a reflection of each other; they are a part of each other. Once you've taken the meaning out of the act of living, you've taken the spirituality out, too. And by "helping" these people to "update" their lives, we are destroying that spirituality we claim to honor.

These private investors have also been shipping the Native Amazonians pharmaceuticals, which clarifies their motives even more. Our pharmaceutical and medical industries have no redeeming value in terms of good health, so, clearly, they're trying to destroy the health of the Amazonians. If the Amazonians are like the Natives of North America before the colonizers came, they have exceptional health and traditional medical care, and they don't need our help to stay healthy. Maybe the pharmaceuticals are intended to fight the multitude of diseases we will import to them as part of the sustainable industries we're helping them develop. More importantly, if the people who say they are helping the Amazonians can make them dependent on our industries (or make them believe they are dependent on our industries), such as our pharmaceutical industry, all the better to draw them into the world economy. Eventually, they'll have to sell their souls. And if the private investors haven't done so already, I'm sure they have plans in the works for shipping drugs which "may cause sterility" as a side effect.

They're also teaching the Natives' children English (I wonder how long until that becomes their first language – and then their only language). It's telling that, whenever PEOCs have wanted something from an indigenous people, the documentation of the agreement (if there is an agreement) is in written English (or Spanish or French...). We are the ones who want something, but we cannot trouble ourselves to learn their language. (By the time we're done with our part of the agreement, there is often no one left speaking their language, because everyone has been killed, or their culture destroyed.) I wish I could bring some of the Amazonian leaders here to talk to North American Natives about the reservations, the Indian schools, everything that lies on the road ahead. There are plenty of people here they can talk to about how much goodwill there is in our culture for theirs.

Supporting Genocide

PEOCs wonder at the German people of the Holocaust years (those who have heard of the Holocaust): How were good, civilized people able to live their daily lives while their government slaughtered people, having more concern, for example, with getting fabric for a new dress, than for the deaths of children? I don't wonder, because I see the same phenomenon every day. In the U.S., the same kind of good, civilized people live their daily lives, with no concern for the slaughter of innocents perpetrated by the U.S. government.

There has never been a time in the history of the United States, even before it became a country, when it has not been engaged in slaughtering people, up to and including today. Yet the people of this country go about their daily business, worrying more about which coffee to buy or the latest sports scores than the deaths of children at the hands of their government. And yet the people of this country claim to be benevolent and generous and are proud about the greatness of their country. How did the German people support their government's atrocity? –With pride and righteousness.

At the beginning of the war against Iraq, I saw all kinds of "power of pride" bumper stickers, often paired with power of Christ bumper stickers. Apparently, even though pride is one of the Christians' seven deadly sins, it's okay in certain circumstances, like when your government has just bombed the hell out of a country which could in no way retaliate or even defend itself, in order to gain control over its resources; and when your government has destroyed the lives of millions of people, all the while telling its own citizens that it was doing a good thing. I know that during the Holocaust the Germans were basking in the glow of their sense of supremacy, cheering their soldiers on as they slaughtered millions of innocents, thinking about how righteous their leaders were in ridding the world of the evil scourge. (Supposedly, in our invasions of Afghanistan and Iraq, we were helping to rid the world of the evil scourge of terrorism.) Not everyone agreed with their government's actions, but those who didn't agree with the war (in Nazi Germany and during the invasion of Iraq) for the *most* part did nothing and said nothing, or perhaps engaged in futile protests.

(Some may object to my comparing our war against Iraq to the Holocaust, but there are enough similarities that the comparison is informative. Without arguing that we are committing genocide in Iraq, I *would* like to point out that the U.S. will not be happy until we have re-ordered the Iraqi society and revised their lives to be what *we* want them to be. We tell ourselves it is for their own good to become a capitalist democracy like us. We do not want them to go back to their old lives, and that is an important point.

Genocide is the act of eradicating a people or a "group." Of course this can be accomplished by killing a significant number of the people. But it can also be accomplished by not allowing them to procreate and carry on their lineage and culture. And it can be accomplished by destroying their way of life and subsuming them, so that that group of people no longer exists as a distinct group. The point is, there are many ways to eradicate a people, and the end result is always the destruction of that "group," no matter how that end result was carried out.[†]

We may not admit that we are trying to destroy people when we wage war, but that is exactly our intention. We want them either gone [killed], or completely dominated and changed into what we would like them to be so that they will be our friends. [Just to clarify, other civilizations and countries are our friends when they are ruled by a person or people who will freely allow us to exploit their citizens and their resources. The citizens may hate us and everything we stand for, but that is irrelevant to our concept of friendship.] For us, war is always about annihilation and/or complete dominance. We may not always accomplish complete dominance the first time we go to war with a people, but we always irrevocably disrupt the people's lives, and we usually go back for a second [and third] round if we don't succeed with the first war.

Perhaps Iraqi culture was already PEOC before our latest invasion; it is certain that the U.S. and Europe have been interfering in the affairs of that country for many centuries [which, incidentally, is how Saddam Hussein came to power – but that's another story]. But PEOCs have been fighting to control each other for ages. Whether or not our war again Iraq is a genocide, it does not change the fact that we have committed genocide against every indigenous culture we have ever encountered – and during all these genocides, the PEOCs in the

---

[†] *Kill the Indian, Save the Man*, selected bibliography.

aggressor countries spent more time worrying about their daily lives than about the destruction of millions of innocents perpetrated by their governments.)

During the Holocaust, the German government told its citizens that Jews and other non-Aryans were trying to destabilize and destroy their country, and the German citizens sucked it up. When they fought their war, the Nazis didn't call it a war of aggression any more than Bush did. (Bush pretended that the war on Iraq was a defensive war, because, according to him, Iraq was harboring and aiding terrorists like those who had attacked the United States on 9-11-01.) Similarly, during all our wars of annihilation against the Native Americans, the United States government pretended we were fighting defensive wars, to protect settlers.

When the Germans cheered on their brave soldiers during the Holocaust, it was a lot like the U.S. citizens cheering on their brave fighting men during the Indian wars, when the soldiers paraded through the streets with mutilated Indian body parts displayed as trophies, after having slaughtered villages of unarmed non-combatants. It is very easy to see how the Germans supported Hitler if you look at the people of the U.S. We have personalized license plates and 20 million possible ring tones for our cell phones, to keep ourselves occupied while our government commits slaughter, 20 million ring tones which make all that slaughter worthwhile. Meanwhile, thanks to all of our wars, those running multi-national corporations get richer, as the government wages wars for their profit, and the people swell with pride about the greatness of their country and its superior economic system, capitalism.

Gasoline prices started going up as soon as George W. Bush was elected, even before he took office. The U.S. suffered an 8-year series of energy crises (supposedly) during his terms in office. I wonder how the U.S. public would feel if they found out that these crises were complete fabrication. The oil companies put out lame press releases explaining the price increases (which the press duly parroted), but these prices were nothing more than unadulterated corporate greed.

If we hadn't already been in two (declared) wars, these crises would have made for a great excuse to start one. If the American people hadn't jumped on board Bush's fantasy of Iraq being an imminent threat to the U.S., I'm sure he would next have tried to convince U.S. citizens that Iraq was the country responsible for the inflated gasoline prices they were paying, and that Iraq was using high gas prices to try to destabilize our economy.

If we hadn't already been at war, he could have said, "If we take out the government of Iraq, gas prices could go down by as much as $1 per gallon," backing up the assertion with any weak, flimsy evidence he could invent, and the U.S. people would have been clamoring to invade. (Of course, it didn't come to this, because the American people had already bought into the weak, flimsy evidence he had invented about Iraq being an imminent threat.) And if, in the end, gas prices only went down by 25¢ per gallon (which would barely cut into the oil companies' exorbitant profits) – for a short while – and if the real effect of our invasion were the annihilation of the Iraqi people's way of life so we could exploit the resources of their lands, the U.S. people would still be full of righteous pride over the invasion, because we don't bother ourselves to find out what is really going on, and we always swell with righteous pride when we start wars. The effect would be that the oil companies would now have control over this whole new energy supply to sell to the insatiable U.S. public. Good for the companies – good for U.S. citizens – not so good for the people we destroyed, but we can live with it; it's an acceptable loss to us. Americans have a sense of entitlement which tells us that, if another country has a resource we want, we have the right to force them to export it to us.

You can protest a war (or a policy) all you want in this society, but it doesn't mean anything as long as you are benefiting from it and supporting the government with your citizenship and your taxes. As long as you are engaging in a lifestyle which makes such wars profitable, your protests are just hollow words. They show that you know something is wrong, yet at the same time you are too lazy or comfortable or gutless to do anything about it. Spouting lofty ideas means nothing – for a country or an individual – it is how you live. I'm guessing the indigenous peoples of the world did not spend nearly as much time spouting lofty ideals as we do. If the value of life is taught with life's lessons, you don't need to keep yelling through a bullhorn how much you value life, because everyone already knows. If people are free, you don't have to keep telling them they are free for them to know it. If you read a narrative of a Native American, describing their life before they were forced onto reservations, you can see how free they were without the narrator ever saying, "We were free."

Some may argue that protests helped get the U.S. out of Vietnam (people were protesting for years and years). Since when are we out of Vietnam? It is a dubious claim, and it doesn't change the fact that we had no business there in the first place, and that, decades later, the people of Vietnam have not recovered. Nor did those protests change the course of our country; we obviously learned nothing from the atrocity we committed. We have engaged in numerous wars and covert actions since. And the damage is still done to the Vietnamese, though I don't think they (or anyone else in the world) want our help in recovering. In fact, if PEOCs would just stay out of everyone's business and stop helping, the whole world would be a lot better off. We sure helped the Iraqis out of food and water; we helped them get rid of that pesky, clean desert, by polluting it with tons of our radioactive waste, and we helped increase their rate of birth defects and other illnesses. Even Kuwait (the country Iraq invaded, which led to the first U.S. war against Iraq) did not want our help. (For those who voted for George W. Bush because they are against abortion: Why was it okay for the U.S. to go into Iraq and bomb pregnant women, thereby causing deaths of fetuses? And why was it okay for the U.S. to use weapons made with spent plutonium, thereby causing deaths – and deformities – of fetuses? Is this one of those times when something which you claim is morally reprehensible is actually sometimes okay, when it's your side that's committing the act?)

We keep harming people the world over, in one self-serving action after another, and then cheering ourselves on about how we are a shining light of freedom and democracy and are spreading freedom and democracy to the world. Can PEOCs understand the resentment? If someone came to the U.S. and killed millions of people and destroyed the infrastructures and blew up the people's homes and left the air and water and ground polluted, then went back to their own people and proclaimed to them and to the world that they had just "liberated Americans from the tyranny of _____" (whoever the current president is) – wouldn't U.S. citizens resent it? I'm pretty sure that not even those who despise the current president would thank them. Yet we do that to other peoples again and again and again.

Here's an infallible gauge, a way of knowing beforehand if our intervention will be good for the people we claim we want to help: *Every* time we have had contact with other people, we have left them worse off. In other words, we need to leave everyone alone. Next time we want to help someone, we need to reign in our arrogance, which makes us think we're in charge of improving everything. I remember our government (and their press) making a point of saying that the Iraqis *wanted* us to come in and liberate them; they even found Iraqis they could parade around on TV to say it; but, trust me, the Iraqis didn't want the U.S. to invade their country.

I hear U.S. citizens say, about citizens of other countries, "You try to help them, and they don't have any gratitude. Let them try to do it without our help" (as if they will find they cannot possibly do "it" without the great and wise U.S. guiding them, and they will come crawling back when the U.S. withdraws its help). If we would let them do it without our help, it'd be great for them, but we cannot do that, because our help makes the selfish, indolent U.S. lifestyle possible. We go and intentionally destroy peoples (usually U.S. citizens don't hear about these sordid details), then force our help on the straggling remnants to recover from the mess we made and are surprised they don't want our help. We don't pay attention to the fact that our help intentionally makes things worse for the people, and yet we congratulate ourselves on being so helpful, so generous, such a good country, such good people – and we wonder how those Germans sat by while their government slaughtered innocent people.

Colonization

The traditional American Natives' cultures had means to see truth. Surely not everyone took the ultimate spiritual path of the shaman, but the cultures were spiritual, as were the people. They were close to the reality of the world. Their cultures included tools for reaching an understanding of their oneness with the Earth and the Creator, because these goals were important to them. If someone wanted to walk the spiritual path, the cultures had techniques and practices to help that person understand who they were, shorn of the cultural trappings. How wonderful is that? They were able to reach a level of profound understanding that is not only beyond the reach of PEOCs, but is also beyond their comprehension.

PEOC culture, in contrast, blinds us to the spiritual world and reality. All the complication of PEOC culture is just layer upon layer obfuscating what lies underneath. Ours is a culture which cannot locate itself, because it has so long been away from truth, and because it has strayed so far. It is like an impenetrable barrier that we don't understand is a barrier at all. Hence, we do not even seek to penetrate it...

*   *   *

The colonizers of the Americas – the Spaniards, the British, the French, the Dutch, (and so on) – did not come to these lands and see "heathens." They admitted that when they came, they met dignified and generous people of wisdom and grace. But they wanted what the Natives had materially, because to them material wealth was more important than the spiritual wisdom they could have learned. And so they *decided* to call the Natives "heathens." Since they were heathens, they reasoned, it was their job to civilize them (by raping the women and girls; by ruthlessly hunting them; by sadistically torturing and killing them).

You may say that this doesn't logically make sense, and it doesn't; none of it makes sense, and their reasoning doesn't follow. But the whole process was not about making sense. It was about being able to indulge in all their vices, from greed to sadism. The Natives treated the colonizers with kindness and generosity and were repaid not only with death, but with brutal death. There are very few books in our culture that actually describe (in part) the unfathomable brutality with which Europeans colonized the Americas.[‡]

Moreover, the colonizers convinced themselves they had God on their side, telling them that their evil, no matter how vile and depraved, was okay, because it was right for Christians to gain control of the Americas, because Christians are good. Since they were living in the superiority fantasy in their heads and not looking at reality, the colonizers called the kind Natives "savage," and, in spite of their own extreme savagery, considered themselves "civilized." In spite of their disgusting filth, both in terms of the squalor of their settlements

---

[‡] For some which do, see, e.g., *Bury My Heart at Wounded Knee, Lies My Teacher Told Me,* and *Kill the Indian, Save the Man,* selected bibliography.

and in terms of personal hygiene, the colonizers told themselves they were "clean" but that the clean Natives were "filthy." The colonizers were cannibals, and yet they called the Natives "cannibals." This is how PEOC minds work, never looking at the truth, always referring to the PEOC fantasy world in their heads to interpret life. It is important to note, because it isn't obvious to U.S. citizens (though it should be), that *none* of the people who colonized the Americas were "good guys" – and *all* of the settlers and pilgrims were colonizers.

In what is today the U.S., our holy forefathers would intentionally destroy the entire crop for a tribe of Natives, the goal being for them to starve to death or to become dependent on the colonizers for food. This is how our hallowed forefathers repaid the mercy the Natives had shown them by teaching them how to find and grow food, and for feeding them while they were learning. In what is today the U.S., the colonizers would intentionally annihilate entire tribes and nations of peoples, slicing them to pieces and shooting them to death. U.S. citizens like to think this is a country conceived in liberty, but it is a country conceived in blood and deceit.

Now look how far the U.S.A. has come, since we are always progressing. Today, we still use "God is on our side" and "God bless America" as rationale to subjugate, starve, torture, and kill peoples the world over. And even though PEOCs are one of the most savage and merciless people on the planet, we still call ourselves the most civilized. Complex social structures meant to control the populace; technology which facilitates our destruction of the planet and the utter routinization of our lives (as with assembly lines, sitting in traffic, renewing your car registration, and so on, ad infinitum); a culture which deadens people to life itself; massive amounts of weapons, which are created only to destroy; a complete lack of moral rectitude – these actually are not indications of advanced civilization – unless the word "advanced" is as meaningless as the word "progress."

And in PEOC culture, the words "progress" and "advancement" really are meaningless, as we use them. When someone in our culture uses the word "progress," what they are really saying is, "We have another way to destroy even more of the planet. We are progressing toward a total destruction of the planet and all of its entities." (The "non-progressive" Natives were wise enough to keep the Earth in pristine condition and to realize that, as it was, it could provide shelter, food, knowledge, and a doorway to spirituality. With all of our progress, we still don't realize that.) "Advancement," in PEOC culture, really means, "We are changing in a way which does not include any true improvement of the human condition but which allows us to become more and more lazy, slovenly, and self-indulgent." Next time you hear someone talking about progress or advancement, know what they are talking about. In this culture, the word "progress" is like a hypnotist's trigger: Someone says, "It's progress," and everyone accepts "it" as something good.

PEOCs are not trying to populate the entire planet as they populated most of the United States, mainly because we have found ways to destroy selected populations who stand in the way of our progress and still retain a slave class of laborers – we have all the wealth out of the land one way or another. But it is instructive to look at what PEOC culture was like before Europeans colonized the Americas to see exactly what they were exporting to other peoples.

Before colonization of the Americas, Europe had continual, constant warring, with more and more advanced (= destructive) warring tactics (wars were never absent from Europe – and now are never absent from the world, since PEOCs infested it), as well as epidemic non-war violence (pogroms, murder, rape, etc.). They had epidemic disease; many of the diseases the Europeans brought to the Americas were undoubtedly man-made in the sense that they arose out of the incredibly filthy, unhealthy, unnatural living conditions of Europe – which is why the American Natives had no exposure to such diseases: They did not have those filthy, unhealthy, unnatural living conditions here.

Pre-colonization Europe boasted famine, poverty, and warped social structures, based on wealth, aristocracy, and privilege. Unlike the situation in the Native Americas, the European civilizations included only a nominal – and optional – responsibility on the part of the "haves" to take care of the "have-nots"; gluttony and starvation living side-by-side in Europe was common; in the Americas it was unheard of and unthinkable. Pre-colonization Europe had religious intolerance, cultural intolerance, racial intolerance, and so on. This is what European culture was like before they decided to search for new lands to conquer and new peoples to torture.

Maybe the Europeans should have cleaned up their own act before exporting it to pollute the rest of the world (which would mean they still would not be ready). Only people raised in such circumstances and in such a culture could ever look at it as in any way superior. Anyone evaluating from the outside would have to conclude that it was one of the saddest, most decrepit cultures the world had to offer.

Though the colonizers took their victories in the destruction of the Natives as signs of God's favor in their cause (which was genocide), the actual reason they won was that, as morally bankrupt as they were, they would stop at *nothing* to win. All sorts of legends have grown up in the U.S., such as "The colonizers won because they were able to divide the Indians." Or, "The Indians broke as many treaties as our government." Or, "The Indians didn't know what their land was worth and sold it to us for almost nothing." (Let's look at that. Here's a common scenario from our early days: Say the colonizers wanted to buy land from a Native nation or tribe that didn't want to sell, because they knew exactly what their land was worth – their land was their life. For the colonizers, this was an easily surmountable obstacle: Nearby lived the remnants of a different tribe, one they had already destroyed, people whose land they had already stolen. The colonizers would approach these people, who had no claim to the land they were now trying to acquire. Since the colonizers had already destroyed their homes, taken their food, and spent the last five months hounding, harassing, and killing them off, the people were worn down. They could be coerced into signing whatever paper the colonizers put in front of them, without any idea of what that paper said [because, of course, the colonizers didn't have the integrity to tell them the truth about what it said]. They would take whatever pittance [= price] the colonizers offered, without necessarily even knowing it was meant as a land purchase. Congratulations to us! We have just purchased land really cheaply "because the Indians didn't know what their land was worth and sold it to us for almost nothing." See? –PEOC fantasy world.)

To say that the Native Americans didn't know what their land was worth and so were willing to sell their homes – for *any* amount of money – is beyond ridiculous and beyond idiotic. Never would the thought have occurred to them, "Wow, let's sell our land." They didn't even have the concept of selling land. And they were connected to their land; they could no more have sold it than sold their legs and arms. The only way these people would sell their land was because they were forced to sell it.

In spite of all of our idiotic legends, the real reason and the only reason the colonizers won is because there was no act, however horrific, however evil, which they were not willing to commit, and the Natives were not able or willing to sink to their level of ruthlessness and brutality: That is the *only* reason the colonizers won. It wasn't that the Natives didn't destroy the colonizers because they were not powerful enough to do so – it was that they were too honorable to do so. To deliberately set up a peace agreement with a nation of Native Americans only so that they will let their guard down, so that you can attack more effectively, is a despicable tactic, but it was a common technique of our colonizers, and we used many such techniques.

Those pioneering folk who struck out to settle the frontier knew exactly whose land they were claiming. They knew that the Native Americans who had belonged to that land had been brutalized and slaughtered and herded onto reservations, and that these reservations had been strategically set up on the most undesirable land so as to keep the good land for pioneering settlers. And in their self-ishness and greed, these pioneering settlers encouraged this behavior to continue. They were, in short, genocidaires.

After we had won the Indian wars (which we waged for over *two centuries*) and had forced onto reservations all the Native Americans who had survived our relentless campaigns of slaughter, we still were not content to let them live the way they wanted on those reservations. We wanted to thoroughly crush their cultures (which, after all, presented a viable and attractive alternative to ours). We encouraged them, usually through force and coercion, to give up their children so that their children could be raised in our culture's residential schools, which were, in effect, prisons. In these schools, the teachers taught the children to hate everything about their cultures and themselves. These teachers presented the PEOC as the ideal model to live up to: The children were made to speak only English and were often forbidden from seeing their families. The teachers and school administrators changed the children's names, cut their hair, and made them wear PEOC clothes. They made them pray to Christ and taught them to try to be something they could never be (according to our culture – since they were non-white) and never should have been forced to try to be.§

These children had to work so that the good PEOCs who had destroyed their tribes and nations and had taken all of their land wouldn't have to be

---

§ *Kill the Indian, Save the Man*, selected bibliography.

burdened with the cost of "educating" the "heathens." They weren't given enough food because the money gained from their work was used to keep the administrators fat and happy rather than feed the children. Because they were worked like slaves and underfed, many succumbed to disease, because there was almost no medical care, not even the weak PEOC version of medical care.

This is not a sad story about people who had the best of intentions to save or raise up the Indians but made some mistakes or had some errors in judgment. Nor is it a tragic story about people whose good intentions got lost in red-tape bureaucracy or in a few people's abuse of the system to their own advantage. This is a genocide story; there were no good or honorable intentions. Our behavior fits one of the definitions of genocide, and this is a story about people who had every intention of destroying the Native Americans. The U.S. government (and the Canadian government) implemented it, and the U.S. citizens (and the Canadian citizens) supported it. If they thought it was right to take the children because they had good intentions, that means they thought it was right to commit genocide, and apparently they need a drastic reworking of their sense of what is right and what is wrong, because I don't know of any culture, not even our warped culture (which has perpetrated so many), which *says* genocide is good.

People may say it's unfair to judge the past by today's standards because they didn't have the concept of genocide then, but that is just our culture excusing itself (which is common). I've also heard of hunting a species to extinction and wholesale destruction of the natural environment (and creation of the atomic bomb and so on) excused because "they didn't know what we know now." This is a disingenuous argument, for (at least) two reasons: 1) They actually *did* know; and 2) We are still committing the same acts today, even though we acknowledge that we now know. (I'm sure future generations will give us the benefit of the doubt, though, and say *we* didn't know.)

If someone destroyed a portion of a forest, they surely knew they were killing trees which were hundreds of years old; they knew they were killing other plants; they knew they were killing animals and disrupting nature. But they also knew they wanted money, and getting money was more important to them than what they were doing to the plants and animals and the Earth.

And how did all the indigenous peoples, who are supposedly so far behind us and who have no "true knowledge," know? How did they know that you cannot commit destruction of nature without hurting humans, too? How did they know that once you've hunted an animal to extinction, it's gone – and all the rest of the planet will be affected? Why were they able to see the damage our lifestyle causes? How is it that they knew how destructive it is to grasp material gain at the expense of our Mother and our brothers and sisters – and why did their cultures shun this type of gain? How is it that they understood the destruction we cause, on a much more fundamental level than our culture can understand, straight through to today? Could it be that they were more advanced than we are? They knew it *all* matters, even if we didn't – and still don't.

Yet we *do* know that we are hurting the planet – and even with this knowledge, we are continuing to do it, for profit and selfishness, same as in the past. Even those who claim to care about the Earth, who have joined the green movement, are hurting the planet; their harm is easy to see, even if they choose not to look. We may not understand on as profound a level as indigenous peoples, because we have our cultural haze clouding our vision, yet we do see that we are destroying – same as in the past, just as they knew they were destroying the lives of the plants and animals and peoples. The Native Americans knew our roads and railroads were harming the wildlife and destroying their homes; they made a point of telling the colonizers repeatedly, so the colonizers knew, too; but the colonizers didn't care. While the colonizers were killing off the dodo birds, I'm sure they noticed that dodos were becoming more and more rare, harder and harder to find. I'm sure they realized that soon the dodos would all be gone – but that didn't stop them from killing them.

When people say, "You can't judge the past by today's standards, because they didn't know what we know today," it's a lying argument, a fantasy. Some claim that people of the past thought African slavery was okay because those people were ignorant and thought Africans were "less than human." – I've got news for those making this claim. When the Europeans encountered Africans, they sure knew they were human. If they changed their minds later because they wanted free labor, that doesn't mean they didn't know. When the slave owners raped their slaves, they knew. It's a lying argument.

And to say the colonizers of the Americas didn't know they were committing genocide or understand that it is wrong to kill off and destroy entire peoples is also a lying argument. To say they didn't know it was wrong to hack people to death, drive them from their homes, and starve them to death, is self-serving dribble. To say that it was not their intention to annihilate Native Americans is a lie. To claim they didn't realize the results of their actions is contemptible. And to deny that this is the true history of the Americas and the United States is disgraceful, but that's what PEOCs do. Of course the colonizers knew that what they were doing was wrong; they may not have had the *word*, "genocide," but they definitely had the concept – genocide was their goal, what they wanted consciously and maliciously – and they surely knew it was wrong.

Similarly, to say that the people who conceived of, implemented, and supported the Indian schools didn't have the concept of genocide, and that they thought that what they were doing was right, is a sham. They were trying to destroy the Natives' cultures, by taking the children and imposing their thought on those children. And, by the way, the Indian schools didn't close until decades after the Genocide Convention was written – by then they not only had the concept; they had the word.

Today, people torture animals in laboratories, and they also know it's wrong. Yet the PEOCs of the future will say it's unfair to judge these people, because they didn't know. PEOCs can rationalize all they want (it's for the good of humankind) (it was for the good of the colonizers), but they still know that they are doing things which are wrong. If people in our past didn't know that what they were doing was wrong, it was only because they didn't *want* to know; in other words, they *did* know but would not acknowledge it to themselves. And we are the same today.

*   *   *

I remember a short lesson one day in school about the ancient Aztecs and Incans. (Obviously, since we think these were the most advanced indigenous civilizations, they are the ones taught in schools. Obviously, too, no mention is made of the fact that there are Aztecs and Incans still alive today, because that would sort of cancel out our use of the word "ancient" for schoolchildren. We like to at least give schoolchildren the impression that they died out long before the Europeans arrived.) Learning about them had nothing to do with learning about their cultures. (But it's not like we actually understand anything about their cultures, after all. Even if some of the Incans or Aztecs alive today might be able to shed some light on their cultures and explain something about them to our brilliant scholars, the scholars don't want to waste their time listening; after all, they can come up with much better theories themselves. Why look at what's actually there when you can make a career of inventing fictions in your mind?) We just learned that they had developed sundials, calendars, and what we consider to be impressive structures, accompanied by the thought: "Pretty sophisticated for such primitive people." The lesson definitely didn't include the information that these peoples had been destroyed by colonizing Europeans, with a brutality that almost defies comprehension.

No, herding people together and slicing them to pieces, or setting up death camps and interring people within to be worked to death or to die of starvation and disease – these are not the tactics of superior peoples, nor, when they succeed, are they signs of God's favor. However, we see that neither

Hitler nor the Rwandan Hutus who committed genocide were original in their methods, because these were techniques commonly used by the colonizers of the Americas long before Hitler slaughtered Jews or Hutus slaughtered Tutsis. And when the colonizers of the Americas won, God was no more on their side than on the side of Hitler or the Hutus, anymore than God is on our side in our current and continuous destruction of both peoples and the Earth.

Anyone who thinks colonization would be any different if PEOCs discovered a new world today, because we are now so much more advanced and enlightened, is suffering serious delusions as well as a deplorable lack of knowledge regarding current events (the war in Iraq being an obvious example). It's sad to realize this land *actually* used to be what we now *claim* it is (the land of freedom and liberty and equality), and that we destroyed it in our greed and cultural arrogance.

The Europeans actually believed they were superior to the Native Americans. Their culture told them they were the most advanced people on Earth – as such, it was clearly a culture which did not value other peoples – just as it tells us we are the most advanced people on Earth today. Today's PEOCs still have the prideful thought that our culture is (and hence we are) superior, and that other peoples of the world should try to become like us or, at the least, serve our needs. This is one of the best reasons, perhaps, to look through the lie that is our culture: Who wants to be a genocidaire? As long as we cheer on our government in its current acts of domination, trying to impose our culture and values on other peoples, we are cheering on genocide; and if you wonder how the Germans who did not actively participate in the Holocaust sat by while it happened, stop wondering. Genocide did not start with Hitler; it did not end with him; it is happening now, and PEOCs, in all their complacency about being superior, still do nothing.

* * *

Forget about a book rating fine chocolates; let's rate the growers of fine chocolates. This first group of growers is actually the remnants of what were formerly many distinct peoples. Their ancestors were destroyed by the Portuguese and the Spaniards long ago: They tried to escape, but were pursued, and their numbers became thinner and thinner. Some were enslaved; some brutally slaughtered; and what you see now are the few who are left, who have no land on which to live and who spend their days farming the land of the wealthy colonizers (descendents of colonizers are still colonizers), while they live in squalor and oppressive poverty.

This second group was destroyed by American corporate interests only ten years ago. They are the last survivors of a once-great people, viewing their homeland devastated so that Americans can export energy from their lands. They are reduced to growing chocolate for those Americans who destroyed their lives. Maybe some Peace Corps volunteers came in after the corporation was set up, to teach the poor people how to farm – because they obviously don't know how to take care of themselves, and they live in such incomprehensible squalor.

How do U.S. citizens think indigenous peoples lived in the Americas (and throughout the world) for so long – that we need to teach them how to farm, or how to take care of themselves – that we need to teach them how to live? How do they think those people living in incomprehensible squalor *came* to be living in incomprehensible squalor? And which group of chocolate growers is more tragic?

* * *

Those who try to change things by working within the political framework are actually abetting the devastation, not ending it. The whole point is that the political framework is part of the culture, and the culture is destruction. It is a culture which cannot improve itself from within, and the political framework does nothing more than add a veneer of legitimacy and propaganda: "See, we have a constitution; therefore, we allow free speech." "See, we have courts; therefore, we have justice." "See, there is a genocide convention; therefore, we are trying to end genocide." "See, we have a U.N.; therefore, we are trying to work together to develop international rights and world peace." Meanwhile, it all doesn't mean anything. The culture which spawned an evil may end one instance (usually after it has played itself out), but it will carry on the act, spawning it again and again. It seems there is nothing our culture can touch which it does not pollute or destroy entirely, a virtueless culture. Although it is a goal of our space program, I hope we never "discover" another planet to colonize.

If I could undo colonization, I would, not just of the Americas, but of the world. But to do so, I would have to be able to annihilate the PEOC mindset, which was already at work so long ago... It is the same mindset which allowed the domestication of animals, the idea being that humans were

313

separate and higher than other animals and that it was okay to impinge on their sovereignty in order to make them serve people. It is the same mindset which promoted the destruction and genocide *within* Europe of cultures alternative to the dominant culture, the mindset which allowed Rome to become a Holy Empire and which told the English it was okay to invade Ireland and Scotland...

If there are two cultures, one in which people are peaceful, willing to live side-by-side with others, and another which seeks to dominate and destroy others, the culture which seeks to dominate and destroy will probably win eventually, because they will always be fighting wars of aggression, inventing new warring tactics, developing new weapons, and harassing the other people so they cannot know a moment's peace. But their winning doesn't mean that the dominant culture is superior, just more brutal. And if the peaceful culture wins by constantly developing defensive technology to counter the aggressive culture's weapons, they have still lost, because their lives are still centered around war. And if they win by becoming as violent and brutal as the aggressive culture – again, they have lost. So you see: Against our culture, no one can win.

Right Colonization

I read a book jacket for a James Michener novel which fictionalized the colonization of South Africa.** The story summary on the book jacket made it sound like the tragedy of South African colonization was a series of inevitable events, and it stated that the colonizers who slaughtered, enslaved, and oppressed the people of South Africa were essentially, in the end, "decent" people, because they believed that what they were doing was right. If that is the criterion, Hitler was also a good, decent person – he thought what he was doing was right. In fact, those responsible for 9-11-01 believed that what they were doing was right, too. And based on that criterion, the Ku Klux Klan is chock full of decent people. Heck, based on that criterion, pretty much everyone who has ever committed an atrocity is decent: Not many people say to themselves, "I want to do something evil. Now what comes to mind?" I'm sure the people of South Africa who were killed and enslaved would be relieved to know that those responsible for their destruction were at least "decent" people – it's not like some *barbarians* from Africa wantonly slaughtered and mercilessly enslaved them. (I wonder: If South Africa's colonizers can be called "decent," what does one have to do to lose this claim?)

** *The Covenant*, James Michener. Random House: New York. 1980.

The idea that, if you believe you are doing the right thing, then you are a decent person doesn't hold water. When self-interest is guiding your principle of what is right – for example, when the colonizers devastated what is now South Africa, thinking it was right because they wanted to control all the valuable resources there – then you can no longer lay claim to being a decent person because you are doing what you think is right. When people decide the right thing based on what will benefit them most, they are rationalizing, not decent.

This is true of all the people who colonized and told themselves they were raising up the entire continent of Africa. (There is no such thing as a "decent colonizer"; that is an oxymoron.[††]) PEOCs treated the continent like it was theirs to own and use, like there were not people already living there who had every right to go on living their lives without interference. They had civilizations; they had spirituality; they had food; they had laughter and enjoyment; they had everything they needed to live good lives. It isn't like they didn't know how to live before PEOCs came along – like this was a whole continent of crazy people, wandering aimlessly through their lives. They *already had* cultures and civilizations. Then PEOCs came in and divided up the continent, for their own convenience (i.e. so they could keep track of who owned what), and they named the newly-formed countries. But these countries mean nothing – they were a fiction of PEOCs.

And, as always, what the PEOCs touched, they poisoned. Today, many countries in Africa are embroiled in troubles, and PEOCs like to tell themselves that Africans can't get it together: They're

---

[††] *The Colonizer and the Colonized,* selected bibliography.

always warring, and the people are all starving (PEOCs tell themselves). They ignore the fact that not all the peoples of Africa are warring or starving – and that those who are, are still suffering the effects of past *and current* PEOC intervention in their lives. It's not like the colonization of Africa ended when the countries received their independence; it just changed its form. If you want to know why some countries can't get it together, ask why PEOC countries are doing everything they can to make sure those countries *don't* get it together. It's not that there is no one in these countries who would try to help their people – it's that PEOCs try to keep them from gaining power – we prefer to support the totalitarians who slaughter their people and help *us*.

The Rwandan genocide was very much a product both of European colonization and of ongoing European interference at the time of the genocide; PEOCs definitely get the credit for that one. It was Europeans who decided that *Hutu* and *Tutsi* were "ethnicities"; it was Europeans who decided that Tutsis were superior to Hutus – guess why – because (they believed) Tutsis more closely resembled Europeans (they determined this based on the approximately two Tutsis they had met). It was the Belgians who were demented and insane (and arrogant and pathetic) enough to actually go through the country, measuring each person's forehead and nose to decide whether to label them Hutu or Tutsi (or Twa – a *very* small percentage of the population) and giving each a card to identify them as such for their entire life.

The Belgians then made the Tutsis, who were much fewer in number than the Hutus, do their dirty work of running the country of Rwanda and of making the Hutus slave away their lives for the greater glory of Belgians. Tutsis could never be Belgians, but they were above Hutus.

Ironically (or not), it was the privileged class, the Tutsis, who first started pushing for Rwandan independence from Belgium. Rwanda eventually got its independence, but the Belgians didn't appreciate the Tutsis' initiating the revolt, and so they appointed a Hutu to be head of state when they left, thinking that the Hutus would use their political power to avenge themselves on the Tutsis. And indeed, for several decades, there was ethnic tension in Rwanda, and Hutus would massacre Tutsis from time to time. (Remember, this kind of thing never happened before PEOCs came into their lives.)

Then a Hutu named Habyarimana took office, and he issued a moratorium on the massacre of Tutsis; he wanted the entire country to work together for the good of all. Violence against Tutsis didn't stop while he was in office, but it slowed down quite a bit. However, he was assassinated, and the rulers who took over after his death strongly promoted violence against Tutsis; in fact, they promoted killing them all, and they started this killing the very day he died. And France and other PEOC countries were happy to support the new party ruling Rwanda, right down to supporting their genocide and providing them with weapons. (The Hutu Christians were also very helpful to the genocidaires, by the way. They would, for example, invite their Tutsi parishioners to come to church, telling them that they would be safe there. Then they would let the Hutu genocidaires know to come with machetes, because they had gathered a group of Tutsis together for slaughter.)

It was the Rwandan Liberation Army which ended the genocide (no, PEOCs didn't do that –

didn't even try to do that; remember, they were *supporting* the genocidaires). And as the genocidaires fled the country ahead of the Rwandan Liberation Army, they forced many, many people to flee with them.

After the war, when the Rwandan Army tried to begin the long task of putting a country back together, PEOCs were there again (still), interfering and making things harder for the people they claimed to be helping.‡‡

Rwanda wanted its people back from the refugee camps – innocent and guilty – but the international community (PEOCs) prevented the Rwandan army from breaking up the camps, in spite of the fact that the genocidaires basically ran them, and in spite of the fact that many of the people in the camps wanted to return home. The problem (from the point of view of the genocidaires) was that, if they let the innocent go home, only the guilty would be left. Things got very bad, and many of the refugees were living in hellish misery. Perhaps this was lost on the PEOCs; perhaps they just didn't care. Regardless, they would not let the Rwandan army break up the camps.

Things got very bad in Rwanda, too, because these camps provided staging areas for further violence against Tutsis. Hutu genocidaires would sneak across the border and continue their killing, then return to the safety of the international-community-protected camps. The only thing PEOCs did was make things worse, supplying the genocidaires with food (which only sometimes got to the innocent refugees) and with weapons.

---

‡‡ For more on the Rwandan genocide and its aftermath, see *We Wish to Inform You that Tomorrow We Will Be Killed with Our Families*, selected bibliography.

This history illustrates another one of the problems with PEOC culture and its causes. We like to say, "See, we have human rights and international aid organizations; this shows that we care about human rights and international aid." But these organizations actually caused the innocent refugees months and months of additional misery and suffering and abetted the perpetrators of the genocide in escaping justice. So the only people they helped were the guilty – and themselves (they were pouring in the money this whole time).

We say we care because we have these organizations – only we don't. We don't bother to find out what's going on and how our actions are affecting people because we don't *really* care, we just like to tell ourselves we do. International relief organizations are just another industry. We tell ourselves, "At least we *try* to help people..." but this is just us telling ourselves we are wonderful again. We *don't* really try: Throwing some money at the "Rwandan refugee problem" and then completely disregarding how that money is used is not the same as trying. If I offered to baby-sit your child but was too busy watching TV to notice as your child dropped out of a second-story window, I couldn't justly claim I had tried to help you, could I?

* * *

PEOCs like to label many of the practices of various African peoples "barbaric." We neglect to realize that many of these practices were not part of African cultures until after the interference of PEOCs (and other Eurasian cultures). We act like we are enlightened people, trying to enlighten others, and ignore the fact that in many cases *we* caused the problems we are protesting. And in many cases, there is no problem at all but what our warped culture interprets as a problem, because we don't bother to understand but still like to judge. Our culture is a little too far from ideal to be making these kinds of calls, and yet we make them. We may think a tradition is savage, or that *that* is not an acceptable way to live, but if *no one* is being hurt by the tradition, or if *all* the people living *that* way find it acceptable, there's not really a problem, is there? They don't need us to validate their lifestyles, and they don't need our puritanical judgments telling them what is acceptable.

And PEOC interference in the African peoples' lives goes on. We want Africa to be a part of the world economy, for all kinds of reasons which are all to our benefit and which keep various African peoples in distressed circumstances. For example, we want the people to harvest and mine raw materials, which PEOC corporations can turn into finished goods. We'll typically only buy raw materials from African countries, because raw materials are much cheaper than goods; in most cases, the profit is in the production. The PEOC corporation may turn the raw materials into finished goods at a slave factory, also in Africa, which is another one of the reasons we want Africa to be a part of the world economy – so the people will need jobs.

Obviously, if the leaders of an African country were to say something along the lines of "To hell with this" and were to work on taking care of their people and on saving their culture rather than trying to be more like PEOCs and trying to be a part of the world economy, everyone in their country would be a lot better off. So, to keep that from happening, we send Peace Corp volunteers to act like they're trying to help the people, and we keep leaders in power who are more interested in their own wealth and comfort than in their people. We support the ruthless leaders who do the bidding of PEOCs, and we keep their armies supplied and trained. Plus, we have most of these nations in debt to the World Bank and/or to PEOC nations, and we use that debt as leverage to make them do what we want.

*   *   *

Like the colonizers of Africa, the people who colonized the U.S.A. undoubtedly thought themselves decent; I'm sure they, too, found ways to convince themselves that what they were doing was right. When someone wants something in our culture, it is not hard for them to find a way to believe it is right to get it. As soon as the Natives' help was no longer wanted, the colonizers found a way to rationalize killing them. They believed it was right to dominate and control this land because they wanted to dominate and control this land.

If they had actually been as decent and as superior as they claimed, why didn't they simply erect colonies and settlements next to the Natives' lands, then wait for the Natives to flock to them, to learn how to live the wonderful and superior white men's life? And why didn't the Natives flock to their settlements, to learn this superior way to live? If we are superior, it should be evident to everyone; if it is only evident to us that we are superior – well, then, the superiority is just another illusion in our heads. Why did the Natives fight to retain their own lives and cultures? Anyone who thinks the answer to that question is that the Natives were too ignorant to know what was best for themselves clearly does not understand anything about the Native cultures (nor the right to self-determination) and so is in no place to say the colonizers' culture was superior: How can you think one culture is superior to another if you only know one of the cultures, and you've started with the presumption that the one you know is superior? How can someone say the colonizers' culture was superior without understanding the Native cultures? You cannot say algebra is superior to geometry if you know algebra but not geometry.

I thumbed through a book about George Washington (i.e. another book glorifying George Washington), in which the author, after glazing over a few of the atrocities waged by the colonizers against Native Americans, claimed that it would be "sentimental" to think that the "primitive" civilizations of the Natives could have co-existed beside the "advanced" civilization of the Europeans. Thus he blithely dismissed our genocide as inevitable. A more accurate statement would have been that it would be sentimental to think the brutal, ruthless, greedy, "superior" Europeans could ever have had respect for other peoples and their right to live as they chose. It would be sentimental to think the colonizers could ever have tried to live with them and learn from them rather than seek to destroy them. No matter how advanced had been the civilization they found here, they would have tried to conquer it.

Many people see the fact that, in the end, we won (i.e., we control the U.S.A.) as evidence that European culture was superior. Let's look at that: The Europeans were unwilling to live side-by-side with other cultures or to tolerate diversity because they were racists, they had no respect for other peoples' ways, and they wanted what did not belong to them and were willing to go to any vile means to get it: hardly signs of superiority.

The PEOC way is to eliminate diversity and force the predominate culture on those who survive their campaigns of destruction. They won the U.S.A. by resorting to lying, thievery, torture, coercion, killing non-combatants, killing unarmed people, introducing Indians to alcohol for the deliberate purpose of destroying the people and their societies, selling captives into slavery, killing and mutilating babies, committing every atrocity they could conceive; all of it a concerted genocide against the Natives in order to destroy the peoples.

Once the wars were won and they controlled the land, after they had forced all the remaining Native Americans onto reservations which they had assigned to them, they forcefully took the Natives' children and imprisoned them in Indian schools, and they forced our governing system and our laws onto the Natives living on the reservations. These steps were meant to completely destroy what remained of their cultures, because our culture cannot tolerate diversity. And we continue, even to today, to find ways to take land from the Natives, because apparently that little bit of land they have is still too much – we want it all.

To top it all off, our history is full of lies about the motivations and actions of all our great American heroes, who were in reality nothing but unprincipled, evil, and cruel people. Can you imagine the gall it took for our Revolutionary War heroes to tell Great Britain, "This land belongs to us; we are no longer your subjects" – while, at the same time, they were killing off the people the land *actually* belonged to and making them into subjects of *their* new tyranny?

In the mind of the U.S. citizen, the U.S. is a nation founded in liberty and freedom, holding the loftiest ideals. But this country never was that country, and we're not working towards becoming that country. Today's citizens, who claim tolerance and were raised in the concept that "all men are created equal," continue the barbarity. Straight through to today, Native Americans and other groups are subjected to oppression at the hands of U.S. citizens.

*   *   *

Some people claim they are *not* guided by self-interest in their interactions with indigenous peoples; they believe they are decent because, they tell themselves, they are guided by the interests of those whom they seek to help. They say they seek to improve indigenous peoples' lives, and they tell themselves this is "right." But they are just kidding themselves; they are no different from all the other colonizers. They are using the same tired but time-honored PEOC technique of rationalization which every PEOC uses, which lets them call themselves decent. These people, too, are trying to impose our lifestyle on others, because they believe our lifestyle is superior. They are just like the Europeans who, wanting the land, killed the Native Americans – or the Christians who, wanting a Jew's money, killed the Jew. No matter what they tell themselves, they are no different. They try to set up a delineation (but it is all in their minds) because, they say, their actions are not motivated by a desire for wealth; they will not benefit from their activities. But self-interest is not the same thing as personal profit, and personal profit is not the only benefit to be derived from colonization. There are other ways to benefit from interference:

Like Christian missionaries, our science missionaries fall into the do-gooder, "we're trying to help these people" category: They believe what they are doing is right and think they are motivated only by a desire to help other peoples and are unmotivated by self-interest. (Perhaps they are too blinded by their tunnel vision to see all the profit some PEOC corporations make off their activities.) Yet, as Christian missionaries have always done, they, too, go to indigenous peoples and destroy their lives. Science missionaries travel the world to teach indigenous peoples what science has discovered about the world that *the indigenous peoples live in* (how idiotic is that?) and to encourage on them the superior (they believe) PEOC view of life. They are just like the Christian missionaries, who swarm the planet to teach the most spiritual peoples on the planet about spirituality (how sad is that?). Again with science missionaries, it is evident that people of our culture believe they have something to teach indigenous peoples, because the hubris of the PEOC mind is unbounded.

These science missionaries may say, "You don't know the reality of the matter. The reality is that, in many [but not all] cases, these peoples' traditional lives were destroyed long ago, and now they are living in poverty and squalor, destroying their lands and the species of plants and animals living on those lands, in an attempt to make money, because they are so desperately poor. They need our help. Moreover, we need to save as many animal species as possible, for the sake of humans. Right now, we have to look at the current situation and make the best of it, and what we are teaching is better than the way they're living now." This is how the science missionaries rationalize their actions, as though the atrocities of the past make it okay for them to commit a whole new set of atrocities. (It's incredible how many ways we justify our interference – and all are supposedly for the benefit of those we harm.)

Scientists' ideas of what is wrong and what needs to be saved and why we want to save that and how to go about the saving are all based on science. But science *harms*, so all of this so-called saving actually harms. For example, scientists actually collect what they call a representative sampling of fish in a representative sampling of areas by electro shocking those fish, then collecting them for study. They tell themselves and everyone who listens to them that this doesn't harm or have any long-term effects on the fish. But anyone who has ever undergone electro shock therapy knows that it has permanent, detrimental effects. These detrimental effects don't just disappear because it's fish who are being tortured instead of people.

It is not to anyone's benefit to be sucked into our culture or our cultural view, to be sucked into serving our needs. Science missionaries actually have no desire to see the indigenes have their traditional lifestyles back, because they believe our lifestyle is better. They just want to change the indigenes' lifestyles in a different way than the Christian missionaries want to change them, and a different way than the U.S. corporations want to change them (and so on). "If we can just show them," their thinking goes, "how to make money without destroying their animal species, and we can get them to accept scientists into their communities so the scientists can teach them, then we are helping them and the planet." Notice how similar this is to the Christian missionary goal of getting indigenous peoples to accept Christians into their communities so *they* can teach them.

Science missionaries sometimes go to harm people whose lives have already been devastated by PEOCs, acting as the cleanup crew, finishing the job the PEOC corporations and PEOC governments and militaries started, nailing down the lid of the coffin on the indigenes' heritage, on their identity *as a people*. Yet sometimes, they get there ahead of the corporations and governments, initiating the destruction and leaving it for corporations to nail down the lid. Everything about our culture is toxic: The Christian missionaries tell themselves they are doing good and teaching indigenous peoples about God's one true religion so they can be saved. The corporations claim when they are exploiting the people that they are helping bring income to desperately poor people in Third-World countries. Science missionaries have joined the ranks, carrying on the age-old PEOC formula: "We are helping these people by destroying their lives." They tell themselves they're different, that *they* aren't destroying peoples' lives; *they* are helping. But that is just what everyone in our culture automatically tells themselves.

In our culture, people want to do whatever they want to do and to pretend the harm isn't there by refusing to look at it. It's similar to a child covering their eyes so you can't see them. The science missionaries want the people to adopt science, and the scientific studies they want the people to conduct and to allow cause harm – but the science missionaries don't want to look at that. They just want to do their thing. Science missionaries are continuing the same domination as all the other PEOCs; they have just found one more way to say to indigenous peoples, "Our world view is superior to yours."

All that is left to PEOCs is what we will never do, and that is to let other people live their own lives and quit trying to control or change them. Their lives are not ours to control or change – even if we have convinced ourselves it is for the better for them. With that attitude, it's obvious we are going into the situation with a feeling of superiority – if not personal superiority, then cultural superiority (we know what's best) – so we obviously cannot truly help. This culture's guidance mantra is like Christianity's (and it is easy to see why Christianity is the primary PEOC religion). In PEOC culture, you have to expound lofty ideals to justify your actions to yourself and others; one cannot rationalize that which claims to be what it really is. If George W. Bush had said he wanted to invade Iraq so that his oil company friends could control Iraq's oil reserves and so he could hand multibillion dollar contracts to his campaign contributors, he would not have had public support. So instead he lied and claimed Iraq posed an imminent threat to the U.S. – viola, tons of public support. After we had invaded Iraq and determined they had *not* been an imminent threat, he claimed, in retrospect, that we had invaded to help the Iraqi people establish democracy – again, tons of public support, because we really like to swell with pride when we help people, and we always claim we are helping.

Similarly with the pogroms in Europe: Christians convinced themselves they were doing God's work in killing Jews, Gypsies, lepers, and so many more, and they spouted the holiest of intentions while committing their destruction. All of PEOC control and devastation expounds the loftiest, highest ideals, but PEOCs never *were* a culture which lived the highest ideals anymore than Christianity was ever anything but a tool of dominance and destruction. And our military men and women are no more serving their country than our missionary men and women are serving God. There is no "right" in PEOC culture.

Honoring Our Treaties

Let's put aside Puerto Rico, Guam, the Virgin Islands – and the rest of the world. In the fifty states of the U.S., today, right now, the Native Americans and other indigenous peoples are colonized peoples. Just because we forced the Native Americans onto reservations and put them out of our minds doesn't mean they ceased to be colonized. The fact that they are now *allowed* to leave their reservations and mingle freely in *our* society does not mean that they ceased to be colonized – nor that we ceased to be colonizers – nor that this country ceased to be an illegal colony. And we are still reaping the benefits of that despicable colonization: for one thing (of many), whose land do you think we're living on?

U.S. citizens like to think they are honorable and just, citizens of an honorable and just country. However, if we are so honorable, why do we not, even today, when we say the errors of the past are past and it is time to move on, honor the treaties signed by our government with the native peoples? If colonization is all in the past (as it is in so many PEOCs' minds), why cannot our government act honorably and return to the native nations land stolen from them in violation of treaties *our* government signed? If our actions of the past included misguided, unfortunate errors, why are we not vigorously correcting those errors today? And why do we tell Natives to "move on" and "get over it" when *we* are unable to do so?

The question is, are we so selfish and dishonorable that we cannot do the right thing? Are we so in love with having control from sea to shining sea that we want to keep everything, so we say it is all over –the past – even as we violate our own and international laws on an ongoing basis and reap the rewards of our illegal activity? Still today, we illegally occupy land which does not belong to us – and yet we condemn other countries for this kind of activity, as we did when Iraq invaded Kuwait, for example. Still today, we hold colonies against the wishes of the colonized, and yet we talk about colonization as though it is all past, something that happened hundreds of years ago.

We tell ourselves we are working past colonization's "unfortunate" (our word) effects and moving on. But we are not moving on. We are just pretending that, since it's past (according to us), everything's fixed. Here is an illustration to clarify the situation: I tortured you every day for four hundred years, then stopped one day. I then declared it was the past. Since I wasn't continuing to torture you, I said the problem was now fixed (though, obviously, if you had spent four hundred years being tortured every day, your problems would not magically be fixed just because the torture stopped). That is the situation in the United States regarding colonization, except for one very important difference: *We* are continuing the torture; *we never stopped.*§§

We think that, if we destroy a people's culture, but then say, "Well, it's the past, and there's nothing

---

§§ See, e.g., George E. Tinker's preface, *Kill the Indian, Save the Man,* selected bibliography.

we can do about it now; but you can become a part of our great culture," that this is the best we can do, and at least we have *tried* to help and make amends for the past. This is what we think, because we don't want to actually consider giving up the rewards of our atrocities (like land) – nor look at the fact that we have committed genocide; that we have taken something that can never be given back or replaced; that we, as a people, have a negative impact on the world.

I wonder (if anyone in the U.S. has the empathy or imagination to fathom this thought) how U.S. citizens would feel if a race of people more "advanced" (i.e., just as violent, unscrupulous, and selfish, with more powerful weapons) came to the U.S. and discovered it and colonized this country. How long would it be before *we* would decide it was all in the past and move on? How long after U.S. citizens were killed in massive numbers, before they decided the whole experience was a good thing, because the new colonizers were decent people? How long after being forced to sign treaties ceding their lands before U.S. citizens accepted that what had happened was progress, because the new colonizers were, after all, superior? How long after U.S. citizens were herded onto reservations until they realized it was all for the best and, after all, "there's nothing we can do about it now"? How long after they were forced to give up their children to be sent to schools in which they were sexually abused, tortured, starved, forbidden to speak English, and brainwashed into believing this new race was superior and they were inferior – how long until all that would become the shining history of a new, better, free and just country? How long until we got over it? And, with our culture destroyed, with our families broken so that we could not teach our children how to live, with our children raised in abusive institutions in which they were taught to hate themselves – how *would* we recover?

The closest fantasies U.S. citizens seem able to imagine are alien attacks: aliens from outer space (we always find a way to kick their butts in these idiotic fantasies, even though the attackers are advanced enough to have traveled across the galaxy); or aliens from Latin America ("What language will your children speak?" is one of the favorite rhetorical questions of the racist U.S. citizens who have configured this fantasy).

In any fantasy, the response is always a fight for our country: We're not giving up our country to _____ (fill in the blank: communists, Mexicans, beings from outer space, pod people – take your pick). But it isn't "our" country. If I kill you for your car, is the car then mine? If I want your house and offer you ten dollars for it, but you refuse to sell, and so I kill you and claim it, will our government accept my claim? –No, it will not. So how can our government make the same claim over Native lands? It doesn't matter how many self-serving laws our government has passed which supposedly give us ownership of the land – it still isn't ours, and our own treaties confirm this.

Some would, undoubtedly, claim that the U.S. is ours by virtue of the fact that we control it. If this makes the U.S. ours, then why did, for example, Ugandans fight for independence? By the logic of control, since white colonizers controlled Uganda, it was theirs. Yet Ugandans fought against their rule, because it *wasn't* theirs. You can see that asserting that the United States is ours because we control it is nonsense.

Some would, undoubtedly, claim that the U.S. is ours by virtue of the fact that there are now more PEOCs living here than Native Americans. However, if percentage of population had any bearing on ownership, then how were European countries able to own African countries, or, for that matter, how does the U.S. own Puerto Rico?

The argument that we *were* a British colony but fought for and gained independence and therefore are no longer a colony also fails, because it was former British citizens (i.e. colonizers) controlling the fate of the new country. To look at a similar situation, South Africa gained independence from Britain, and yet colonizers continued to run the country. Thus, the black South Africans again had to fight for independence, this time from white rule.

We may think we do not have an apartheid regime, and so the situation of the U.S. is different, but we are just lying to ourselves. Native Americans can attest to the fact that we do have an official policy of discrimination. For just one example of this, look again at the fact that we completely ignore the treaties we signed with them – because, according to our government, they are not entitled to equal protection under our laws.

U.S. citizens can and do ignore the reality, but it still remains that we are illegal colonizers, daily oppressing those we have colonized. At the time of American independence, the Native Americans did not receive *their* independence. All that happened was that Great Britain ceased to be the colonizer, and the newly formed U.S. government took over the job.

Try this: Imagine that, when the Europeans came to the New World, the indigenous peoples had been more advanced (according to our warped definition of the word) than the Europeans. The Natives acted kind, but only to fool the colonizers into going home and returning with more people. The Natives then enslaved the adults who came, to work in their factories. They took the children to work their fields, teaching the children that Natives were superior to Europeans and that they must try to act like Natives, though they would never be as good because they were white. Meanwhile, they did not feed the children enough and gave them only spoiled and rotten food. They beat and molested the children and taught them that their religion was evil. Massive numbers of the children succumbed to disease and starvation, just like their parents working in the factories. (This is our culture's definition of more "advanced.")

This is what *our* culture would have done (and has done), and we congratulate ourselves on it, claiming superiority because, after all, we *have* factories. The Natives were more truly advanced in their cultures, values, and spirituality, but we like to paint our own picture of ourselves and to believe this distorted portrait.

If colonization is all past, and we've learned our lesson; if we say we wouldn't engage in such acts anymore because we're more enlightened now and understand the consequences of our actions; if the errors of the past were unfortunate excesses or kindly meant but misguided actions, then why do we not now: 1) Cease these kinds of actions; and 2) At least *try* to do something *real* about those excesses and misguided actions we have already committed? (Obviously, they can never be corrected.) Why do we not return the land which belongs to Native Americans to the Natives? Why do we not also declare null and void those treaties which were coerced or otherwise fraudulently obtained, and return the land we thus stole to the native nations from whom we stole it? (Payment for the lands would not address the issue: If I am unwilling to sell the land where my ancestors lived, obviously you cannot justly buy it, and the same holds true for the Native lands. And governmental rights of way would not apply, because these lands do not belong to any U.S. governmental authority to establish rights of way.) In fact, if we really want to make the point that we have learned a lesson, why do we not even cease to occupy the land which has no claim by Natives anymore, because we killed them all? After all, do we want to benefit from past misdeeds? If we killed all the Natives to whom the land belonged, we should not reward ourselves by occupying their land – at least, not if we are just and honorable.

Why hold on to what you have gained through dishonorable and unjust means – unless there were never any good intentions, and the goal then was exactly in keeping with the outcome today? And since we will not do what is honorable and just, why can't we at least cough up enough integrity to quit claiming those titles?

Illegal Immigration

Once upon a time, so the story goes, some straggling people, who had sailed from Europe, arrived on the shores of what is now the United States, looking for freedom of religion, opportunity, and a better life. Regardless of the veracity (or lack thereof) of our sentimental history, it is certain that, at that time, this land was occupied by people who were not obsessed with owning every square inch of the Earth. And so they welcomed the newcomers, helped them get settled, and left them alone to live their own lives in their own way. The point is that the only reason Europeans were able to come here and live was because this land once was, indeed, a land of freedom and liberty.

In the farthest stretch of your imagination, can you conceive of our supposedly free government having the strength and liberty to allow a group of people from another culture to come to the United States, settle on some land which is not in use, and live freely the way they choose? Obviously, this would never, ever happen. We didn't even let the people who were already here live their own lives in their own way. This whole story just illustrates, once again, that we are a country of tyranny, calling itself the land of the free; nothing more.

*   *   *

The U.S. government, in its infinite wisdom, decided that we should build a wall between the

United States and Mexico and make it a felony offense (punishable by imprisonment) to be (or to aid) an illegal immigrant in the U.S. During the debates over whether to build the wall, some people organized protest marches, and, regarding one of these marches, I heard someone joking that we should meet the protestors with buses and ship them all "back." His punch line went something like this: "If they want to come to this country illegally and protest, we'll show them by sending them all back home." Not much of a punch line, but hate isn't funny.

Did this joker actually think everyone in the march would be an illegal alien, or was he just going to ship everyone, even U.S. citizens, over the border? Maybe he thought that being shipped over the border is the punishment U.S. citizens should face for the crime of supporting the aliens and disagreeing with our government. Or was he just going to ship the Latinos? Maybe he was thinking it'd be worthwhile to illegally detain 100,000 marchers for a few weeks to check their identities. If someone didn't bring ID, we could assume they are illegal and ship them home.

Obviously, the joke was idiotic and the man was racist, but enough people in this country agree with his feeling (i.e. are racists) that we actually built a new great wall, laced with barbed wire and electrified – wow.

Clearly, keeping terrorists out of the U.S. is not the issue. Didn't most of the alleged 9-11-01 perpetrators cross into the U.S. from Canada? I have heard that there are border crossings between the U.S. and Canada where you just get out of your car, open the gate, drive through, and close it behind you; and there are many places to cross without ever even hitting a border crossing. Yet U.S. citizens have determined that our northern border is secure, and the only one we have to worry about is the Mexican border.

One readily apparent question in this debate, but one which no one in America has thought to ask, is, "Where do we get off declaring a border?" The whole idea of declaring a border which X persons may not step across is very repulsive, but, clearly, PEOCs don't see that; we believe in ownership and control and "our country."

Notice that people in the U.S. rationalize, excuse, and deny the PEOC genocide of Native Americans, which we committed because we wanted to take everything they had away from them. But, at the same time, we scorn "Mexicans," who just want to work here, not kill us. (Of course, many of the Latino people who come here are not from Mexico, but many ignorant people in the U.S. use the term "Mexican" as though it is a generic term for all Latin Americans. For the U.S. citizen, someone need not ever have lived in Mexico to be Mexican. But, beyond that, it is worth noting that many of the immigrants coming here from Latin America are not Latin at all: Some are Natives of the Americas, and some are descendents of African slaves.)

How is it that, though the European colonizers came to this country with every intention of taking control of it, we consider that praiseworthy – and yet we think it despicable if someone else wants to come here? The Europeans bred and apparently filled the country up, and now, evidently, there is no more room. The difference between the European immigrants and the Latin American immigrants is that the Europeans wanted to control the

United States and were willing to commit (and did commit) every imaginable atrocity to take it away from the Natives. They set up their own government and declared the land theirs (thereby allowing them to determine who else is allowed to enter). The Latin Americans, on the other hand, just come here to take jobs. And many come because we helped their people in the past, so they are now starving, or are persecuted by the puppet governments we set up, or are worked to death by our corporations. Who's more criminal?

I guess U.S. citizens have determined that all the things they have (for which people around the world die daily) are just for them, and those nasty "Latins" don't deserve to live as well. We'll take their oil and natural gas, and we'll destroy their homes to get to it, but we don't want the people.

Perhaps the most tragic (and ironic and ridiculous) thing of all, is that the fight against illegal immigration is just another fiction of our government. The wonderful part (from the point of view of those in power) is how easy it is to manipulate the people into thinking this is an actual problem that they're aggressively addressing. I've seen tons of political campaign literature on "What I have done to fight the problem of illegal immigration."

There is no fight against illegal immigration. It's equivalent to our war on drugs (and, for that matter, our war on communism, and so on). Notice how we never won the war on drugs (this is obvious because we have more drug use now than we did when we began the war), and yet you don't hear about it any more? That's because the lie served its purpose and allowed our government to justify all the horrible activities we wanted to commit in Latin America at that time, and now we've moved on to a new fictional enemy. How the rest of the world must have laughed at us when they heard that our government, one of the biggest drug dealers in the world, was declaring a war on drugs. I can imagine what a kick they got out of that – all except those who had incurred our disfavor and were offered up as sacrifices to show we were making progress in our war on drugs. But, the point is, these people did not incur our disfavor for drug trafficking; drugs had nothing to do with the war on drugs.

This war simply served our purposes: With the fall of communist USSR, our government needed some new fictional enemy in order to rationalize for U.S. citizens our frequent illegal incursions into Latin American. They could no longer blame our activities on communism, and so they invented the fictive war on drugs to mask our real goals when impinging on the sovereignty of other peoples. The war on drugs also served to fill U.S. citizens with their usual false pride about how we were doing good things as we engaged in our illegal actions. It is a lot easier to bring together the troops when you tell them they are ridding the world of an evil.

By saying we were fighting a war on drugs, our government had a convenient excuse for all of its illegal activities in Latin America (and throughout the world). It gave us an excuse to arrest Manuel Noriega and bring him up on charges of breaking U.S. laws. Apparently the laws of the U.S. are so just and universal that people who don't even live here must obey them. But, after all, we didn't arrest Noriega because of drug trafficking. Noriega's arrest allowed us to install a puppet plutocracy to govern Panama, one which would allow U.S. businesses to come in and do their damage. This change in government was a wonderful thing for American businesses, and was, after all, the real reason for Noriega's arrest.

And this brings me back to the make-believe war against illegal immigration. Things wouldn't be so bad for those who try to come here if the PEOC countries and their corporations and their tools (such as the World Bank) would leave them alone. If we did not do so much to make life unlivable for so many people, they wouldn't want to come here. Why are the people who are so strongly opposed to illegal immigration not protesting the policies of our government and our corporations, which make people need to leave their homes? I have spoken to many immigrants, both legal and illegal, and most would rather live in their own countries, but they cannot make enough money to live. And it is PEOCs who have spent hundreds of years now trying to re-order the world, trying to re-organize the whole planet so that everyone has to work, to earn money, to live.

Many immigrants work to send money home, because of our unrelenting efforts to make this a cash world. But we want it both ways: We want to be able to destroy their means of self-sustenance, to make them dependent on jobs, and also to be able to tell them they can't come here for jobs that pay livable wages, they have to stay in their own countries and work for near-slave wages. We want them working for just enough to keep them barely holding on, and though many die, we don't care. We want them to believe that 10¢ a day is worth trading your life for (though in reality $1000 a day isn't worth trading your life for). We do everything in our power to make the people of the world dependent on us and enmeshed in our economy, not because this is what they want, but because it serves our interests. But if we want them to hold jobs and make money to live, it's hypocritical to complain when they come here to take jobs and make money. And yet we do complain. And though we consider ourselves the most generous people in the world, we begrudge them the chance to earn livable wages at their jobs.

And beyond everything else, we can't have death squads terrorizing people, destroying homes and villages, and killing people, and not expect them to want to escape. And yet we do organize and train death squads. I suppose U.S. citizens would prefer it if Latin Americans would stay put and take the bullets when they come; hang around and let the soldiers rape their children. We're obviously not concerned about the death squads, because we continue to support our government and our military, which trains the terrorists, and we continue to believe any ridiculous lie told to us to justify our government's actions.

But the fact that the immigrants do come here is, after all, an added benefit to corporate America. Think for a minute: If for one day, all the illegal workers in this country didn't show up for work – the country would close down. Many of those senators and representatives who voted to build a wall have illegal workers in their employ. They don't want to end illegal immigration, they just want a rallying cry for U.S. citizens – and what a great one, appealing as it does to the huge amount of latent racism here. Look at all the scare reports about whites becoming a minority in "their own country" and Latinos the majority.

Just think of all the money these illegal workers pay in taxes and never get back. (They are not all paid cash under the table.) Look at all the money they pay into social security that they will never collect. How great is it (from the corporate point of view) that any company in the U.S. can hire an undocumented worker and pay terrible wages, thereby increasing profitability for the company? Why is it not a criminal offense, punishable by imprisonment, to *hire* undocumented workers?

We put up a wall, and if more people die trying to cross the border, we really don't care; to us, their lives are cheap. (Do most U.S. citizens even know how many people die each year trying to cross the border?) During Hurricane Katrina, the good, generous U.S. citizens poured money and supplies into the charities which were assisting some of the people who had lost their homes – some, but not all of the people. Like many U.S. cities, New Orleans had many undocumented immigrants, most of whom had been living there for years and who were what we call "contributing" members of their communities. But according to us, they don't belong, and so they got no help – they were left to swim or die.

Just think of the windfall for the contractors who have built that wall (at taxpayer expense). I'll bet some contractors made heavy contributions to political campaigns in order to get in on the building of that wall. And the contracts, indeed, went to those contributors, because that's how our great democracy works.

And if, in ten years, we have increased our prison population by a few hundred thousand – or a million – immigrants, all in the name of this lie, that's another added benefit, because it means a huge economic boost to the prison industry. Remember, in our culture, *everything* is advancement.

Wisdom

Lenses

One of the greatest conquests of PEOC culture and control is to have made its lenses accepted, or, in other words, to have destroyed the lenses of other peoples and to have forced our lenses on them. After the Civil War, when the slaves were emancipated, to a large extent they accepted the PEOC society, and they tried to cut out their places in it, to be a part of it, and to define their self-worth and success by how well they were able to do so. (Of course, the playing field was never level; not only those in power, but even ordinary people, made sure the former slaves would not have equal opportunities or rights.)

The emancipated slaves would have been better off rejecting a culture capable of slavery, perhaps joining the Natives in their fight against the colonizers. The Natives' ways would have been much closer to the ways of their ancestors. But our culture had succeeded in forcing our lenses on them, and so, for the most part, the emancipated slaves didn't see joining the Natives as an option. Rather, they accepted and adopted our assessment of the correct way to live and, sadly, our assessment of them.

* * *

If our culture were to (figuratively) point at a ceiling and say, "That is the sky," then, without looking up, PEOCs think it is the sky and that everyone else is too foolish to see. Non-PEOC people view our ceiling and clearly see that they are looking at a ceiling, regardless of how positively we assert it is the sky. But we think our culture is the ultimate authority; our logic (our "thinking") is nothing more complex than this: "We have defined that as the sky – and so it is the sky because we say it is." But that doesn't stop it from being a ceiling. Of course, since we are so sure we are right, we hold fast to our superior "truth"; it is much easier than troubling ourselves to look.

*　*　*

People in our culture often pose two questions. The first one is, "What makes humans different from animals?" In Christianity, this is answered, "God created the world for humans and He created humans in His own image. He made them lords over all the animals." The second question is a variation of the first: "What makes humans different from other animals?" A common response to this is, "Humans have larger brains." No one in our culture has (as far as I know) ever answered these questions by saying, "The other entities of Creation are the souls who have become angels," or "The other animals are farther on the road to enlightenment than humans, and the plants are those who have reached enlightenment and are here to guide us..." The point is, the answers to these questions can be entirely different when you are not viewing through a PEOC lens, and the PEOC lens comes with a boatload of assumptions which make both the questions and our answers meaningless. These questions presuppose our view of the world; they assume, among other things, that humans are a species which is separate and different;

that there even is such a thing as a species; and that humans are somehow different in a way that no other species is different and are, in fact, higher. We take all these assumptions to be self-evident; we do not even realize we're already 200 steps from reality before we even begin to ask our questions.

Another common and yet painfully foolish question PEOCs ask is, "If a tree falls in the forest and there is no one around to hear, does it make a sound?" The question is supposedly profound, which is why people keep asking it, as though it holds the key to some secret of the universe. But in truth, the question just illustrates our ignorance and arrogance. If it's a forest, there are obviously other trees and plants around, along with an abundance of wildlife. Do they not hear? We ask the question only because we are so arrogant that we think something makes a sound only if heard by *humans* – or it only counts if humans are involved. It never occurs to us how obvious the answer is because of our blinding arrogance.

People in our culture automatically use our culture's lenses and let them determine the view they see. They use these lenses because it is the only way they know to look at the world; they don't even realize they are using lenses. This is one way we limit true difference of opinion, thoughtlessly: Everyone has basically the same point of view, because everyone views the world with the same lenses, and all of the lenses show views which fit neatly into the culture. Whether you pick business or spirituality or anthropology or superiority or democracy, you're going to get a picture that stays within the culture. Beyond that, you have to use the lenses of our culture, or yours is not a legitimate opinion, it is "only subjective," or it's superstition or insanity. And if you want to effect change, you are supposed to go through the proper channels, which all funnel right back into the culture.

*   *   *

The Europeans came to the Americas, and, without bothering to listen or learn, without bothering to consider whether this was where they had come from, they decided they had discovered a New World (it was new to them, wasn't it?). And all our scientific and social scientific theories support that point of view, and people believe them, no matter how many missing links there are (evolution isn't the only theory with a missing link). It makes sense, doesn't it – we were more advanced, more evolved (our culture tells us); therefore, our culture must have been around for a good long time before their cultures even started developing (for us to be so far ahead of them). And we were far too blinded by our culture to see just how advanced they were – but not in the same sense of PEOC advancement, where progress is always followed by poverty, hunger, disease, and devastation. They had made actual progress in the lives of their peoples, physically and spiritually: Their health surpassed ours, and their wisdom surpassed ours.

*   *   *

In A Adu Boahen's book, *African Perspectives on Colonialism,*[*] a book about the European colonization of Africa, the author asserts that, although the continent at the time of colonization was not as

---

[*] *African Perspectives on Colonialism,* selected bibliography.

modern as Europe was, it was developing in that direction. (Remember, the continent of Africa had been subjected to hundreds or thousands of years of European interference before the period people refer to as the actual colonization.) According to Boahen, the continent's peoples had developed international trade (as though that is a good thing), and though they did not have nation-states on the European model, they were heading in that direction. And he continues on and on about the progress Africans had made.

The problem is, he is viewing the situation as though it would have been a positive thing for Africa to become like Europe, if the people had been allowed to develop that way on their own, without being colonized. In other words, he is viewing everything through PEOC lenses. Instead of arguing about their progress (according to PEOCs), he *should* have been arguing that the Europeans should have left them alone, that they should never have come to Africa to begin with, and they had no business coming to buy people, ivory, and other "goods." If he weren't viewing through PEOC lenses, he would have straight out stated that Africa would have been better off without any European interference; that they were progressing how they wanted to progress; and that there is nothing inherently superior in nation-states on the PEOC model to what the peoples of Africa were already working with. The only superiority is that PEOC culture thinks it is superior in all things, and it is built on nations-states: therefore, nation-states are superior. The author should have flatly declared that even if the continent of Africa had never developed nation-states, that would have been a perfectly legitimate choice.

It is very sad that people view their traditional cultures through the lenses of PEOCs and, through these distorted lenses, see flaws in their cultures that were never really flaws. It is very sad that there are people who have been devastated by PEOCs and, because of this, feel the need to be apologetic about their cultures. It is sad that Boahen felt a need to argue that the African people were becoming more like Europeans. It was a little like he was saying, "We were becoming civilized; Europe did not need to invade to civilize us" – as though European colonization had to do with anything other than greed and power.

*   *   *

People in our culture see the positives (what they consider positives) and ignore the negatives – they put them out of mind or contribute money to a cause or tell themselves experts are working on solutions. They deaden themselves to the problems they are aware of but do not see so many others that no one in the culture is working to solve. Nor do they see that the positives are really negatives.

Our lives are made up of self-indulgence. One of the primary goals of working is to make money for self-indulgence, and we consider the fact that we have so much self-indulgence to be an indication of our superior lifestyle, a "positive." But it isn't. From the time we are young, we are taught to meaninglessly entertain ourselves. We listen to stories, then read stories, watch TV, play games, develop hobbies. (Notice how we teach children, through stories and television and classroom instruction, to passively absorb information that is being fed to them, rather than letting them interact with the world and learn something real from that interaction. Even our interactive games and school labs spoon feed information to children, as though we do not even know how to let children learn.)

In our culture, someone develops a product, and we call it "advancement." Or people destroy the land, and we call it "progress." Or someone starts a charity to fight childhood leukemia, and people pour tons of money into it, and scientists work for decades, and we say we are "progressing towards a cure." These are all cultural lenses which allow us to ignore what is really there. If you can take off your blinders for a minute, this culture looks like a huge, relentless, devouring monster that destroys everything it encounters and then congratulates itself on its virtue and superiority. There is nothing benign in our culture; our destruction isn't accidental:

Picture a plantation owner prior to the Civil War. The slave owner eats fine foods and sometimes gives parties to entertain his friends or potential business partners – they laugh the evening away or talk about current events. The slave owner purchases fine china or beautiful fabric or a new wagon and strong horses; perhaps he reads all the classics and the works of the great thinkers; perhaps he indulges in hunting parties. He buys toys for his children's amusement and indulges in a multitude of "harmless diversions"... And he thinks to himself, "I am cultured and refined; I am successful and deserve my wealth; I am an important person in the community, and I support the economy of my country."

For this, thousands upon thousands of African people were kidnapped from their homes. For this, they were transported in worse-than-deplorable conditions to the Americas. For this, they and their descendants were sold. For this, they slaved away at hard work for long hours in the plantation owners' fields. For this, they lived in decrepit housing and were unable to create family lives because a spouse or a child could be sold at any time. For this, grown men and women had to say, "yessir" and yet be called "boy" or "girl." For this, they could be shot if they tried to escape to pursue their own destinies. All of this so that slave owners could indulge in a thousand ways in their lives of luxury. There is *nothing* harmless or benign in this picture.

Let your focus become blurry so the image changes slightly, so the plantation owners start to look like the colonizers of, say, Uganda: The clothes have changed and some details in the background are different, but the composition remains basically unchanged. Again, wealthy PEOCs are indulging their greed and selfishness at the expense of the thousands and tens of thousands who live in misery; and again, there is nothing benign or harmless in the picture.

One more time let your focus become blurry, nudge your eyes a little, and then re-focus on modern-day United States. Once again, some slight details have changed, but again the composition remains strikingly similar. Non-PEOC people pay for all of our self-indulgence, as do the Earth, the plants, the air, the water, the animals, and the rocks: our cars, our fine chocolates, our designer clothes, our trinkets, our spa treatments, our dollar-store goods... Many of the raw materials which are made into our things come from Third-World countries, and the people farming and mining those raw materials are living in decrepit conditions. Our corporations love to set up factories where people (some of them children) get paid a few cents a day after 12-14 hours of work – and then they bring those products to the U.S. so we can have some trivial things to buy – so we can indulge ourselves. People in Third-World countries are still dying for diamonds ("certified diamonds" typically meaning only that the trail of blood is more carefully hidden). People the world over farm our chocolate and coffee and produce – and they often cannot afford to eat. We are the slave owners and the colonizers. And there is nothing benign or harmless in the picture.

A lot of people think, "I work hard all week – I've earned the right to indulge myself a little." (Is it sometimes okay to indulge yourself at the expense of others?) There are ways to enjoy life without indulging yourself at others' expense, but no one makes money off those ways. If these were the only forms of enjoyment Americans used, the economy of the U.S. would fail. We are a country built on costly self-indulgence, which other peoples and the Earth and her other children pay for. And our mindless self-indulgence helps some Americans become rich and keeps some people employed, which leads to further self-indulgence at the expense of the Earth and her children...

* * *

If every country in the world developed to be like PEOC countries, I doubt humans would make it even to one year before they were gone from the Earth. We cannot export what people of the culture consider to be the positives *sans* the negatives. They are irrevocably intertwined. And this culture has a built-in preclusion for any fundamental self view. That's one lens our culture doesn't have. You've got your scientists and philosophers, your psychologists and sociologists, etc., but they're part of the culture, oblivious to the fact that they are as integral to the problems as every other facet of the culture, oblivious to the fact that they all build on the same faulty foundation. They shoot each other down – in other fields, in their own fields – but they fail to see their own faulty bases. Maybe they are facing different directions as they look out to sea, but they're all in the same leaky boat.

Every solution to a problem creates new problems, and our culture, which has neither hindsight nor foresight, is incapable of taking a step back to say, "This was not a good idea." Cars have caused horrible destruction: destruction of massive amounts of the Earth's surface to build roadways and parking lots; congestion; smog spewed into the air and onto roadside plants; 50-100 thousand accidental human deaths each year (not to mention human injuries and *non*-human deaths and injuries); the ever-increasing need for gasoline, for which we destroy indigenous habitats and peoples; millions of used tires which, if burned, would release toxic fumes, and so are being used to repave our roadways, where the toxins can be released over time as the cars drive over them, day-in, day-out; destruction of soils and dust production on unpaved areas: countless problems. Yet this culture will never say, "Wow, cars were a bad idea. Let's get rid of them." Instead, they look for solutions to the problems they have created, and those solutions cause new problems, like using old tires to repave roads.

Factory farms came into being as a solution to produce more meat more cheaply – and basically to make their owners richer. They are immensely cruel to animals; create unsafe, diseased meat (how do you like eating an animal that's been sick its whole life?); create massive amounts of what becomes dangerous waste: They have their own long list of problems. But those who own them have enough money to thwart efforts to close them, and citizens are so happy they can go to the corner and buy a burger for just a buck that they don't care it is contaminated meat.

*   *   *

If we are trying to cross a street, we look both ways, but we don't actually look at what's there: We just verify that there are no cars coming. This is a cultural lens. In some cultures, people actually *look* at what's there, but we're focused on checking for one particular thing – same as science and Christianity and philosophy and so on.

*   *   *

"Going green" is one of the latest marketing tools companies are using to increase profits. Sadly, going green isn't a way to save the planet; it's just another marketing tool for exploiting it. This catch phrase is used by corporations pedaling everything from natural gas to household chemicals. It's a meaningless label, meant to make a product more attractive to PEOCs who want to tell themselves they are helping to save the planet while they continue to be as self-indulgent as ever. It's patently ridiculous to think anything involving mass production can be green, but that doesn't in the least deter PEOCs.

The greenies promote what they call sustainable energies, which science says can save the planet. Since their sustainable energy sources damage the

Earth and harm her children, just as traditional energy sources do, it is clear that scientists and greenies promote harm to the planet. (Just for starters, manufacturing all the windmills and solar panels involves destruction, and, moreover, the Earth has to make way for the placement of the panels and windmills.)

When fossil fuels began to be used, scientists (and PEOCs in general) knew their use involved destruction of the Earth, but they didn't care, nor did they foresee the extent of the damage (which they still don't and culturally can't understand). But, the point is, they knew they were harming; they knew they were destroying. It is the same with what greenies call "renewable" energy. These sources still harm the Earth, and scientists and PEOCs know they harm the Earth – but they don't care, nor foresee the extent of the damage...

If PEOCs stopped everything they are doing with traditional energy sources and switched to what science calls a sustainable lifestyle within the next six months, it wouldn't solve our problems. Everyone would learn, once again, that there were unforeseen consequences to the technology; that the technology hadn't quite solved our problems as intended; that the scientists had oversold the cure.

The sustainables tell themselves that *this* damage doesn't count, *this* damage is insignificant, but that doesn't make it true. I am as unimpressed as folks like George W. Bush with their facts – but I'm unimpressed because I *do* care about the Earth – and *they* are unimpressed because, like the sustainables, they do not. Both the "traditionals" and the "sustainables" believe some damage and destruction are acceptable.

Dams were once thought to be a means of providing clean energy. This fantasy, too, was based on the mentality that some destruction is a-okay and that it is acceptable to completely disregard the plants and animals and waters whose lives will be destroyed in our insane quest for more energy. But it turned out that dams aren't a clean and green energy source at all.

There actually is no clean, renewable, sustainable source of energy, as we use it. In fact, I guarantee you that the scientists who are pushing alternative, sustainable energies already see, in an admittedly very limited way, some negative effects of these energy systems, but they're willing to overlook them.

Beyond that, the things we power *with* all of these energies also cause harm. Finding an alternative source of energy to power these things isn't going to solve that problem. For example, systematically growing and annihilating plants to power our cars isn't going to eliminate the need for roadways, Freon, and toxic tires. Powering our TVs with windmills isn't going to eliminate the need to produce plastic to manufacturer the TVs, nor the need for landfills to throw them into when they break down. The millions of fish who get mutilated, killed, and maimed each year by motorboats will not find comfort in knowing that the boats are powered with supposedly green energy. Obviously, all of this is not a reason to continue using traditional energies – it's a reason to clear our eyes and stop using energies.

Note that "sustainable" isn't the same as "self-sustaining." Everything we create breaks down: The massive infrastructure needed for sustainable energy will always need regular maintenance and repair. And these sites will have accidents, which will kill animals and plants and perhaps people.

Note also that there will never be enough. Sustainables seem to think that, once the systems are set up, they'll be completely self-reliant, as though our society doesn't indulge in an ever-increasing desire for more energy; as though we won't have to be building more and more sustainable energy sites; and as though those who own the sustainable energy companies won't encourage more and more energy consumption, in order to increase their profits. We see the greed of those who own and run traditional energy companies, and we see their maniacal, relentless destruction of everything they are able to destroy, in order to get more energy to sell. But there are people with financial interests at stake on the sustainable side, too. Many traditional energy companies also have investments in sustainable energy, and even the upstart companies have financial interests.

If, someday, we have a fully-developed sustainable energy industry, it will be run by people who are just as ruthless and brutal as those running traditional companies; it won't magically be run by kind people who really care. The new reign would promote energy usage just as much as today's energy industry leaders. Do you think the people running today's traditional energy companies think of themselves as merciless, ruthless, greedy people? Do you think they realize how morally vacant they are? I have no doubt that they believe they are not only decent people, but, beyond that, that they are virtuous, the good guys. I'm sure they believe that they are doing not only what is best for themselves, but what is best for the country as a whole; that they are providing the energy which makes our [indolent, self-indulgent, selfish] lifestyle possible (which they believe is a superior lifestyle). Beyond that, I'm sure they've provided themselves a rationale for all the price gouging they engage in, telling themselves it is a virtuous act.

People on the sustainable side of the coin (it's all the same coin) make it easier for traditionals to continue their devastation. The sustainables don't argue against destruction of the Earth, nor against harming the entities of Creation – rather, they argue against the type of destruction caused by traditional energies, preferring, instead, their own type of destruction. It's pretty easy to shoot holes in this line of thinking.

Moreover, by using science to prove the damage caused by traditional energies, people are just giving traditionals something *arguable* to go against. We can all see the Earth torn apart, blown up, dug up, drilled... And we see some of the effects (like smog and nuclear waste). The devastation itself is not arguable to anyone who truly respects the Earth and her children, but the science *is*. Science *can* be argued –it's not exact; it's a sliding truth; it's open to interpretation. Anyone can look at what we do and see it is wrong and be alarmed and saddened and hurt, without needing science to prove it is wrong. As soon as you make it a matter of proof, you've lost – because anything that can be proved can also be disproved.

Those who do believe in global warming think science is an objective field, that is isn't a matter of faith, because it's empirical. They can't understand that there are people (like me) who are so dense (they think) as to *not* believe, because they believe so fervently, just as some Christians do. And the near hysteria of some on the sustainable energy side allows traditionals to pretend that all the people opposing the traditional energy industries are cuckoos, like there is no "legitimate" opposition to what they do.

If you don't believe it's important to care for the Earth and her children for *their own sakes* (and sustainables don't believe this any more than traditionals do) rather than for the sake of humans (as though we are somehow separate from the whole), then anything is okay. If you see that we are one, you realize that, if you are hurting the planet, you are automatically hurting humans, too, but the science actually makes it easy to argue *against* this view. In science, *some* destruction is acceptable without its hurting humans. As I said, it's easy to argue against this slippery, sliding truth.

But this is how our culture works. We are not all on the same side, with a common goal of doing what is best for the whole, the entirety of Creation. We have opposing sides, and they all have self-interest at heart, even though they tell themselves they don't. We have no common sense of caring for and being guardians of the Earth and her children; we have an adversarial culture in which people are always arguing that they see more clearly than the other side(s), but in which they are all actually as culturally blind. They all use the same lenses; they all have the same cultural world view, and it is this culture which makes both the destruction and the meaningless argument about the destruction a reality.

* * *

I read a PEOC book about the black plague (in Europe), in which the author noted that no pre-modern city was ever clean, and he went on to describe the filth of a typical pre-modern European city.[†] He is correct about pre-modern cities – when applied to *Europe*. He seemed to think, however, that today's PEOC cities *are* clean. Yet every modern city I have seen is still filthy.

We have countless surfaces that hundreds of people touch daily (door handles, shopping carts, tables, vending machine buttons, money...), and we've all seen people touch these things right after wiping their noses with their hands or scratching their behinds. We have litter everywhere: discarded food; used diapers; broken glass; Styrofoam and plastic cups, the contents spilled all over the ground; used napkins and tissues; bloody bandages; scraps of paper; cigarette butts... Look at the ground of the average parking lot – or at a grocery shopping cart, for that matter – they are filthy. Our cities and structures and things are all designed for optimal filth accumulation and retention. There is plenty of litter in even the richest neighborhoods. (And, sadly, even if you go to a "pristine" area in the mountains or forests, you will almost surely find litter. Moreover, from sea to shining sea, our oceans and lakes and rivers are strewn with trash and the waste of fishermen; discarded fishing lines and hooks and floats line the shores. If you walk barefoot, you risk catching a hook with your foot, and the lines and hooks kill animals who become entangled and cannot escape.)

Our cities also have waste: a pile where someone took a dump because they didn't want to walk to or know where to find a restroom (so many

---

[†] *The Great Mortality: An Intimate History of the Black Death, the Most Devastating Plague of All Time*, John Kelly. HarperCollins Publishers, Inc.: New York. 2005.

businesses limit their restrooms "For patrons only," which I guess is our version of pay to piss) – and, face it, it's not like using a restroom, where the sewage all drains to one area, is a better option: Here you have human waste from hundreds of thousands (or millions) of people, all collected into one place – what a revolting thought. You see pee on walls, sidewalks, and park benches; vomit; snot; spit; a stain on the sidewalk where someone hocked; another where someone blew their nose; a used condom lying on the grass in the park; a backed-up sewer pipe with sewage leaking.

Our modern cities also have their share of dead animals. In nature, these bodies could go back to the Earth; in city places, they often become a stain on the pavement. If it's a dead dog or cat, someone will probably collect it after a few days to put into pet food (because that's what goes into the "nutritionally balanced" and "scientifically formulated" products you feed your pets: road kill that's been lying around for 2 weeks; factory farm animals that died and laid in animal feces for a month before anyone noticed; pets who have been put to sleep, together with their collars and the chemicals used to kill them – real healthy).

We can pretty much assume they had all this, in one form or another, to a greater or a lesser extent, in pre-modern Europe. But into our mix we have added dust particles raised by the continuous razing of land for development and by our wonderful invention of automobiles, driving on unpaved lands. And we also have smog, toxic chemicals from innumerable businesses (from dry cleaners to computer manufacturers), and pollution spewing from factories. We have pharmaceuticals making their way into the water supply (in some places you may be on pharmaceuticals, whether you take them or not); food laced with toxic fertilizers; and insecticides, herbicides, and pesticides, all of which make their way into our surroundings. Plus, some cities have nuclear waste radiation in the air and soil.

We have airplanes flying overhead, leaving behind trails of noise and of their spent fuel and exhaust, to fall on those below or to hang in the sky, creating artificial clouds on what might otherwise be clear days – and dumping the contents of their restroom tanks. And we also have cruise ships dumping massive quantities of waste into the ocean (okay, that's not in the city, but it's still filthy – and if your city lies on the ocean, realize that water is not a static entity– and the water doesn't have to reach you for the pollution to affect you). We have debris from torn-down buildings and torn-up sidewalks and roadways, junk piles on vacant lots, and illegal dumping (of human waste, motor oil, Freon, etc. – the list is as endless as our waste).

This short description barely scratches the surface of our filth. Ours is a society that generates waste, lots of waste (it's an integral part of our market economy), and much of it becomes the filth of our modern cities. Most people are so used to it, they don't think twice about it, don't even realize how filthy our modern cities are; they are blind to it, kind of like (I imagine) the pre-modern peoples of Europe were. Modern filth in our cities is at least as filthy and toxic as pre-modern filth.

And then we have people's homes. They have to be constantly cleaned, or they become dirty in no time. Again, this was also true in pre-modern Europe – and our homes are full of many toxins, just like theirs were. Our water is treated with chlorine, and, in many parts of the country, with fluoride – both of which can kill you (maybe you trust the safe levels science has determined are acceptable for humans, based on experiments on animals). The cleaners and cleansers most people use are loaded with toxins. Our microwave ovens make our food toxic – and don't stand nearby while that microwave is running. All of our technology is physically unhealthy – and spiritually unhealthy, too.

The point is, the author of this book on the plague grew up in a culture which says, "Our modern cities are clean and so much more advanced than pre-modern cities," and he believes it without ever taking a look around. This is how our culture works – don't look at the color, don't look at the world.

The author of this book also takes time to describe the hunger and wretchedness of the people of pre-plague Europe, and he depicts it as "finally, progress" when people began to cut down the forest to plant crops. After this progress, for the entire period covered by the book (hundreds of years), the people suffered one famine and disease after another, culminating in the plague. How was that "progress"? Progress would have been for those people who were "huddled" in the forests to finally realize that the forests weren't and never had been alien or enemies – that just as they were, they could provide food and shelter for all. This world is wonderful that way: Without any improvements by PEOCs, it's capable of sustaining life; no one has to go hungry. When the climate changes and one food source becomes scarce – there's another food source available.

We think it's progress when people struggle against the natural world the Creator has given us because that is how we live today; it resembles our "advanced" lifestyle – not because it results in any actual forward movement for the people. The author is blinded by our culture's lenses into seeing the destruction of the forests as progress, only because, in our so-called advanced society, we destroy nature. Ironically, the prolonged famines which followed the supposed progress do not in any way deter him from viewing the destruction as progress. The whole mess culminates in massive death from the plague, which is where the book ends, but not the wretchedness, which survives to this day. Notice that even with all of today's progress, millions of people in PEOC countries still go hungry and still live lives of wretchedness, still work long hours but can't pay their bills, etc. Real progress requires the ability to look backward and forward, and we are utterly incapable of that, because in our culture, it all gets called "progress"; it all becomes one forward march – regardless of reality.

*   *   *

I did not read in total *The Feminine Mystique* by Betty Friedan,‡ but I did read parts. Friedan wrote about how (middle income) women had, at that time, been restricted to the role of housewives, in part because of a body of work which had as its basis Freud's theory of women having "penis envy." It's hard to imagine any indigenous people giving credit to such drivel, but in PEOC culture, which is so removed from reality, theories are engaging and compelling – and if this is the latest knowledge, then everyone will jump on board and create a body of work.

---

‡ *The Feminine Mystique*, Betty Friedan. W.W. Norton & Company, Inc.: New York. 2001.

Friedan was appalled to find out that the point of the subjugation of women to the role of house-wives was the profit of U.S. corporations. That is to say, as long as women were defining themselves as housewives and were deciding their self-worth based on what they owned in the way of modern appliances for taking care of the house, and as long as they were bored out of their minds by this life to such an extreme that new appliances seemed exciting, corporations were selling a boatload of products that no one really needed (but which the culture, of course, defined as "progress"). Such is the PEOC mentality – a whole segment of the so-ciety can be sacrificed for money (and many seg-ments are).

Like many other groups, women are victims of the culture, but they also are a part of it; they be-lieve in it. And so, instead of arguing to reject a society capable of sacrificing women, Friedan ar-gued instead for women's right to join this society more fully. Although she is a victim, she also be-lieves our culture is great, and she wants to be *more* a part of it. And so she did not reject out of hand Freud's theories, which were used to prove that women belong in the home; instead, she decided to re-interpret those theories, to prove that women should *not* be subjugated to the role of housewives. Rather than picking and choosing which parts of Freud's theories (and the body of work that his theories built) held merit, she *should* have suspected any water from a polluted source, so to speak, and have realized that the whole body obscures the truth. Instead, she used the same lenses which were used to show that women belong in the home to show that they can be equally effective in the work-place. (Remember, anything that can be proven can be disproven). Even though our culture is patently idiotic, sexist, and turned on its head, as a child of PEOC culture, she did not see that it is patently idiotic, sexist, and turned on its head, and she looked at the men's world as something to strive to join, not to scorn. Rather than strive to be equal to those who hold power in such a culture (which, in spite of her optimism, has not happened – and won't), she should have argued to reject it and look for truth outside of such a culture.

* * *

I read a book about American Natives in the U.S.A. today,[§] in which the author argued for bringing modern medical facilities to the reservations and lamented the fact that most Natives do not have as much education as whites. If Native culture is so devastated that they no longer have traditional healers, and their knowledge is lost forever, I feel sorry – for humanity as a whole. I am sorry that so much native wisdom is lost, and I am sorry that this loss leads anyone to want our medicine. However, the PEOC medical industry does more harm than good, and I wouldn't wish it on any culture. I would not go to a modern hospital. I can understand why a people would want change after having been visited by the devastation PEOCs cause, but I can't understand why they would want to change to become more like us.

Similarly with education; our whole educational system is set up to preserve the status quo – that is one of its purposes. The intention is not and never was to enable poor people to rise up and be anything they wanted, nor to level the playing field in

---

[§] *Anti-Indianism in Modern America,* selected bibliography.

a land where all men are created equal. Moreover, the premise of our educational system is that what you need to know can be taught in a school (even though what you need to know isn't taught in school at all) and that knowledge is a series of subjects you study, rather than something you gain through interaction with real life. When you start college, they teach you how to take notes and study and take tests and prepare assignments, but there is no talk of putting everything you learn into a comprehensive view of the world. And so the only comprehensive view of the world the students end up with is the view that "Euro-American culture is the most advanced culture," and "We have more knowledge than anyone else because people specialize in subjects, so they are able to go deeper," and other such drivel. Obviously, if none of these subjects can lead to real knowledge, being able to go deeper doesn't lead anywhere. So what PEOC education has to offer, what it gives us, is children who have become thoroughly indoctrinated into the culture, who are qualified to take their places as workers in this society. Kids don't really need to absorb much to be able to do most of the jobs in this society – and those elite jobs that require more knowledge are still just a matter of learning to think like this culture and of believing that going to a job each day is what life is about. I wouldn't wish this system on anyone.

The traditional methods by which Natives taught their children seem so much wiser, as were their methods of child rearing in general. In their cultures, children were expected to explore, to push themselves, to gain knowledge which had not been spoon fed to them. (Though, in our culture, one cannot take their child to the wilderness and leave them for an hour – or a day, depending on how old the child is – in order to give them an opportunity to sit quietly, observing the life all around. In our culture, we would be worried about our child being kidnapped – or about the state taking our child away because of "child abuse.")

The point of their education was to guide the children to understand the world. This is the opposite of our culture, in which the point of education is to get a job, and we place no value on understanding the world. In our culture, children are taught exactly what they are supposed to think and are held on a tight leash. People say, "Spare the rod, spoil the child," and although some people have devised other means than spanking, child rearing is still built on a foundation of punishment for not being good. (Our culture is very fond of punishment as a means of control.) What child doesn't hear "no no no" thousands of times before they ever begin school. Thus we begin educating them at an early age.

Someone might think, "If a Native American wrote a book arguing for PEOC education and PEOC health care, that just shows that our culture's education and health care are better. Now that we have control of the country, they see we have a superior lifestyle, and they want us to share it." One problem (of the many) with this thinking is that we deliberately destroyed so much Native culture. It isn't like, after we forced the Natives onto reservations, we left them alone to live how they wanted. It's not like we allowed them to pass down their traditional health care and knowledge of herbs. Nor did we allow them to raise and teach their children their cultures. We enforced our culture onto the Natives on the reservations and often forcibly took their children so we could force our culture on them, as well. These children were underfed, overworked, abused, and tormented – in other words, these children were not raised in their cultures, they were raised in ours.[**] Some children were sent to live with Mormons (because the Mormons couldn't let the Christians wreak all the devastation) to be indoctrinated into *their* religion, which, after all, is the same culture. Some children weren't sent to schools, but they had parents who were. So their parents' childhood experiences included large doses of self-hate and abuse, and this is what their parents learned to pass on to their children. It isn't something superior in our culture which makes others want it. Those parents who had their children taken from them did not want our culture for their children; we forced it on them.

Nevertheless, one distressing aspect of this adoption of PEOC lenses by people we have harmed is that it reinforces in the PEOC mind the PEOC fantasy of superiority. We don't look at the entire situation; all we see is that someone is arguing for our health care, and if people want our system of health care – it must be because our health care system is superior. When someone argues for education, medicine, and development, or equal access, the average PEOC reads that as meaning that the PEOC culture is indeed superior, that we made this country great, that everyone wants to be like us, and, by extension, that we deserve to invade other countries and are helping the people when we do so. And since the PEOC mind isn't tethered to reality, we just keep going with that line of thinking: We deserve to be the most powerful

---

[**] *Kill the Indian, Save the Man,* selected bibliography.

nation on Earth, and, because we are so great, we can do no wrong, etc. ad infinitum. (Yes, we force our lenses on peoples and then, when they use them, we take it as confirmation of our superiority.) The next logical step in the PEOC mind (I have heard it many times) is that, though the colonization of the Americas (and Africa, and Australia, and so on) had "unfortunate" aspects, in the end it was all for the best, because through colonization PEOCs were able to spread their "superior" lifestyle to inferior peoples. But this is not what really happened – it's just what the PEOC lens looks like.

I can imagine someone arguing for medical care and education on reservations saying, "You don't know how bad things are on reservations. Western education and medicine may not be great, but they're better than what we have." But I do have an idea about how bad it is on the reservations; my culture imported to and imposed on Native peoples many, many problems. I know Native Americans and have been to reservations; I have read and listened. But as soon as you say, "We have to live in today's world, and in today's world, Western medicine and education are all we've got; we have to find a way to work within the system to make it work for us" – then you've thrown in the towel. If Western (or PEOC) is all we've got, then the Earth as we know it is doomed – humans are doomed.

You may argue to bring Native American problems into the public eye, or to develop an advanced degree in Native American issues, but if you think that getting the current plight of Native Americans into the public eye will help, that my culture will somehow become kind and people will care, I don't think that will happen. Even if you raise awareness and get people to care, my culture won't help; my culture doesn't solve problems. Either the people who try to help are misguided and don't help at all (and often make things worse), or they get derailed by more powerful people. If you expect help from PEOC culture, I don't think it will come; if you think you can make this culture work to help you, I don't think it can be done: PEOC culture doesn't peacefully coexist – it devours.

Those in this culture who say they are trying to save the Earth are helping to destroy the Earth. They think that saving the Earth is something that can be done from within this culture, and the avenues they take are within the culture. Since they are working within the culture, they get sidetracked, or they are too busy trying to raise money to have time to fight the battles, or they lose the battles, or there are too many people on the other side, arguing *for* destruction. (People need jobs, and if you're out of work and hungry, you may support destruction of a forest so you can work as a logger, even though you know it's wrong: Too many forests have been destroyed already; too many trees have been killed.)

The illusion these environmental groups provide is that something is being done: It looks like we have every side represented in the development process. Environmentalists file lawsuits, which a judge rules on, so if it's *really* important to save some particular land (people think), the company wanting to develop that land will be forbidden by a court injunction. If the court rules that the company can develop, it's because it wasn't really a critical piece of land. It looks like all sides are being represented and a judge is making an impartial ruling, balancing the needs of the companies and workers versus the needs of environmentalists, etc. But it's a façade. For one thing, most judges give very little or no weight to saving the Earth for its own sake. There has to be a question of a threatened or endangered species living there; even then, the judge will often just tell the company wanting to develop to "be careful." For another thing, there are many pieces of land which companies develop without ever being taken to court. Also, sometimes if a company is forbidden from developing land, that company will just wait until time passes to try again; or, to neutralize opposition, it will put advertisements on TV asserting that destroying this land will be great for the community; or it'll just wait until someone appoints a judge who will rule more favorably.

So we have people fighting to save the Earth but at the same time supporting destruction of the Earth, both through their support of the culture which is destroying the Earth, and by creating the illusion that something is being done and the "important" land is being saved. They are supporting the culture causing the destruction without really accomplishing anything to stop it.

What should be happening is, every person who wants to save the Earth should be saying, "No":

"We want to build a new housing development to make homes more affordable." (Who are they kidding?)

–"No."

"We want to put up a mall."

–"No."

"We want to explore for oil and end our dependence on foreign energy." (Does anyone actually believe that is the goal or will be the effect?)

–"No."

"We need to mine for uranium – this is vital to our national interests." (Does anyone actually believe that?)

–"No."

And that atrocious Mt. Rushmore-like monument, which is supposed to "honor" Crazy Horse...

–"Oh hell no." (Think for a minute: Crazy Horse would not allow his likeness to be taken – don't ask me whose image they are blasting into the mountain. Crazy Horse considered the Black Hills sacred, not something to be blasted apart. Crazy Horse did not like us and had no interest in being honored by us – along the same lines as I would not like to be honored by the KKK. There is no way in which Crazy Horse would feel honored by this monument[††] – this is our warped culture's concept of honor).

Along the same lines, next time someone comes out with a new technology, you can say, "I've gotten along fine without it up until now – I'll pass. And while I'm at it, I think I'll get rid of all this old technology, too. It hasn't made my life any better."

The Earth isn't being saved; the course of destruction hasn't changed. Our culture does not save, it destroys. So if you decide, "We have to live in today's world, work within the culture which is here, and make it work for us," you won't save the Earth; you won't save your people as a people. What is the answer? I don't have the answer, but I know that, if we have a future, it lies in the past of indigenous peoples; it doesn't lie in PEOC culture. If there is hope, the answer lies in the ways of those who don't destroy the Earth, not in the culture that does. I am not native; I am a

---

[††] For more on this monstrosity, see *Anti-Indianism in Modern America*, selected bibliography.

child of my culture, and I know there is a lot I do not understand. Yet I'm praying for the Native Americans who remain and all indigenous peoples to find a way to save their languages, their traditions, their cultures – and to continue to share. In fact, right now I would like to say thank you to all the Native Americans and all the other indigenous peoples of the world, past and present, who, in spite of everything the people of my culture have done, have taken the effort to share the histories, the values, the traditions, and the current plights of your peoples. By sharing your wisdom, you have given us something we could never have learned from our culture nor seen through our culture's lenses, and I thank you for the priceless gift.

Wisdom

For indigenous peoples, wisdom was accumulative. Knowledge gained by the old ones and added to by each generation was passed down, so the people did not have to start anew in discovering roads to living and spirituality. They had wisdom about everything from how to prepare dangerous plants to how to stalk and kill an animal. They taught how to live as part of the Earth as caretakers, doing no harm to the natural paradise they inhabited, and how to reach a personal relationship with the spirit world and the Creator.

For us, there is little meaning in life. We pour molten steel into molds and think we are so much more efficient than other cultures, but for Natives, making a tool was a life lesson, imbued with wisdom. Ours is a society without wisdom, and so wisdom has no value. We do not value what we do not understand, and since we have no real understanding – science doesn't provide understanding; our religions don't provide understanding – we value nothing.

And so, for PEOCs, survival is meaningless work, a series of empty tasks to be got through so we can "live." People imagine that by automating these survival tasks, we freed up time to devote to more important things: to search for truth, to make more money, to love, to raise a family. But what if it is these tasks of survival that were meant to show us that truth we seek; what if they were a doorway; what if they are what we need to be teaching our children about life? When we lost the meaning and wisdom behind the essential tasks of living, we left truth behind. People do not have more time for living now; automating survival tasks did not reduce time spent on survival. Now people have time for meaningless tasks like endless household chores, spending time in traffic and in lines at the supermarket, and watching TV. We don't have more time for love and family than the Natives had, and I do not see the higher truth that we freed up our time to look for on TV or in the bars where people go to relax after a day of empty tasks. Truth is not in the theories of science; it is not in the ordering of our society, which is riddled with social diseases. Where is it? We have lost it.

Here is an interesting story: In the southwestern United States, there used to live a nation of indigenous people called the Hohokam, who, for some reason, vanished. I once visited a museum (obviously a PEOC museum – museums are inherently PEOC) which had exhibits about the Hohokam and their mysterious disappearance long ago. Of course, in the exhibits, they proffered theories of possible reasons for the Hohokam's disappearance, none of which actually made sense.

The PEOCs think maybe the O'odham are descendents of the Hohokam, but the O'odham know that they are, and this is a part of *their* story about the disappearance of the Hohokam.

The Hohokam had created elaborate structures, in terms of architecture, irrigation for their crops in the desert, and so on. They had also developed cities in their region. They had become very advanced, according to PEOC thinking. But what happened is what the Hohokam came to understand. They realized that the lifestyle they had created, the irrigation of the desert and their cities, was harming the desert, their home. They realized that they were taking water from the animals and plants, who also needed that water. Even to today, you can still see some of their irrigation channels, and they realized they were harming the Earth, their Mother. They realized that their lifestyle could not survive, that they had strayed too far from their Mother and their Father and themselves. So they gave it all up and went back. To me, it is notable that they had the wisdom not to try to fix the damage they had done, but rather left that to the Earth to heal.

Beyond the shear beauty and wisdom of this history, one can see it is the truth: It was not made up; it was passed down. And this is one kind of knowledge indigenous peoples have always considered it critical to pass down. They had learned a hard and important life lesson, and many of those with whom they shared life on Earth had paid dearly for the knowledge. The lesson could not be forgotten, it had to be passed on. Everything about this history makes sense, yet it was not one of the theories presented at the Hohokam museum.

Notice the difference between this history and the PEOC version of history, in which we are always the good guys, we are always progressing, and anything negative is whitewashed or attributed to good intentions that went astray. They actually learned something; we just tell ourselves we did.

*　*　*

Look at the difference in names in different cultures. In ours, people choose a name for their child because it sounds pretty or because it sounds good with the child's last name. I know the name Matthew comes from the Bible, but the word matthew doesn't mean anything and says nothing about the person. So our first names and our last names are just a way to identify us apart from everyone else, and, perhaps, to keep track of our descendents. In Native American cultures, their very names mean something, so someone has a name such as Woman-Who-Runs-with-the-Deer or Man-Who-Speaks-to-the-Wind, instead of Susan or Bob.

How wonderful a culture in which children are more than just cute, they are a responsibility. You teach them carefully; your actions are a model for them, and so you act in a way that you want your children to learn is a good way to act. When they learn to do things, it is not just to get them done with, in the quickest way, no matter how poor the workmanship. Instead, they are taught to understand what they are doing, and why, and the importance of that thing to themselves and to the entire people and to Creation. In this way, they understand the importance of taking time and doing a good job, of taking care that something is done in the best way, not the most efficient way. The culture is truly accumulative, a constantly changing pattern of ancient and modern. You teach them the culture and the traditions, knowing that some day they will be carrying on this information and that it is important for the wisdom of the past and of each generation to be passed down, so that future generations don't have to learn anew, so they already have tools for life and spirituality which will give them a start in the right direction on their own journeys. Like all the other entities of Creation, children have their paths and their rights and responsibilities. They truly are the future, and it is your responsibility to make sure their future will be what the Creator wanted for them.

Our version of this is:

1. Say we believe children are the future.

2. Decide ways to occupy their time until they are school-aged by what is convenient for us (maybe setting them in front of TVs), not by carefully considering what they should be exposed to. Tell them how to solve their problems and answer their questions in such a way that they don't bother trying to figure things out for themselves.

3. Get them into school as soon as possible, schools being convenient warehouses for storing your children while you are at work, until they are old enough to go to work themselves and become productive members of society. (Schools are not places for your children to expand their minds and learn about the meaning of life; kids definitely come out with their minds much more closed than when they entered.)

4. While they're in school, prepare them for the real world (there's an especially ironic example of our abuse of language, "the real world" in question being the make-believe world of concrete, computers, and 8-hour workdays that we encourage for our children throughout their young lives). Treat them like a bunch of cute but non-distinct, non-individual people: Process them. Teach the culture through subjects, like history and social studies. Accuracy is not important; consistency is not important. The war waged by the U.S. against Iraq can start by being a wonderful thing when they're in 7th grade and become a "well-intentioned error in judgment, but no one's to blame" by the time they reach 12th. –This just teaches them that

truth is a constantly changing thing in our culture and that we are always right or well-intentioned, even when we destroy people.

People who fought on both sides of the Civil War can be called good, even though they were ideologically opposed. Even though the Confederates were fighting to keep slavery (among other things) and believed in the rights of slave owners to the point that they were willing to kill for them, and we now say that slavery was a bad thing (because the North won; if the South had won, slavery would still be "good"), the Confederates were still "good" people. This is because *everyone* in the history of this great country was good (except the traitor Benedict Arnold). No matter if the Confederates were actually morally vacant – we will never call them that.

5. Do not teach the children alternative points of view. And definitely don't teach any Native American traditions. Heaven forbid the children learn that you can carve a stone into an arrowhead using another stone, and why someone might do this; or that you can start a fire using a couple of sticks, and that this act has meaning. In our culture, that's not real knowledge, anyway, it's just "crafts," and if the kids are going to be doing crafts, crayons and sequins are a lot easier and are in keeping with the cultural mindset we're trying to impress on the kids.

6. Destroy as much of the world as you can while the children are growing up, so that the world they inherit is toxic and it is unhealthful for them to go outdoors. Make sure you generate tons of nuclear waste for them to deal with. Buy them things they don't need in order to teach them to consume and to keep those landfills filling up – those landfills are their future. Rack up an insurmountable national

debt so that when they go to work, they can pay twice as much in taxes as you did and therefore have to work even harder than you to get by. That extra portion of taxes will be going to pay interest on the insurmountable national debt, thereby increasing the wealth of those who own the banks; maybe their wealth will "trickle down" to your kids – but don't count on it. Continue voting into office those who advocate destroying the environment and increasing the national debt (which includes pretty much everyone who runs for office in this great democracy, and certainly everyone who gets elected – after all, to win takes money, and that money comes from the people who want to destroy the environment so they can make more money: this is how a great democracy works). Vote them into office because they lie well and say they want to help the environment and are doing what's best for the future of the country, and because crack U.S. news reporters have determined that you'd like to invite them to a backyard barbeque – after all, if you'd like someone at your barbeque, then he (she) must be qualified to hold office.

7. Graduate the kids and put them to work so they can carry on the culture and be the future.

* * *

In our culture, which doesn't and can't question itself, people are too busy marveling that we can pick up so much trash so efficiently to wonder why we generate trash.

* * *

PEOC culture does not have problems that need to be cured or fixed. Alcoholism, incest, pollution, and genocide – these are not problems with PEOC culture; they are a *part* of PEOC culture. It is like a jigsaw puzzle: all the pieces are part of it and they all fit together. This culture cannot exist without all of the problems. It would be impossible to cure the problems without *fundamental* changes to the culture; put another way, it would be impossible to cure these problems and still have *this* culture.

*　　*　　*

We train ourselves, and our culture trains us, not to look, so we don't see, and we congratulate ourselves on our faith. Some believe Christianity will save the world because they do not look at the harm it causes, and the same is true of those who believe in New Age or science or any of a hundred other religions which our culture has spawned. We call it faith, but what is faith if it is necessary to *not* look in order to believe? Shouldn't what we encounter in the world support our spiritual revelations?

By using PEOC religion, we limit our spiritual depth, just as we limit our abilities because science says this or that is impossible, just as we limit the meaning of our lives by letting our society define going to work as a meaningful necessity of life. Men who can't find a job and "provide" often say they feel inadequate. Both men and women who have undesirable jobs often feel unhappy. Why, if work is so meaningful and necessary, and our society is so well-ordered, is there not a good job for everyone, one they find fulfilling and worthwhile and that pays enough for those things our culture has determined should be bought (food, shelter, health care)? Why are there bad jobs if work is meaningful? There is not something wrong with you if you find cleaning toilets unfulfilling.

*   *   *

In our culture, when people hunt, they usually try to get the biggest specimen. For example, they try to kill the mulie with the largest rack of antlers, as though this shows their prowess or proves their manhood; this is in spite of the fact that their hunting techniques have nothing to do with real prowess or skill, and that killing the biggest or strongest might not be the best thing for the animals and the Earth. Native Americans didn't have these empty ideas of prowess and manliness, based on your luck in coming upon the biggest animal and the power and range of the weapon you bought at the store. For them, it was more honorable to do what was best for the animals than to have the largest rack of antlers to mount on the wall.

Look at the difference between the hunting techniques of Native Americans and PEOCs. The Natives would stalk an animal, killing it close up, realizing that the animal had given its life for their survival. They had to have the knowledge to know how to find the animals, the patience to stalk, and the skill to kill the animal as swiftly as possible to minimize its pain. PEOC hunters, on the other hand, sit in stands, use high-powered weapons, and bring binoculars – no real skill involved, no understanding of the world needed. Many times they don't kill with the first shot, and the animal is left to bleed out while the hunter searches for where it fell.

Similarly, when PEOCs fish, they do it in the easiest way, sitting in a boat or on the shore, waiting for the fish to bite the hook so they can pull it out, tearing its mouth and letting it die an agonizing, suffocating death. This is because we do not have (nor desire) the real skill it would take to stand above the water with spear in hand, waiting patiently for the right fish to swim by, and then swiftly killing it in one stroke.

*   *   *

Notice how the modifier "crude" is often used before the term "stone tools" to describe indigenous people's tools, as in, "People of this tribe, using *crude* stone tools, were able to fashion basic weapons for hunting," or other, similar nonsense. This is approximately the same way people of our culture describe pre-historic man. They're assuming indigenous people wanted the same thing we want, that they wanted an efficient way to make something quickly, without any meaning behind the making of the item or its use (note how much waste our efficiency entails) but that they were just not evolved or advanced enough to get it. The thought never occurs to us that an indigenous person learned something in the making of that stone tool and in its use. We are so lazy and fond of doing things in the easiest way that it never crosses our minds that other peoples wouldn't want the same. Using "crude" and other such terms is a value call, but people in our culture don't see that.

*   *   *

PEOCs brought about the conditions which make wildfires so prevalent today and which help them spread so quickly, causing so much destruction. How many PEOCs know that?

*   *   *

This is a true story: A woman got lost while hiking, so she started a forest fire to bring help,

389

thereby burning down millions of trees and bushes, killing animals, and destroying their homes. All of this because the woman could not function outside of our society's grasp and panicked when she found herself without our culture's technology.

Far away from this woman, at approximately the same time, a Native American fireman, who desperately needed work, started a forest fire, burning down millions of trees and bushes, killing animals, and destroying their homes. All of this because he needed money and he, too, could not function outside of our society's grasp. The two fires joined, and it became one of the largest wildfires in Arizona's history. Charges were brought against the Native man but not against the white woman.

*   *   *

It's clear the power of the Earth – go look at the ocean or watch a storm. If you can tap that power, which is a part of us, so much is possible. This is the kind of knowledge indigenous peoples passed down, not the limits of science (if you throw a rock into the air, it will fall down). Anyone who was willing to dedicate their life to the ultimate spiritual path, which was available to *all*, could learn these truths. Our primary religion gives us only the hollowness of "And Jesus said…" – where there is no way to connect to the Creator (though you can pray and have faith "He" hears). In Christianity, you can look forward to joining "Him" when you die, but you do not live with "Him," and there is no doing "His" bidding while you are alive on Earth, unless you believe it's all written in the Bible: God doesn't have anything in mind for you particularly – just do what everyone else is supposed to do: preach, proselytize, commit genocide. Perhaps pray to God for guidance in your life, and then do exactly whatever it is you wanted to do to begin with, all the while telling yourself it's God's will; it's what God had in mind for you. (God wanted you to kill "His" children indiscriminately.) You can see that the Natives' ways of connecting to the Creator and doing the Creator's will actually worked if you just look at the way they lived, just as you can see that the Christian way doesn't work if you look at the way they live.

Indigenous peoples lived in all kinds of climates and survived; but they weren't just barely surviving: They were living good lives, developing themselves in a real way, enjoying their lives. They taught how to really care for the Earth, not remodel it; how to live in, for example, a desert or the arctic, without destroying it for all the other life; how to take your part in Creation, of which you are a part. In our culture, we don't really feel like we're a part of Creation; many don't feel like they're a part of anything.

*   *   *

Anyone who cannot understand the concept of infinity has never paid attention during a single day of their life, has never looked at a tree or a bush. If you don't get it, get to know a tree. When you know that tree, you'll get it.

PEOCs try to order the world in their search for reality and truth, using abstract theories and natural laws (which are also abstract theories). Too bad for them, reality is infinite. They'll never be able to see it by ordering it.

*   *   *

Here's an easily-imaginable scenario for our future: Drinkable water becomes very hard to obtain in the world. In spite of its scarcity, PEOCs continue to waste it, because we cannot sacrifice anything. We solve the problem by forcing others to export their water to us, just like we currently force them to export their food and natural gas and oil. Also, we desalinate ocean water, thereby leading to major problems with ocean ecologies.

At this future time, we know that water is rare and that people in some countries are dying for lack of it, and our scientists jump in to study the problem so they can save the day. After a few decades, these scientists hypothesize that the lack of drinkable water in the world is a result of the actions of PEOCs: Millions of gallons of drinkable water are trapped in plastic bottles which PEOCs have thrown into landfills and onto roadsides; this water will continue to be trapped for thousands of years to come. We tell ourselves that we could not have foreseen this consequence to our use of plastic bottles for water and sports drinks. And we are lying to ourselves again. –How many people bothered to take an instant to consider, *before* they started using them, "What might the consequences of using plastic water bottles be?" It is not that we could not have foreseen the potentially dire consequences; it is that we made no attempt to foresee.

*   *   *

Setting up a wildlife preserve is like saying, "It's okay to destroy ('develop') everything that's not in this area." Too bad the wild animals aren't told about their new reservation, and they end up getting killed if they stray off of it.

When I was young, I used to see huge flocks of bids, flying in "V" formation, covering the sky. Now I see ragged, straggling flocks, and I wonder: How large were the flocks five hundred years ago?

*   *   *

In our culture, appearance is very important: hair, teeth, clothes, etc. In below the surface terms, we are still interested in appearance over substance or truth. People don't try to be better people – they try to give others the appearance that they are good. That's one of the functions of PR. We may know we don't really want to help certain people, but we will try to give the appearance that we do. (Hence for example – and this is only one example of thousands – the pharmaceutical industry airs ads asserting that they are selflessly working on new drugs to improve our health, when, in fact, they have no desire whatsoever to see us healthy. They want only to sell more drugs, and they can't sell them to people who know they're healthy.) And since our culture is so shallow and focused on appearances, we usually believe the PR; appearance is actually more important to us than truth, which we find irrelevant or believe doesn't really exist, because, in our culture, there is no truth. And so, often, we never bother to look and see that the appearance is a façade.

People dye their hair purple or pierce their bodies in an attempt to express themselves or to show a rejection of the dominant culture, to show they are different. But what they are really showing is that they are dominated by their culture, which says that dying your hair purple is a way to show your rebelliousness. They are showing that the only way they can find to express themselves is on the surface, superficial like their culture. The idea of expressing themselves by understanding the world and their part in it, by being aware of the plants and the winds and the rocks and understanding how *they* are interrelated to all of these entities, by becoming aware of how *they* uniquely interact with the other entities of Creation, does not occur to them – and, sadly, our culture does not know this kind of self-expression.

* * *

It's hard to understand that we would be *happier* and more fulfilled without all the luxuries of today's world, that our lives would be more meaningful, less lost. We are comparing, in our minds, the lives of the Native Americans to the lives of our pioneers; we are imagining that giving up what we call "modern comforts" would be like taking a big step back 100 years. But it is farther back than 100 years, and the lives of the Native Americans were nothing like the lives of the pioneers. We are fearing and condemning what we do not understand.

* * *

It's beautiful to look at the natural world (and what a relief for the eyes from the man-made ugliness around us). You don't need a book with someone else's knowledge or interpretation. You are already part of it, and there is more knowledge inside of you than in any book. See a giant cactus growing from a small bit of soil amongst the surrounding rocks of the mountain: How the cactus and the rocks grow together, as part of each other, part of the beautiful mountain. So many desert plants seem to die during a long stretch without water – and then seem to be reborn when the rain comes, re-growing leaves and blooms. Then the water lives in them; they are a part of the water, together with the rocks and the air.

How wonderful to view a pine tree shedding old needles as it grows new ones, its branches growing out; the layers of bark, rough yet smooth;

the lovely flower of a pine cone. Feel the shade and peace under its branches. Next time you observe a pine tree, know that it is also observing you. Look at the way light and shadow mingle under the tree – and know you are part of it. View the same tree each week for a year – you will see at the end of the year that it is not the same tree – nor was it ever the same tree – nor are you the same person. I know this will strike a chord in some readers, who, when they were young, felt the plants and had friends amongst the plants – until they grew up in our culture, which told them this was nonsense.

See the splendor of a pile of leaves fallen from a tree in the autumn – if you look, you'll see it's marvelous. Gather some leaves fallen from an elm, and look at the beauty from one leaf to the next: The colors, the patterns, the infinite variety may astound you. Forget about raking them; learn from them. Those leaves keep our Mother and her children warm through the winter.

If you pass an overgrown field, it's fascinating to look at the grasses – how many types there are, their different forms, how they look when they are not mowed down every week. There are so many bugs buzzing around, taking their nourishment here and flying there. It's funny to see a huge wasp perched on a tiny stalk, going after the pollen of one flower then another. Do you think that wasp is not enjoying itself, delighting in the smell and touch and feel, being a part of the flower?

When you walk through a field with moths floating all around, or with grasshoppers flying, it is easy to relax and feel joy and peace. Try this: Next time a bug lands on you, resist the impulse to knock it away, and use the opportunity to look closely and see its beauty.

It's astonishing to realize the variety of plants in just a small area: in a neighborhood, on a short hike in the mountains. Some of the plants you see are older than you – older than your grandpa's grandma – can you imagine the wisdom they have to share?

You may say, "All that nature watching sounds great, but I have a job to do and bills to pay. I can't spend all my time watching nature; I wish I could." And, sadly, in our culture, observing nature and being aware of the other entities is considered a luxury rather than an essential way of life and a form of respect for Creation and the Creator.

You may say, "I'm not at all interested in nature. I'm far too sophisticated to spend hours a day looking at plants and animals." But your sophistication is just something pulling you from reality, another veneer hiding truth.

Or you may say, "Nature watching might be okay once in a while, but I need some mental stimulation." But you could spend your whole life observing nature and not learn everything the Earth has to teach. This kind of mental stimulation leads to real knowledge; it has more value for your life than learning calculus.

Learning from the Earth might be compared to learning a new language. When you're learning a language, if you just relax and listen to the sounds, you can hear them – but if you are blinded by your language (or your culture) to interpreting and hearing only "relevant" sounds, strangely enough, you often can't even hear words you're familiar with.

If you've never had a pang looking at the beauty of a tree: the form of its branches; the shapes of its leaves, their textures and colors; the textures of the bark; the canopy of the foliage and the sky;

the contrast of the older leaves and the newly budding leaves; the veined seed pods, some opened, spilling their contents; the way the bark and leaves go together; if you've never felt this pang, you are missing something exquisite.

We have so many plants that we label "weeds," which people never bother to look at: how beautiful, how delicate, how detailed they are. Nor do they know that many of these weeds are healthy foods and have medicinal value as well. When I view plants, I see how they are a gift just in their life. They are so painfully beautiful, and they provide so much life to the other plants and animals. They are a wonderful gift, and I hope that someday people of our culture will see that wonder and stop torturing them, trying to control where and when and how they grow. How can you revere the Creator without revering Creation?

We look at plants and, because we cannot see them (or ourselves) outside of our cultural interpretation, we've simplistically (and arrogantly) decided that we are more complex than they are. We believe we are more evolved or are superior or that we alone were made in God's image (isn't it strange that God has an unchanging form – and it's just like ours). If you really want to see the form of God, look at the world.

Ending PEOC destruction is not a matter of fixing what we've done. Neither the Earth nor the universe is waiting for us to fix anything. Ending the destruction is just a matter of stopping, not of then trying to undo and return something to its original state. Well-intentioned actions meant to help and undo the damage would just be a continuance of the destruction. Nature can heal and fix and balance; PEOCs do not have the wisdom for this.

Respect and Dignity

People cut limbs and leaves off plants, or uproot weeds, and leave the pieces lying around like it is nothing – and they treat people the same way. No dignity and respect.

* * *

As I walked down the street, I saw a landscaping boulder which had been moved from the other boulders and left to lie in the gutter, maybe because someone wanted to pass the time. In our culture, we have none of that sense of respect and reverence which would tell us that it's not our right to disturb the other entities of Creation without a real reason.

* * *

One day I saw a caterpillar which was clearly in pain, regardless of what our culture says about caterpillars' ability to feel pain or whether their pain is important. I couldn't do anything to help it, and I contemplated for a moment whether to kill it to put it out of its misery. But the incredible arrogance of that thought struck me, as though I have the right to end another being's life for something other than survival. Besides, as the Native Americans teach, death provides valuable lessons, and who was I to take away from the caterpillar its wisdom? In our culture, we don't understand that we can learn something profound in death. We drug animals and people to numb them, or we help them along to end their lives quickly and painlessly, like death is something to be got through and not a valuable part of life. You see, we have no respect for death.

*   *   *

Some pre-Columbian Natives were hunters and gatherers, and some were farmers. Because they view everything through their culture, PEOCs think that indigenous peoples who farmed were more advanced, and they think that indigenous farming was basically the same thing as PEOC farming. But in practice and spirit, it was not the same thing at all. PEOC farmers tear up the Earth – the more efficiently, the better – throw the seeds in, dump the Earth back, maybe spray insecticides – all for the crop at the end, which they reap. In there minds, there is no other point to all of these actions than the harvest they reap at the end. This bears no resemblance to indigenous farming.

*   *   *

In our culture, which places humans as the center of the universe and which defines life based on humans, people believe that rocks and water are not alive. How blind we are.

*   *   *

Here is a beautiful old tree, which has lived through so much: the cutting off of its limbs, the tearing down of plants and earth all around, the paving of the land, years of animals living in its branches, birds landing and returning, people walking by, the changes of time. And here you see in this hole in the tree: Someone has stuffed trash inside.

*   *   *

The term "organic" has nothing to do with the humane treatment of plants. The idea of treating plants humanely would not occur to our culture. People will cut down a 100- 200- or 300-year old plant without a thought that they have taken the life of another living being.

Some people congratulate themselves on helping the forests by planting trees to replace the ones they cut down. They believe it is okay to kill a 1000-year-old tree because they are planting two young trees to take its place. This is like saying it would be okay to kill an adult as long as they had two babies to replace the adult they killed.

Once you start ranking any life, you devalue life. People developing a plot of land may decide to save some trees but decide that the smaller plants and weeds are expendable. I imagine most murderers do not consider themselves expendable, but the people they kill are. But it all ties together in this culture's world view, deciding the value of one life over another.

*   *   *

You may decide that you are willing to give up some modern comforts, but, at the same time, there are other things which you're just not willing to surrender. But it's important for you to understand that, by making this choice, you are taking the choice from your children. If I wanted to work for 30 years and save every cent, and if I wanted to overlook the fact that I find land ownership morally objectionable, I *might* be able to buy 5 acres somewhere, but it wouldn't be free of the clamor and pollution and restrictions of our society. And there's no way I could take a journey from one end of the country to another without ever hitting pavement, waste, the noise of engines... It's not an option that's available to me anymore. My choice to live a natural life in this country, free from the noises, free from plastics, free from litter, and free from pollution was taken away from me long before I was born. I realize that those of us who *would* make this choice may be a minority, and we live in a majority-rules democracy. But what if *your* child decided he or she would like to spend some time in nature – not to be lazy, but as a voyage of discovery and self-awareness. If your child wanted freedom, would that make it important?

* * *

Scientists do not want to save the rainforests for the sake of the trees and plants and animals living there, for the sake of the rainforests. If they decide they "have to," they'll cut down rainforest trees to study them, in the name of saving the rainforests. They don't care about the rainforests; they want to save them for the sake of people, because they believe we need them to create oxygen.

Scientists also study animals in an attempt to save them when they have become endangered. But they start with the preconception that the animals are below humans, so respecting the animals is not a part of the process. They study them and attach tracking devices and correlate and analyze data but cannot understand. Their primary goal, after all, is not to save the animals – as with the rainforests, it is to save the animals for the sake of humans.

* * *

Someone is cutting down a very old tree, a tree which towers above the homes and surrounding trees, a tree which is older than any of those people killing it. Why? Because they want to put in a flower bed? Because they want to put an addition on their house? Because its roots have intruded on their sewer line? (Although the tree was there first, so it would actually be their sewer line intruding on the tree's roots.)

They are taking their time killing it, many days. This morning, one trunk is gone; another, stripped of its branches, stands upright; a third, stripped of its branches, is leaning unnaturally after suffering all night. When they stop, the tree works on nursing itself; the next day, they cut off more branches, creating new wounds, leaving it there, living but dying. The tree knows it is being killed, but they can't get the killing over with, they just take their time, leaving it in its terror and pain. This is the way the missionaries treated the Natives when they came to the Americas, putting them to work as slave laborers, without enough food or rest, killing them slowly.

What will they do with this tree once it is down? Will they at least use what they have killed? No, they will feed it into a wood chipper, shredding it as its blood still flows, like they do to farm animals, cutting off their skin and sawing off their limbs while they yet live, in absolute terror and pain.

This old tree, who spent its life providing food and shelter to the animals and shade and beauty to the neighborhood, is treated like it is nothing important.

To Avoid Misrepresentation

Because the future is a mystery and I don't know how my words will be used, and because PEOCs and people we have influenced like to use words; to avoid misrepresentation of my writings, I'd like to give a short example.

Some people who hate Jews may try to claim that this book offers further justification for trying to destroy Israel, as though this book provides proof or confirmation that everything PEOC is fair game for destruction. One problem here is that these people who are intent on killing or driving away all of Israel's Jews have no moral high ground to claim. Their actions are as PEOC on this issue, meaning as immoral and self-serving (among other things) as Israel's. They have no right to claim moral superiority; this book is not a justification for them to commit genocide. Their actions are as atrocious as Israel's. They put on a good show and good PR for the viewing public – as I say, they are very PEOC on this matter – but the show is not the truth, and the truth is that they are violent, brutal, and merciless; they use people as pawns to get what they want, and what they want is genocide: They are very PEOC. Perhaps that's because, living so close to Europe, they encountered PEOC culture many ages ago and learned well from what they encountered. Or perhaps Europeans and Middle Easterners used to all be one people and simply split because they couldn't get along and thought they were always right. Who knows? But the people who hate Jews cannot use my book as justification for their holy war.

This is just one example of many ways in which my words could be used. In fact, if you want to use my words for anything, please don't: Don't use them to support your theory or to prop up your argument or to make your point… Whatever you would be doing would be within this culture, and so you are misrepresenting the meaning of this book.

Look

Perhaps you've gotten to this point, and you're thinking that I twisted everything around to make my point; that I turned everything on its head. Alas, it is I who have untwisted things to unveil the truth.

*   *   *

One of the great gifts of beauty and wisdom of so many indigenous cultures is that they had doorways leading out of their cultures. For example, the act of revering the Earth and understanding it leads you beyond any culture, because the Earth is not of one culture – it is of the rocks, and the wind, and the sun, and the moon, and of fire... Beyond that, they had practices *intended* to lead people through the doorways, as though they realized that any culture has limits, and one must be able to pass those limits to truly understand. Their cultures helped those who wanted to pursue ultimate spirituality to go beyond.

The PEOC way of life, every part of our culture, keeps the seeker within our culture, where there is no truth or knowledge to be found. We define the rules as to how truth can be proven, how God can be encountered, or how knowledge can be discovered, and within those rules, there is no way to exit the culture.

Our culture is like a huge building, filled only with ghost images and mirages, which seem to us to have substance – but they only seem that way because we believe them and because they are all we know. Their substance is *only* in our minds; outside of our minds, this substance doesn't exist. We attach to these images and feel ourselves superior because of them, and hate those who are not attached to them also – or we want to "help" them see our mirages.

Our mirages may change and twist, but reality is always outside the building, and no one can even see that they're trapped inside.

To reach true spirituality and knowledge, you have to find a way outside of our culture – and that's what this book is about: a look at the building and the images and mirages floating inside. If indigenous cultures were built, at least their buildings had exits – and if you can take a look at the building of our culture, maybe you, too, can find an exit.

Change

I have no doubt that, should someone desire, they could find a way to disprove what I have said in this book – but that wouldn't make their proof real, nor would it make what I have said false. Someone could discredit a point I have made, showing, for example, how our scholarship proves that such and such is the case; but that scholarship will itself be disproven in ten or twenty years.

If I am wrong about PEOC culture's inability to change, PEOC culture can prove it, not by arguing that I am wrong (which will only prove I am right, that PEOC culture cannot look at itself), but by *changing*.

When a year (or a day) goes by in which no woman is raped, no child molested, and no one murdered; when we no longer have prisons and do not have enough criminals to sustain them; when we don't need laws about lying anymore, because no one lies; when we do not have slums;

When no one is starving because they can't make enough money to buy food; when no one is dying of cancer or heart disease; when we realize that medicines, diets, and exercises are not cures for our unhealthy lifestyle and that the only cure is an elimination of our unhealthy lifestyle;

When cars are gone because we realized they were a bad idea; when we are no longer fervently, desperately seeking new ways to generate energy in our pathetic reliance on our society and its technology; when we realize that our pathetic dependence on our society and its technology was never advancement;

When we are no longer a consumer society, and we are no longer thoughtlessly and carelessly destroying the planet in our insatiable desire to purchase something, anything;

When the PEOC concept of land ownership has been eradicated; when gone is the idea that I own this land and can do with it what I want, even though I may live only a hundred years, and the devastation I wreak may last thousands; when the thought is, instead, "This isn't my land – I am just living here for now, and the next person deserves just as much as I";

When I see diamonds lying on the ground next to the other rocks, because they are not more precious, just more bloody; when we stop training death squads; when I never again hear the phrase "God bless America";

When spirituality is no longer religious dogma, and there is no "one way," because we realize that everyone has their own way;

When PEOCs quit using marginalized populations as guinea pigs for their experiments; when we have to refer to memory to recall that calling people "guinea pigs" was a reference to lab experiments on helpless animals, because we no longer perform lab experiments on helpless animals, because we no longer torture or exploit any animals;

When I see the land agreed by treaty to be Native American land returned to the Natives and coerced treaties nullified, and we are able to live side-by-side; when U.S. citizens speak several Native languages in addition to English and Spanish;

When the children (and adults) of the U.S. are taught a proper sense of shame and sadness about the origins of this country and the history of this culture, and when those living in other PEOC countries stop pretending that the harm they cause to other peoples is a thing of the past;

When we have not been at war for 100 years (or even one); when there is no World Bank and nothing to take its place, and there are no debts; when PEOCs stop interfering in other peoples' lives, so they can choose their own fates;

When the colonials living in the countries of Africa, who tell themselves they are no longer colonists because "this country has independence and isn't a colony anymore," acknowledge that they are still reaping the benefits of colonization; when they truly cease their colonization by letting go of everything they own, because it all came (and still comes) at the expense of the indigenous peoples living there;

When Australia's indigenous peoples and New Zealand's indigenous peoples and those of Canada and of all the islands, and all the peoples of the world are freed from the tyranny of PEOC colonization and interference;

When we've learned that all our causes are one cause, and you address it all or accomplish nothing...

When all of this comes to pass; when any one of these things comes to pass, PEOC culture will prove that it can change, and I will be proven wrong. So prove me wrong.

Selected Bibliography

Much of what is in this book came from my conversations with many people of many cultures; much came from inside of me, my instinctively felt view of the world, the act of the Creator, all that has gone into the making of me. And some of what has gone into the making of me came from my readings over the years: newspaper and magazine articles now forgotten; books whose names or content I no longer recall or which do not bear directly on what I have written. Here I list works whose content I can specifically contextualize in these pages.

Please note that I know not one of these authors. I make absolutely no representation that these authors would in any way agree with what I have written or would agree with the conclusions I have drawn regarding PEOC culture, nor that I agree with their conclusions.

This said, these are books I have read, in whole or in part, whose content informed this text.

"I Will Fight No More Forever": *Chief Joseph and the Nez Perce War*, Merrill D. Beal. University of Washington Press: Seattle and London. 1966.

Lies My Teacher Told Me: Everything Your American History Textbook Got Wrong, James W. Loewen. Simon & Schuster: New York. (Touchstone Book.) 1996.

Kill the Indian, Save the Man: The Genocidal Impact of American Indian Residential Schools, Ward Churchill. City Lights Publishers: San Francisco. 2004.

The Wisdom of the Native Americans, Kent Nerburn, editor. New World Library: Novato, California. 1999.

We wish to inform you that tomorrow we will be killed with our families: Stories from Rwanda, Philip Gourevitch. Picador: Farrar, Straus and Giroux: New York. 1998.

The Colonizer and the Colonized, Albert Memmi. Beacon Press: Boston. 1991.

African Perspectives on Colonialism, A. Adu Boahen. The Johns Hopkins University Press: Baltimore. 1989.

Anti-Indianism in Modern America: A Voice from Tatekeya's Earth, Elizabeth Cook-Lynn. University of Illinois Press: Champaign. 2001.

Bury My Heart at Wounded Knee: An Indian History of the American West, Dee Brown. Henry Holt and Company: New York. (Owl Book.) 2001.

www.ingramcontent.com/pod-product-compliance
Lightning Source LLC
Chambersburg PA
CBHW051811090426
42736CB00011B/1433